# Children of Kali

Other titles by the same author

*Eating the Flowers of Paradise:*
*A Journey through the Drug Fields of Ethiopia and Yemen*

*Chasing the Mountain of Light:*
*Across India on the Trail of the Koh-I-Noor Diamond*

*Hunting Pirate Heaven:*
*In Search of the Lost Pirate Utopias of the Indian Oceans*

# Children
# of Kali

*Through India
in Search of Bandits,
the Thug Cult,
and the British Raj*

KEVIN RUSHBY

Walker & Company
New York

First published in the United Kingdom in 2002 by Constable, an imprint of
Constable & Robinson Ltd; first published in the United States of America in
2003 by Walker Publishing Company, Inc.

For information about permission to reproduce selections from
this book, write to Permissions, Walker & Company, 435 Hudson Street,
New York, New York 10014

Art credits for photo section: "thugs strangling a victim," reproduced by the
British Library; family tree reproduced courtesy of William Sleeman; "thugs
demonstrating their techniques," reproduced by permission of the British
Library; portrait of Major-General Sir William Henry Sleeman courtesy of
William Sleeman; photo of Koose Muniswamy Veerappan
© PA Photos; five final photos © of the author.

Library of Congress Cataloging-in-Publication Data
available upon request
ISBN 0-8027-1418-8 (hardcover)

Visit Walker & Company's Web site at www.walkerbooks.com

Printed in the United States of America

2  4  6  8  10  9  7  5  3  1

For Sophie

# Contents

# Acknowledgements

Many people helped me with the researching and writing of this book. In India: Professor Anandkrishnan, Bhaskar Bhattacharya, Gulshan Grover, Narendra Luther, Om Nath Mehrotra, Hussain Zeidi and the Cox and Kings travel company. In England, assistance came from Anubha Anand, Jenny Balfour Paul, Suman Bhuchar, Asha Gupta, Deputy Assistant Commissioner John Grieve of Scotland Yard, Caitlin Rushby, Amandeep Singh, Harbinder Singh, the staff of the India Office at the British Library, Bruce Wannell and my agent Carolyn Whitaker. I am also grateful to Mr William Sleeman for permission to reproduce the portrait of his great-great-grandfather. With the text itself Carol O'Brien and Maggie Body were bastions of good sense and sound advice. I would also like to thank Sophie Carr, without whom this book would not have been possible and to her it is dedicated.

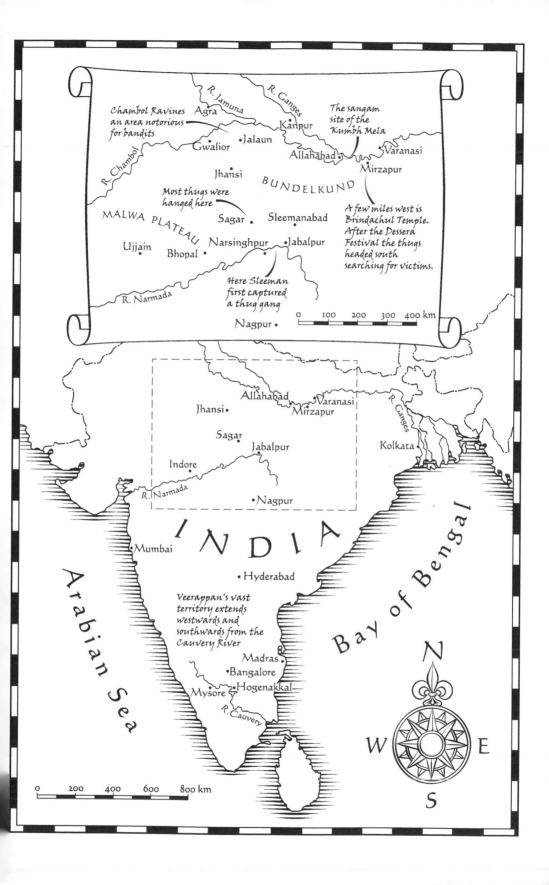

R. Jamuna

R. Ganges

Chambol Ravines
an area notorious
for bandits

Agra

Kanpur

The sangam
site of the
Kumbh Mela

R. Chambol

Gwalior

Jalaun

Allahabad

Varanasi

Jhansi

BUNDELKUND

Mirzapur

Most thugs were
hanged here

MALWA PLATEAU

Sagar

Sleemanabad

A few miles west is
Brindachul Temple.
After the Dessera
Festival the thugs
headed south
searching for victims.

Ujjain

Bhopal

Narsinghpur

Jabalpur

R. Narmada

Here Sleeman
first captured
a thug gang

0    100    200    300    400 km

Nagpur

Jhansi

Allahabad

Varanasi

Mirzapur

R. Ganges

Sagar

Jabalpur

Kolkata

Indore

R. Narmada

Nagpur

I N D I A

Mumbai

Bay of Bengal

Arabian Sea

Hyderabad

Veerappan's vast
territory extends
westwards and
southwards from the
Cauvery River

Madras

Bangalore

Mysore

Hogenakkal

R. Cauvery

N

W        E

S

0    200    400    600    800 km

# PART ONE

# HEROES AND VILLAINS

I have never heard of such atrocities, or presided over such trials, such cold-blooded murders, such heart-rending scenes of distress, and misery; such base ingratitude; such a total abandonment of every principle which binds man to man; which softens the heart and elevates mankind above the brute creation . . . mercy to such wretches would be the extreme of cruelty to mankind . . . blood for blood.

F.C. Smith, Agent to the Governor-General of India,
Calcutta, 1832

Interviewer: Mr Gandhi, what do you think of western civilization?
Gandhi:    I think it would be a very good idea.
(This exchange is said to have occurred when Gandhi disembarked at Southampton in 1930, though a variation substitutes 'modern civilization' for 'western'.)

# 1

# A Million Murders

THE FIRST MURDERER I EVER MET was an old man who walked on his hands and feet like a crab. He lived in a nest of sticks on the edge of an African village and scavenged scraps of food, without much success. Nobody cared for him or about him, but there were sufficient free meals in that place: mangoes lay on the ground uneaten; tall stands of cassava went unclaimed and groundnuts grew wild. It was a time of war and there were spaces between people: empty huts and abandoned gardens, cracks in the surface of village life into which an outcast could crawl.

He had been a tall man once, a typical Dinka, with skin as black as burned timber, a likeness furthered by the ashes he threw over himself to deter mosquitoes and tsetse flies. I used to pass his place occasionally and if I had a piece of bread or fruit with me, I would give it to him. Not always, mind you, because he was a troubled man and would sometimes rush out shouting, or throw stones, or simply rock himself and weep silently. I can't say I ever went inside the nest he had constructed, a sort of geodesic pastiche of a dome-like tribal hut with scraps of found plastic and string to tie the sticks together. If he was calm and approachable, he would be lying outside propped on his elbows, his long legs bent at the knee, for all the world like a tired athlete. I would stop my bicycle and call to him. Then slowly, very slowly, over a period of months, with great long gaps for madness, I gathered the scraps of his memory and tied them together.

His original home had been in the flat bushlands on the west bank of the White Nile. The Dinka life is to move with their cattle herds, living for part of the year on a mixture of blood and milk – a hard life, but he was not disabled in those times. Like many others, however, he had been dispossessed by the Sudanese civil war, his hut burned and cattle stolen. When his wife died of sleeping sickness, he had taken his only daughter and fled the fighting, south towards the town of Rumtek. On the way they found nothing to eat or drink and the girl grew weaker. One morning she did not get up. When he shook her, he found she was dead.

During the following night, while he lay by her body, a hyena pack tried to get her body from him and he fought them off with stones. It was a short-lived victory, however. An army truck came by and, seeing the mutilated body, accused him of murder. He did a few years chained to a wall in the local jail, then was let out. Crippled by disease and beatings, he had washed up in that tangle of sticks on the edge of some alien village.

When I told my neighbours the old man's story, they laughed. The old man was a liar, they said. He had been a townsman, not a nomad, and he had fled with his daughter when the rebels attacked. Somewhere on the road south of Rumtek he had been found. Hunger had driven him to it, perhaps, but there was no doubt as to the crime: the man had strangled his child and eaten her.

In the beginning, so the story goes, the first crime was the disobedience of Eve who leads Adam astray. After that, the first child to be born of a woman commits murder because God is displeased with his offering. Cain, the farmer, kills Abel, the

[4]

herdsman, and denies it with the first lie, 'Am I my brother's keeper?'

However, God is not deceived: 'The voice of thy brother's blood crieth unto me from the ground.' A mark is set on Cain, so all will know him, and he is sent out to be a fugitive, forever travelling to the east of Eden. All Cain's lineage become vagabonds, nomads, musicians and workers of metals, all those who breed suspicion and mistrust.

Many generations later, God tests Abraham by asking him to place his only son Isaac on a funeral pyre and sacrifice him. Abraham dutifully raises the knife and God intervenes. In another version of the story, that found in the Koran, Abraham is called on to sacrifice Ishmael, not Isaac the supposed ancestor of the Jews, and Ishmael agrees to his own death. Satisfied by the display, God grants life to the son and Muslims celebrate that every year at Eid al-Adha.

Murder and sacrifice were always fatally intertwined: there is the action of a vicious and jealous man, a savage who cannot control his passions; and there is the action of a noble and holy individual, a prophet who proves his righteousness by blood sacrifice, of his own child if necessary.

I went back to the old man who could not walk. I told him that I had been in the same jail where he had done time. This was true: four years before I had found myself in that town (spelled Wau and pronounced Wow) and needing to get off the street at night because of rebel gunmen. The guards had invited me into their office where they slept on their desks. There were only enough for them, no spares, and I dossed down on the floor with the rats. Outside, I could hear the sounds of snoring and groans where the prisoners were chained to the walls. Further off again was the sound of gunfire.

The old man and I swapped reminiscences of the good old days in Wau Jail, then I told him what people said about the killing and eating of his daughter. He began to cry miserably. He had a huge long head and his skin was permanently filthy with dust and ashes; the tears cut dark gashes like cicatrices down his cheeks. Desperate hunger, he told me, had driven him to do it.

One man, one victim, one rather mundane motive. I wrote that story down in my diary, then forgot all about it until I found myself in a secondhand bookshop in York with murder on my mind. The librarian of Wakefield High Security Prison had asked me to give a talk to seventy life-sentence prisoners on the subject of 'The Benefits of Travel'. At first I thought it a bizarre new punishment dreamed up by the Home Office: gone are the whip and the wheel so we'll give them Rushby chatting about beaches and island paradises. In fact, I was informed, it was part of a reading scheme.

I was looking for something to give me a clue as to how to start this tricky talk without causing a riot, but all I could think about was murder. I told the bookseller about the first murderer, not Cain but the crab man, and when I finished, he said, 'Man is fascinated by hand murder.' He peered at the shelves. 'The hand-on-throat . . . ah! Here it is.'

He took down two slim green volumes and weighed them in his palm. 'Fine condition. Constable's Oriental Miscellany series. You should get the original with the wonderful prints and end papers. Find it for around six hundred.'

'Beyond my means.'

'False economy.' He squinted at the book. 'Greatest murderers in history?'

'That's the title?'

'No, no. I am asking you: who were the greatest set of murderers in history?'

'The Nazis?'

'I mean always with the hand. One to one. No weapon except what you might find . . .' he smiled to himself '. . . in your pocket.'

I didn't do very well guessing. He read the spine. 'Sleeman: *Rambles and Recollections.*'

This triggered a distant memory. 'India and the thugs,' I said. 'Thuggee Sleeman.'

'Thug, or is it thag? It's Hindi meaning deceiver. Strange that the name for a religious cult of stranglers should become synonymous with football hooligans. They were such clever killers too, not bully-boys at all, actually the best kind of murderer: silent, cunning, ruthless and never caught – not for hundreds of years.'

'And then came Sleeman?'

'In the 1830s. You could say he was the first undercover cop. Suppressed them. Hanged them. To be precise, he hunted them down and exterminated them.' He passed the book across. I opened it at the contents page and read off the chapter titles with increasing amusement and interest: 'Insalubrity of Deserted Fortresses', 'Witchcraft', 'Men-Tigers', 'Interview with the Raja who Marries the Stone to the Shrub', 'Thugs and Poisoners'.

'They were stranglers,' explained the bookseller, going to his desk and checking how much he had paid for the books. I think he knew from my reaction to the chapter titles that the sale was made. 'Always attacked travellers and always regarded their killing as a sacrifice to Kali. Have you seen the film *The Deceivers*? It starred Pierce Brosnan, pre-Bond days, of course.'

The shop door opened at that moment, annoyingly, and an old friend of his came in, carrying a box of books. I saw it was time to go and paid what I owed. He wrapped the books carefully in green cartridge paper, then showed me to the door.

'Sleeman wrote another book,' he said as we stood on the step. 'Much harder to get hold of – called *The Phansidars or Thugs*. I could get you a copy, maybe pay around seven hundred pounds.'

'I'll try the British Library.'

'False economy. Think of the investment.'

It was starting to rain and I tucked my package inside my jacket. 'By the way, what was it they had in their pockets? The thugs.'

'Ah, the terrible murder weapon!' He grinned as he closed the door. 'It was a pocket handkerchief, of course.'

It was Sleeman's grandson James who did the calculation in 1933. One thug strangling eight men per month and active for twenty years, multiplied by all the thugs in India for all the years before anyone knew anything about it until its final demise in the 1840s equals, at a conservative estimate, one million murders. And most of those achieved with nothing more than a pocket handkerchief. *The Guinness Book of Records* adds that a single thug named Buhram managed 931 of the total on his own account.

The man who eradicated this criminal conspiracy became a hero of the British Raj. During the 1830s and 1840s, William Henry Sleeman, supported by seventeen assistants and about a hundred sepoys, hunted down and captured over 3,000 thugs. Of these 466 were hanged, 1,564 transported and 933 imprisoned for life. When the five-month siege of the British Residency at Lucknow was ended in November 1857, one officer remembered the portrait of Sleeman hanging in the building. Such was the importance attached, he risked his life to go back and save it. Listen to Lieutenant-General Francis Tuker, biographer, waxing lyrical about that same portrait in 1961:

> The mouth is firm, as we might expect of a man we know to be one of India's great servants, yet also it is mobile, well able to express at need a haughty or gentle mood, and to be stern or humorous at will. That mobile power is the key to character. We notice it especially in the eyes, the most remarkable feature of all. They are large, wide apart, and beautifully shaped: omnivorous eyes, observant in seeking to understand, because wanting to act out a purpose.

Despite such merits, however, Sleeman was no self-publicist: the task of selling the tale to the public was left to others. The day after visiting the bookseller in York, I followed up the thug story and ordered, over the internet, *Confessions of a Thug*, first published to great acclaim in 1839 and still in print. Written by Colonel Philip Meadows Taylor, a colonial officer in Hyderabad at the time of the thuggee campaign, it was not only the first successful novel set in India, it powerfully reinforced in the minds of the British public their picture of 'Hindoostan' as a place both passionately exotic and irredeemably savage.

Meadows Taylor had originally contributed a short article on thuggee to *New Monthly Magazine* in 1833, prompting its editor Edward Bulwer-Lytton to suggest a full volume, something the young English captain was well placed to do. In his memoirs, he records: 'Those famous discoveries in regard to the practice of Thuggee had recently been made at Jubbulpore and Saugor by Captain Sleeman, which made a sensation in India never to be forgotten . . . I volunteered my services in the labour of collecting evidence, and they were accepted. Day after day I recorded tales of murder, which, though horribly monotonous, possessed an intense interest.' Not only that but he had married an Anglo-Indian woman of Mughal royal blood and had plenty of opportunity to see India at its most romantic and exotic.

He set to work and, between tiger hunts and military exploits, a manuscript emerged. Once finished, he set sail for England, escaping death at Aden only to be incarcerated in Malta during an epidemic. Desperate to get his manuscript to England, he passed it through the bars of his isolation cell and it was spirited away to England by a Mrs Austin.

When Taylor finally arrived at Dover in 1839, it was to find himself at the centre of a growing literary sensation: Queen Victoria herself demanded to see the page proofs as they were made ready. On publication, long extracts appeared in national and local newspapers, in addition to glowing reviews. The Duke of Wellington called him to Apsley House, keen to reminisce about his own exploits in the first Mahratta War. Such was the impact of the book, the word thug itself was punched deep into the language, albeit soon to take on the modified form of 'ruffian', rather than the original 'deceiver'. The cult itself quickly became one of the most pressing issues facing British India.

The plot of *Confessions of a Thug* is simple: a murderous anti-hero strangles his way to fortune and fine women, some of whom he loves and some of whom he kills. Ameer Ali is evil certainly, but thrillingly so, a camisole-quaking menace, a dark-eyed man-tiger prowling the skirts of civilization. I imagined him as tall and thin with a wiry build and a wry smile under a bristling moustache, a man both brave and cunning. He was said to have been based on the real thug leader, Feringhea.

Ameer Ali tells his tale to his captor, a British officer like Meadows Taylor himself, but there is little moralizing on his exploits; in fact, the reader begins to rather like the man, finding him an entertaining companion in the same way as his victims do – until they get his handkerchief around the throat.

Ali constantly undermines our preconceptions of morality, behaving with principled decorum, then utter brutality. It is his fanatical devotion to the Hindu goddess Kali (Meadows Taylor uses the alternative name, Bhowanee) which leads him astray, that and the ritual eating of jaggery, or ghoor, the dark sugar cake with which Kali seals her pact with her followers. Beautiful women, children, nobles, honest peasants, they all fall under his spell while travelling; he spins yarns and draws them into liking, even loving him. Once that task is complete, he destroys them, as though the crime would have no piquancy without the element of treachery.

It is Kali, however, who deserts him in the end, enraged by his dereliction of her rules. Without her protection he is soon captured and condemned to die, realizing too late that the British are even more powerful than the goddess.

*Confessions of a Thug* was not the only account to astound the British public during the 1830s. The *Illustrated London News* offered sketches of thug crimes and there were popular books detailing Sleeman's work by Edward Thornton and Caleb Wright. In the *Quarterley Review* of 1837, Charles Trevelyan thundered, 'If we were to form a graduated scale of religions, that of Christ and Kalee would be the opposite extremes.' Thrilling first-hand accounts of thug territory and the work of Sleeman came back too. Mrs Fanny Parks included visits to a notorious thug temple in her diaries and did sketches while on tour with her brother-in-law, the Governor-General, Lord Auckland. He had an armed guard of

12,000 men, and yet the sheer horror of it all, the exotic cruelty, the desperate fragility of civilization in the face of such savagery were all well drawn. Such was the furore raised by thuggee, a small boy in a remote homestead in the Mississippi valley would hear of the cult of stranglers and recall the fact half a century later when visiting Benares, having by then become famous under the name Mark Twain.

It was not only rumours that spread around the world: seven thug heads, taken from executed men, were handed over to the learned scientists of Edinburgh by the Chief Secretary to the Government of India, George Swinton, in 1833. Careful measurements were taken and the conclusion reached that 'the mass of the posterior and basilar regions is large; the coronal region is too small to enable the moral faculties to exercise sufficient restraint over the propensities; and hence the natural tendencies of the individuals were to selfish and immoral courses of action.'

The doctor who supervised removal of the heads offered the information that thugs, while on the road, 'indulge in every carnal propensity'. And again, according to the measurements, 'the sexual feeling, as the table shews, must have been strong in most of the seven thugs.' This was scarcely surprising as 'the Hindoo cerebellum is uniformly well-developed.' 'The heads and characters,' concludes the report, 'exactly correspond.' (One story circulating at the time claimed that various dimensions sent from India had been mixed up and when the learned scientists chose the very worst example of thuggery, they actually selected the measurements taken from the Chief Superintendent for the Supression of Dacoity and Thuggee, Major William Henry Sleeman himself.)

Soon the thugs and their pursuers were appearing in further fictional works. In 1844 a French naval doctor named Eugène Sue published *The Wandering Jew*, a best-selling tale of oriental chicanery in which the thug leader, Feringhea, appears. Unlike Meadows Taylor's crime blockbuster, Sue's novel is now badly dated but remains interesting for its smouldering portrayal of Indians, their eyes heavy-lidded, their passions quickly aroused by the women of Paris. Feringhea appears as something panther-like:

[11]

his manliness touched by femininity, his power of love only excelled by his power to deceive. Feringhea was a genuine thug captured by Sleeman and his name, meaning Frenchie, came about when his mother gave birth during an attack on the family's village by foreign troops.

Feringhea's fictionalized literary career did not end there: he appears in the 1988 film mentioned by the York bookseller, the Merchant Ivory production *The Deceivers*, based on John Masters' 1952 novel. I managed to find a video copy – with difficulty as the picture was not a great success – then watched with fascination. It's worth summarizing the plot as it neatly encapsulates the generally accepted history of Sleeman and the thugs.

William Savage (a thinly disguised Sleeman played by Pierce Brosnan) is a British officer in charge of a remote and peaceful area where his local ally is the Thakur, a charming and bejewelled Eastern potentate. One night Savage witnesses a murder by a thug gang and manages to apprehend them. Under duress, one suspect, Hussein (Saeed Jaffrey) confesses that there is a religious cult of killers who sacrifice travellers to the 'six-armed goddess of destruction, Kali'. The cult is spread all over India, he says, and has murdered millions over hundreds of years. Savage goes to his superiors but is unable to persuade them to fully investigate. In fact, they point out, he has been over-zealous in locking people up without trial and must be relieved of his post.

With this blow, Savage decides to go undercover disguised as a weaver, Gopal, and join Hussein on the road. He will discover thuggee from the inside. It is a reckless course of action, and unfortunately the kiss of death for the film: Brosnan looks like James Bond in an out-of-season production of *Aladdin*. However, passing over such implausibilities, Savage heads off and is tutored by Hussein in thug ways. He teaches him the secret language, Ramasee, and how to handle the handkerchief with devastating power. (A knot in the centre to break the larynx and a bunch of coins tied in the end to whip it around. Brosnan does at least manage that with aplomb.) Then there are the omens: these are very

[12]

important as they are Kali's way of informing the gang whether she approves their mission. A crow cawing on the left is favourable, but two owls hooting are very inauspicious. Hussein warns Savage, however, in no circumstances must he accept the ghoor, the sacred sugar of Kali, because its magical qualities will ensnare him. Savage, of course, sneers at such Indian mumbo-jumbo.

It is here that Feringhea appears as the leader of the thug gang Savage and Hussein join. Remarkably, considering the 144 years between, he is Eugène Sue's creation: dark, menacing and panther-like with hints of ambiguous sexuality. At his instigation, Savage eats the ghoor and falls under the spell of the evil goddess Kali. The Englishman is drawn to the exotic and sensual menace of the Orient: seduced by a dancing girl, he goes on to murder his first victim and takes pleasure in the kill. Quickly the east drags him down, his morals are upended and his qualities perverted. His bravery makes him a great thug and his charm is a lure to unwary travellers. All hope of Savage returning to his senses is gone: he has gone native in the worst manner possible for an English officer and a gentleman. He has strangled for Kali, had sex with locals and given make-up artists a bad name. Wisely, Hussein makes a dash for it, alerting the East India Company en route.

Savage's comeuppance is on hand: at a thug gathering he is confronted by his old friend the Thakur. As all Indians in the movie are portrayed as either weak-willed or cunning liars, it is hardly a surprise to discover that this amiable prince is a thug, and has been protecting his own gang for years under the noses of the British. The Thakur challenges Savage to prove his allegiance to Kali by strangling an informer – 'an approver' – and brings out Hussein.

Only in this extreme situation does Savage return to his senses. Hussein must be saved and the thugs exterminated. Fortunately for him Hussein's message to the Company was heeded and the cavalry charge to the rescue. Savage survives and is promoted to being in charge of 'Thug Extermination'. The film ends with the epigraph: 'It took twenty years to wipe out thuggee. Rather than betray the cult, over 400 thugs put the hangman's noose around their own necks. Thuggee had claimed almost 2 million victims.'

For all its shortcomings, *The Deceivers* was what I wanted. It put flesh on the bare bones of Sleeman's own published writings, the man being rather shy of personalizing his story. In addition to a single chapter in *Rambles and Recollections* there were several collations of thug interviews, statistical tables and lists of names, but very little storytelling. No matter, I could Sleeman out there in the soft night of central India, lounging next to the camp fire in pyjama, kurta and turban, eavesdropping on the tales of bravado and murder, then later compiling his relentless lists that would one day bring the criminals to justice.

If the word 'thug' itself has been sidetracked into the cul-de-sac of hooliganism and bully-boys, what remains of thuggee is the image of an oriental evil, addicted to its grotesque idols and murderous sacrifices. As James Sleeman put it in the 1930s, the thug is 'that fiend in human form, luring his victims to their doom with soft speech and cunning artifice'. The thugs were the personification of evil, the embodiment of all that was alien and immoral in the nascent British Empire and, by extension, the enemy within that had to be destroyed if that empire was to survive.

My first question was how could Sleeman have so completely eradicated such a tenacious and ancient cult, a cult that he claimed went back to the time of Alexander the Great? Had he in fact succeeded? Perhaps their descendants were out there, a remnant of the secret cult, sacrificing the occasional traveller to keep Kali happy in her dotage. I wanted to follow William Savage down that dark and terrible road. I wanted to find the Ameer Ali for our times.

Then, a few days after I had finished *Confessions of a Thug*, on an English summer's day, I opened the newspaper and saw him.

Not literally, of course, but the man I imagined him to be. A thin face, black hair and soulful eyes over a huge handlebar moustache, in his hand a rifle and behind him the jungle. The headline read,

'Indian Star Seized by Bandits', but the film star was not the man in the picture, that was the bandit and his name was Veerappan.

I already knew the name of India's greatest living criminal, a man thought to have murdered at least 120 people in a career spanning twenty years. In 1991, while travelling in India, I read some minor news items about the problem of sandalwood smuggling and ivory poaching. The biggest bandit was a Tamil, Koose Muniswamy Veerappan, whose fiefdom was a huge swathe of jungle to the south-east of Mysore. It was not that which made him newsworthy, however, it was his ruthless nature, gunning down any police officer or wildlife ranger who dared cross him, including five in a single incident in April 1990. His case interested me, but at that time Veerappan did not seem such a bizarre phenomenon. India was creaking towards economic liberalization with all the speed of an ox cart and the old India easily encompassed a bandit chief of almost mediaeval style. After all, bandits, or dacoits, had been a part of the landscape for centuries and there were many others who seemed more dashing and glamorous: Man Singh, the king of the impenetrable Chambol valley ravines during the 1940s and 1950s, and the 'Bandit Queen', Phoolan Devi, who emerged from the same ravines in 1983 to become a member of parliament. (She represented Mirzapur, home to a renowned Kali temple, until her career was cut short by assassins.)

At the start of the new millennium, however, times had changed; the country was a major computer software producer with a growing middle class who preferred swanky new Toyotas and Suzukis to Raj-era trams and cast-iron bicycles. The age of Gandhi was over. Not only was his party, Congress, out of power, but his ethos seemed forgotten. If he was lucky, the Mahatma might get to be a question on *Kaun Banega Crorepati*, the Indian version of *Who Wants to be a Millionaire?*.

The new power was with the middle class and they supported the Bharatiya Janata Party, the BJP, a party that had won them over with its modern toys and Hindu assertiveness. Perhaps more

[15]

significant, however, were the other people won over by the use of quotas for castes. Coveted government and railway posts now had quotas for Dalits and other low-caste groups. Until the time of Rajiv Gandhi it might have seemed that caste as an issue was very slowly withering away. (The 1977 election results were clearly divided geographically, for example. Writer Vir Sanghvi found himself scrawling 'none of your business' across a form that asked his caste in 1979, partially out of necessity as, like many others, he didn't know.) Now the issue was back with a vengeance: in first-class railway carriages you would hear urban legends of Brahmins forced to apply to be reclassified Dalits just to make progress in their career, while in third-class the injustices and tyrannies of centuries were not being wiped out by a few quotas for railway conductors. There was a new note of stridency in India, and with it came intolerance.

As the country changed in the nineties, so did the bandit Veerappan. He discovered kidnapping. It was much better paid than elephant-killing and less risky. With the new wealth around there were soft targets too, particularly the quarry-owners on the fringes of the jungle who had become rich supplying the building boom. He did not have to fear being turned in either: the average villager had no sympathy for the fat cats of Mysore, Bangalore and Coimbatore, or their political masters. Veerappan was careful to cultivate the ordinary man, he was one of them too: the son of a woodcutter, without education or contacts, born in the jungles he inhabited. That was the other thing about Veerappan, he had gone into the jungle, rejecting any amnesties and offers to come back into the mainstream. Just as Ameer Ali had stood for the old India of 1830, the one that the British would prefer to do away with, Veerappan's life had become a rejection of everything the new India of 2001 stood for. Not for him the mobile phones, the cars and the middle-class toys, Veerappan had an old Mauser rifle, a handlebar moustache and the instincts of a wild animal. He lived in the densest jungles, moving from camp to camp; if you crossed him, he killed you. For some, Veerappan was Colonel

Meadows Taylor's hero sprung off the page, an elemental force, the man-tiger prowling the edge of civilization; for others he was a madman, an ugly reminder of the past, desperately in need of caging or, better still, extermination. And then, just as India's Prime Minister announced that the twenty-first century would be an Indian century, Veerappan pulled off his master stroke: the kidnapping of Rajkumar, one of the country's top film stars.

I could have gone then, of course, chasing Veerappan. But there were other murderers to cope with first. At Wakefield Prison I was shown around the bleak exercise yard with its single mulberry bush – the origin of 'Here we go round the mulberry bush'. Then I stood with one officer by the corridor of razor wire and waited. After a minute a door opened and a man came walking up towards us, heading for the canteen in the immense forbidding block behind.

'You'll know this one,' said the screw, mentioning a name that I recognised. 'Serial killer.'

'Is he part of the reading scheme?'

'No.'

Sigh of relief.

Most serial killers get a book written about them at some point, a film may follow, a few are remembered beyond their own deaths. Some attract a kind of following: prison visitors who see something redeemable, presumably, in the caged beast. But they are bogeymen, demons, in that they are deranged, for us outside serving the same function as fairground freaks once did. Veerappan is not of that ilk, though his tally of victims is long enough. On the web I found hundreds of sites dedicated to him, even lists of Veerappan jokes. (I searched hard for one worth repeating but failed: example, 'How do you start a letter to Veerappan?' Answer: 'Dearappan.') There was also a mention of a new Bollywood film, *Jungle*, mythologizing his life. Veerappan was fast becoming a man whose political and social context obscured the growing pile of victims. In interviews I found prominent Indians

[17]

who would no longer denounce the man, but rather point to the crimes of his tormentors and the sufferings of the jungle folk from whom Veerappan had once sprung.

Surveying the world of crime in 1969, historian Eric Hobsbawm declared, 'On the whole social banditry is a thing of the past.' But here was a man, apparently intent on reviving the tradition, a man heading for that hallowed ground reserved for the heroic outlaw. The Tamil woodcutter's son was becoming Robin Hood.

At an Asian video shop in London's Archway Road I asked for *Jungle*, directed by Ram Gopal Varma and was told they had sold out.

'Veerappan has released Rajkumar,' said the assistant. 'Officially no ransom was paid but we do not believe that. Certainly, lakhs of rupees, maybe crores, have changed hands.'

The Indian numerical terms seemed as incongruous as an ox cart might have, had it thundered past behind the 135 bus. I asked if he knew the area where Veerappan operated.

'That is very terrible jungle area on the Cauvery river below Mysore.'

'Is it closed off? Do people go there?'

'How will you go there?' He laughed dismissively. 'There are no buses or Underground trains. You must walk long distances and there are many lions.'

'Tigers,' I corrected him. He was right, however, to infer that I was planning to go. Discussions of the thuggee cult and Indian crime had led to a list of names and numbers in India, people who might help, or had come across Veerappan. A few months of chasing demons in India beckoned. I decided to go, quite suddenly, with a ticket to Mumbai and a plan to get down to the jungles of the south, investigate the Veerappan phenomenon, then work north, into the heartlands of India where the supreme robber band of all time had once reigned: the Kali-worshipping thugs.

The talk to the Wakefield prisoners went reasonably well, despite a rebellion from the slide projector which jammed and refused to show beach scenes. There were seventy category 'A' men, mild-mannered and friendly, many of them smiling up at me encouragingly. Encircling us, about one hundred prison guards stood shoulder to shoulder, a few of them smiling encouragingly, most looking rather tough and not-on-a-dark-night, thank you very much. In retrospect I think it was the projector problem that led me to launch inadvertently into a story of gun-running in Yemen and where best to procure weaponry. The guards stopped smiling encouragingly at that point.

Afterwards, I presented certificates for achievement in reading and the prisoners crowded around, eager to talk. A few were socially awkward and clearly had to steel themselves for the ordeal of asking a question, others were charming and quick with amusing stories. In their blue trousers and shirts they could have been any group of male factory workers, relaxing after a lunchtime pep talk; it was peculiar to think that the hands I shook were responsible for more murders and rapes than there were people in the room. I was reminded of photographs taken by Samuel Bourne in 1863 in which imprisoned thugs are seated on a carpet and appear as a rather ordinary group of Indian men.

Among the Wakefield inmates, one individual waited politely while the others had their say. He was in late middle age, of kindly appearance, and only when a lull came did he edge closer. 'I'll be out next year,' he said. 'And I want to travel, go for years, maybe never come back – just keep going.'

'How long have you been here?'

'A long long time. I killed my wife.' He smiled ruefully, looking away. 'It was a demon in me. Madness. I loved her, completely loved her. But I killed her.' He sighed and looked me in the eye. 'But I'll be out next year and I'll go, straight away, I'll just go.'

# 2

# Bollywood

I took a room in the Colaba area of Mumbai, a hundred yards from the sea. It was a street of shady trees under which taxi-drivers slept next to their black and yellow Padmini cabs. The buildings were dignified old blocks with cool dusty staircases and balconies full of terracotta pots and line-hung laundry. On one building was a large sign: 'Mere Weather Pumping Station', and the pump worked day and night to produce fine clear days with a sea breeze. People strolled out to the esplanade to enjoy it in the late afternoon when the heat was gone, replaced by a warm golden light that made them look and feel good. Perhaps that's why Mumbai became a film-producing city, as did Los Angeles; it faces west towards a big ocean and the sunlight comes hurtling in across the waves like a bouncing bomb and explodes over the frontage, the long teeming reef that is Mumbai.

Each day I jumped out of bed and greeted that sun on the balcony, forever delighted by it, then took the suburban commuter train out of Churchgate station, returning before dark usually and by cab. I learned to ask not for my hotel but for Merry Weather, and I thanked Mr Merewether, whoever he was, because the words always tasted good in the mouth.

On the map, if the city resembles anything it is a long pitted tongue, lolling down to lap at the Arabian Sea. It is narrow, less than a mile across in places, never more than four, and covered in growths and excrescences: bits added on by landfill, islands joined up by causeways. The sea infiltrates everywhere with inlets, mangrove swamps, dockyards and bays. It surrounds the city and yet is ignored by it. Nobody swims, but everyone strolls besides this quiet, waiting sea, and if a wave ten-feet tall ever did come along, it would sweep Mumbai right off its reef and into the shallow salty waters of Thane Bay.

I had arrived in town at night, but there had been luggage delays and it was mid-morning by the time I managed to get a taxi, sharing with an Indian couple from South Africa on their first visit. They had just flown in on an internal flight from Calcutta and had a few days shopping before final departure.

I asked for their impressions and they smiled thinly. 'We are glad our forefathers had the foresight to go,' said Mr Patel.

'Hick-tick,' said his wife who had an accent stronger than biltong.

'When our great grandparents pitched up in South Africa, they got work on the sugar plantations,' said Mr Patel as we chugged out of the airport. 'Mum and Dad never did come back, but we always had a dream to visit home.'

I was in the front, arm stretched along the single seat, looking at the plastic model of Krishna with its flashing red lights and garland of jasmine. Padmini taxis are a Mumbai speciality, sleek and dangerous, like greased rats with white-walled tyres. I liked the fact that the meter was a clockwork giant outside on the near-side wing, but the dashboard shrine used the latest in digital LED displays. I liked the sign that read, 'This cab is hypothecated to Mercantile Bank'; it reminded me of Salman Rushdie's novel, *The Moor's Last Sigh*.

'Our frinds told us we're cray-zy,' said Mrs Patel, 'to come out here on our own steam. They said we'd be murdered in our bids.'

The great-grandparents must have come in the nineteenth century, I thought, when the great menace of thuggee was still remembered and travelling was considered, as a result, the most dangerous activity possible. Of course, my new-found friends' ancestors may have been thugs themselves: many were transported, though most went to the hated Andaman Islands or Penang.

'We consider they over-estimated the dangers,' said Mr Patel. 'It's just . . .'

He searched for the word.

'Hick-tick,' his wife said.

We made it through Mahim: a narrow bottleneck where the road and railway pass across a causeway and the squatters' shacks squeeze right up to the wayside. Through the holes and cracks I could see people sorting out waste paper they had collected. Then we were into the close-packed shops of Dadar but they were all shut.

'Is there a holiday?' I asked the driver who frowned at me, blankly uncomprehending.

'Do you speak Hindi?' I asked the South Africans. 'Or Marathi?'

'Oh, sure,' said Patel, leaning up to lean on the seat and engage the driver in conversation. His head waggled earnestly. 'Christmas, huh? Eid shopping open closed, huh?'

The driver face cracked into a broad smile. 'Aha! You Indian fellow, is it?'

I had never spent enough time in Mumbai, always rushing through on the way somewhere else, but this time I was forced to slow down. I'd dashed away from England with one pair of trousers and no haircut. I wanted to sit and read a bit, collect my thoughts, see if I couldn't worry up a few contacts to visit.

There was an internet place in an alley close to the hotel. An internet place, not an internet café: a narrow dark room with computers and people squashed elbow to elbow, young men mostly, all writing application letters for computer college. I hadn't realized at that point, hadn't cottoned on to what they were really doing.

I walked up there every day for five days, past the street dwellers: women on their haunches surrounded by naked children, doing their long beautiful hair in the gutters, all the serenity and shit of India in that small daily ritual.

On the fifth day I got the email I needed, from a friend in London. 'Why don't you call this guy Gulshan,' she wrote. 'You are interested in crime and he's a Bollywood star who always plays villains. Isn't that what you want – villains?'

Later I sat on my verandah and wondered whether to follow this one up. There were several film connections: Veerappan's life story was already in film, his hostage Rajkumar was a star (though of the Karnatic film world, not Bollywood), and the Mumbai Mafia finances many Bollywood blockbusters. Three good reasons. I rang the number, a mobile, and a young man answered.

'Yah!'

'Can I speak to Gulshan?'

'Sorry, he's in make-up. Who's calling?'

It was my first bit of Bollywood glamour: the personal call-minder. I left my hotel number and Gulshan called back that afternoon.

'Kevin!' he said, a richly toned Indian voice. I could hear the traffic behind him. 'We've just finished my interview up here at *Times of India*. I'm on my way home for a bite to eat, then we have a night shoot out at Juhu.' He said something to his driver. I gathered that my friend in England had warned him I might call. I wondered how she had described me.

'Come on out to the shoot,' he said. 'It's in a five-star hotel that we've taken over. I'll introduce you to some people.'

I had been out to Juhu once before, to see the beach, a lovely long stretch of sand where the Mumbai glitterati like to hang out. Not that anyone should think this is the South of France: even glitterati hangouts in India have their paan-sellers and their little wooden carts selling chat, down-home nibbles served on plates made from leaves.

Travelling out to Juhu, I thought, was simple. Take the train. I walked through Colaba to the Churchgate terminus and took the commuter train with ten thousand others, out along Marine Drive, stopping at Grant Road and Mahalakshmi where the oncomers simply charge at the packed crowd in the open doorways, brief-cases in their arms like rugby balls. Some managed to stick, others bounced off and had to wait for the next train. I read the ads: 'Squeeze-to-Please Tomato Sauce', 'No Sex Before Marriage Organization'. I missed my stop at Vile Parle because I could not move and had to get down at Andheri further up the line. By the time I got out to Juhu it was dark.

Juhu is dominated by well known glitzy international hotels, but it took some time to find the Horizon as it had closed for business a year before. When I finally walked in the gate I could see the dark mass of the unlit hotel above and the huddle of film company trailers and cars. There were lights on in reception, the brilliant spotlights of a film set, but the steps up to the door had been rebuilt to form a balcony. I followed the cables around the side and in through a gap in the wall. People were moving quickly: carpenters carrying wood, men holding walkie-talkies, two youths measuring distances across the lobby, a pariah dog scuttling across with a samosa in its mouth. I wandered up some steps and into what was once the lounge bar, a room twenty yards across and packed with equipment and people, all intensely focused on a backlit screen in the corner. In front of this were two men, both dressed in piratical head scarves and with heavily made-up eyes, one of whom was toying with a huge dagger.

'Silence!' bellowed someone out of the darkness. The room settled, but not fast enough. 'Bloody Indians,' added the voice to some laughter. Then, 'And action.'

Very slowly one of the men lifted the dagger dramatically and held it high, the camera glided forward, the knife was lowered, very slowly, into the hands of the other. They both glanced over their shoulders, eyes flashing. There were some hissed words of Hindi, entirely superfluous: every exaggerated gesture, every black line of make-up, every stitch of cloth, all reeked of shifty character and dastardly crime.

The two men hung there for a moment, then slunk away in opposite directions.

'Cut!' shouted the director. Instantly there was activity. Two youths dashed forwards and mopped the brows of the actors, two more handed them cold drinks wrapped in napkins, another took the knife, two more handed them their mobile phones, another measured the distance from the tip of a nose to the camera. As he was talking one of the actors spotted me and raised his hand. With the acolytes still dabbing at his forehead, he came around the camera.

'Kevin! Hi, I'm Gulshan. We're just doing a take. Let me introduce you. Akashti!' It was the director: plump, bearded, sensibly in shorts and tee-shirt for the heat. 'Akashti, Kevin Rushby – top writer, very famous, from UK. Kevin, Akashti – top Bollywood director, many famous films.'

The director shook hands and sped away.

'Tea?'

There were two youths bearing tea cups behind us. We took tea and went to a sofa where a plump middle-aged man was sitting with a smooth young man in red shirt and slacks. The young man was talking on his mobile and smoking affectedly.

'Kevin, let me introduce Raj – one of the top scriptwriters in Bollywood, many famous scripts. Raj, Kevin, top writer from UK and very famous.'

We shook hands. The mobile phone conversation next to us finished and the young man casually held the phone away from his ear; a boy jumped forward to take it.

'Sharat!' The young man turned his head slowly, so as not to disturb his quiff and cravat. 'Meet Kevin, top and famous writer, come here from UK. Kevin, Sharat, top Bollywood star, the real thing, a Bollywood star.'

[26]

We shook hands.

'Be cool,' said the star, already rotating away from me. 'Just be cool.' A boy dived forward with an ashtray to catch his dying cigarette. If acting, and over-acting too, is a staged deception, then a star, I decided, was clearly a person who is never off-stage – like a good thug really.

Gulshan was having his hair brushed. 'I have to do a take now, Kevin. Stay and chat with Raj.'

The star was called away too and I sat with Raj.

'I am branded as a gangster writer,' he told me.

I asked how he got his ideas: did he do much research? He gave me a mildly amused look. 'Research? I read the newspaper, I live in Mumbai, I grew up here.'

'Don't you try to meet gangsters?'

He gave me a smile that was hard to read. Did it mean, 'We don't deal with reality,' or did it mean, 'In Bollywood the gangsters come to us.'

'How long does a script take to write?'

Again he looked amused. 'Sometimes there is no script when they start shooting. Sometimes we use the same one we used before.'

Do they change it a lot while shooting? Do they ask him?

'Sometimes. If I am here they may ask, out of politeness. The scriptwriter is badly paid and not important.'

The man was as laconic as a gangster movie and our conversation petered out. I was relieved to see Gulshan coming across from his second take. 'That one was a wrap. Why not come and see the set.'

The scriptwriter was up and away immediately. Sitting alone was clearly dangerous; people might think you were badly paid and unimportant.

We walked through the mêlée of people and stopped at a double doorway. 'You see they took over the whole building, so this long corridor has been rebuilt for our next take, five minutes in a single shot with a steady-cam, lots of co-ordination needed.'

[27]

He had a great voice, richly toned and slightly plummy, weightily enunciating each word.

'Who are you playing?'

'The village snake.'

'You're always the villain?'

'Always – I've played the villain more than three hundred times.'

He turned and a boy handed him his tea, another mopped his brow. My own boy was there too, bearing my tea. I took a sip and, copying Gulshan, handed it back to him. We set off strolling down the corridor, the tea boys following discreetly. The more important you were, the slower you moved. The star of the movie, though apparently around twenty years old, moved like John Wayne at fifty. Gulshan, however, did Wayne at eighty. The electricians, the grips, the mobile phone guards and tea wallahs – they all did the six-year-old. Slowing down your body language created the effect, illusory perhaps, that you were a steady centre around which the crazed energetic universe revolved. I'd seen gurus do the same thing in ashrams.

I asked about the film.

'It's big budget – good backing. We're shooting all night here, then I am off to Hyderabad to shoot something else.'

'You're doing two films at once?'

'No, I am doing fifteen movies at once.' He enjoyed my surprise. 'That's normal in Bollywood – different to Hollywood. I've worked there – on *The Second Jungle Book*.'

Around us were gilt-edged mirrors, grand plasterwork, chandeliers, rich colours – all faked up. There is no realism in Indian cinema, no attempt to pretend that this bears any relation to the average bus driver's life; it inhabits a world consisting entirely of fake mansions, the type seen in *Dallas* and *Dynasty*. If it gets outdoors, it is into high Alpine meadows in spring. Once that was Kashmir, but the troubles there have forced them out to Switzerland recently.

'What's the difference between Bolly and Hollywood?'

[28]

'There they have a script and everyone is involved! Over here you have one big fat man who knows all and doesn't feel the need to share it with the others until he's forced. So costume don't know what the stars will wear, the sound man hasn't a clue what he might need to record. Even the actors know next to nothing.'

'Why?'

'Fear of copying, but also when Bollywood started actors were just mouthpieces. They were dropped if they asked any questions.'

'And how have villains changed over the years?'

We had come out of the building and were crossing a lawn towards a second building.

'Initially the villain was the landowner, the zamindar, and the farmer was the hero. It was exploiter and exploited over crops, land and water. Then the farmer got so oppressed, he took to the hills, picked up a gun and became a dacoit, a Robin Hood. Then the city audience became bigger and they never saw a man on horse carrying a gun and shouting "*Jai Bhawani!*"'

Bhawani is one name for Kali: *Jai Bhawani!* Victory to the goddess! Her name is on every page of Indian crime, like a monogram on a pocket handkerchief.

'City people wanted city villains, so we had the gold smuggler in white suit smoking cheroots. At that time gold smuggling from the Emirates was big business. Then we had the businessman as villain. After that corruption became big and we had the policeman as villain. Then there was a run of assassins. I played that so many times: the man who is totally evil, just comes on with a gun and kills. Next we had the dons.'

'You mean godfathers, like the one out in the Emirates – Daud Ibrahim?'

Gulshan didn't like bringing things around to reality, he wanted to stick with the movies.

'The dons became boring. We had the same three photos in the papers for years and most of them moved abroad.'

'What about Veerappan? What do you think of him?'

'They asked me to play him but I turned it down.'

'Why?'

'Not enough money and it's not fair to play a real person when I don't know much about him.'

'Were you afraid to do it?'

'Not at all.'

'He's the real thing though, isn't he? A charismatic baddie?'

'He's an embarrassment for India. We are trying to be a modern country and along he comes and makes all our advancement look like a piece of shit.'

We climbed over a low parapet and entered a large country house.

'Look at this – all wood – built on the grass.'

I touched the walls. It was indeed all false, a brilliant pastiche of a tycoon's residence, full of fabulous carving and workmanship – all the skills of Indian temple art now being put to good use by the Bollywood directors.

'If you want to talk about the way things are,' said Gulshan, 'speak to Mahesh Bhatt – top director and producer.' He held out a hand. 'Cellphone!'

The mobile phone appeared in his hand and Mahesh was soon on the line, talking – he was a top talker too. 'Kevin! You picked a great subject. Crime in India. You know India is anarchy that works. Take this fellow Veerappan, the bandit, how can that happen in this supposedly modern society? All the politicians taking the balcony view of a complicated terrain and claiming to have solutions while this man is out there; he doesn't exhaust himself with self-questioning, there is a place where he confronts the dark side. He kidnaps a big movie star, Rajkumar, a big top star, and we see how incapable we are of locking horns with the terrorist.'

I felt I had to direct this conversation a little. Gulshan was now in discussion with a youthful man with a clipboard.

'Mahesh,' I said. 'Have you ever met a gangster yourself?'

'Now, Kevin, they have decided to take Bollywood by the

[30]

jugular and break organized crime. They have the media going and they come down on producers who are then paraded in front of TV cameras, sending the message we are inches away from breaking the backbone of organized crime. If you dissent you are anti-nationalistic or marginalized by ridicule. It's a fascist state and they give lectures on democracy to Pakistan. These gangsters use satellite phones and internet and operate like multinational corporations with proper management and agendas, not eye-patches and cutlasses.' I could see people moving past and around me. That's the bigshot English writer, on the cellphone to Mahesh Bhatt, with a tea wallah waiting on him. Mahesh piled on.

'This rotten corrupt government reflects me. It reflects every other Indian. We are all rotten and corrupt to the core. India exports gurus and talks about introspection but hasn't the audacity to stare at its own ugliness. That's why I don't make films any more, Kevin, all that candyfloss and happy endings. It's exploitation and I can't do it any more. Give me Gulshan.'

I handed the phone back to the minder who took it across. When they had said goodbye, Gulshan and I toured the pastiche palace, met several top actors and top directors and top producers, then I watched the five-minute steady-cam take. This was sophisticated film-making, a balletic co-ordination of hundreds of people as Gulshan and another stalked through the hotel, the camera moving around them, extras flying past. Only the characters were outdated, but India throws nothing away, not if it works. Like the Ambassador cars in the street outside, unchanged since first invented as the Morris Oxford in 1948, the stock villains and heroes of Indian cinema continue to do good service.

I said goodbye to Gulshan at midnight in his trailer, two minders helping him into his Armani shirt and Levi 501s. He apologized for not inviting me to his apartment for a beer, but he had to be at the airport by four next morning.

Next day I took the newspapers with me to the esplanade and sat on the sea wall reading. There was an interruption about every thirty seconds: shoeshine boys, hashish-sellers, a chai wallah with an urn on the back-rack of his cast-iron bicycle – he was the only one I took anything from.

The shock waves of Veerappan's kidnapping and subsequent release of Rajkumar were still spreading: no ransom had been mentioned and some of the negotiators were being accused of Tamil Tiger connections. To what extent Veerappan had actually embraced the Tamil nationalist cause was unclear, but his rapidly growing status as a champion of the oppressed was attracting the attention of politicians and myth-makers. One article quoted a source as saying Veerappan walked backwards in little kangaroo hops in order to throw followers off his track, another said he could talk to the birds and they warned him of approaching dangers. Now a Special Task Force, the STF, was being reassembled (they had failed to catch Veerappan before) and the jungles in question sealed off. Helicopters, night vision equipment, satellite tracking by CIA, tribal trackers, trackers with dogs, commandos with 'special training in jungle warfare and tracking', every kind of tracker known to man – except perhaps those with crafty kangaroo experience – were going in. The papers were full of big-bellied blustery senior policemen making big blustery statements about Veerappan's imminent demise at their hands and how they had learned from previous mistakes. And they were expensive mistakes: apart from all the people killed by the man and his gang, the cost of searching for him was estimated at two million dollars a month for almost a decade.

I thought of the man himself out there in some jungle camp, sniffing the air and listening to the calls of birds, a man, I imagined, quite at peace with himself. As Mahesh Bhatt had said, 'He doesn't exhaust himself with self-questioning.' But all this attention obviously made a search for him well nigh impossible. Maybe I'd be better looking for people who knew, or had at least met, the man. And from what I read in the press those people were not in the jungle, not the green jungle at least, but down in Madras.

[32]

# 3

# A Working-Caste Hero

A FORTNIGHT LATER I WAS ON the railway platform at Madras with a second-class ticket to Salem in my hand and a steely resolve to get out of that city as fast as I could. The truth was I had no idea if Salem was a good idea, but I had to get out of Madras.

The platform was busy with people: a man scuttled along like a cockroach, his arms and legs horribly mangled and I remembered the crab man of Southern Sudan and a snippet of conversation once overheard on an English station platform. Two ladies staring idly across the tracks and one said, 'We're not designed to stand on two legs, you know.'

A long and thoughtful pause before the other added, 'We're not designed to go on all fours either.'

I avoided the soldiers with bags stencilled 'Happy Journey' or 'Good Luck', picked my way through several families of more than a dozen members seated on Samsonite suitcases with camouflage covers and found the right carriage. The bookseller's cart next to it stocked the *Deccan Chronicle* and *Times of India* so I bought both, plus *Frontline*, the Indian political magazine, plus a book that caught my eye, *Letters for All Occasions*. From the food stall I took a bottle of water. A cow wandered past, heading up the platform. A mother adjusted the grubby knitted bonnet on her child and wrapped a shawl around its shoulders; perhaps it was feverish, the temperature was climbing and sweat dripped from my nose. My bag was too heavy and I didn't like that, but books in India are my chief vice. I had Meadows Taylor's autobiography, Sleeman's too; I had a dream interpretation manual that ought to be thrown; I had *Anil's Ghost* by Ondaatje which I'd finished and might give to the right person if I found them, plus a series of Kali texts; I had *Common Wayside Indian Trees* and several language primers, and I had *Reef* by Romesh Gunesekaran. This marvellous book had tried very very hard to tear me away from the mood of Madras, the sheer bloody-minded, byzantine, buggeration of Tamil politicking. It had perched in my room at the broken-down nawab's palace-cum-guesthouse and sung sweet melodies of southern breezes and deep subtle pleasures. I had lain under the fan on long sweltering afternoons, drinking in the sensual simplicities of the tale. But in the end, it failed. My Veerappan quest had taken me too far in the bowels of the beast; I had heard too many times those cautionary incantations of the inveterate schemers: 'Do not speak of these things. Do not say you met me here. Beware of him. Do not trust that man.'

They had sucked me down into the swirling deeper waters and I had clutched at *Reef* and missed. Now I was here, running from Madras with a notebook full of dodgy contacts: men who had been implicated in the murders of other men, including that of Rajiv Gandhi, men who believed that the Tamil nation were fighting to the death for a homeland and that Veerappan was one of their number. I was expected in Salem. The jungle was not neutral, it was sealed off and my only hope of entry was via these men, or so they told me. I did not want to go to Salem; I did not trust any of them. I did not even trust my main informant in Madras, a man who had warned me about the others: 'Do not be trusting those fellows – not even with ten large barge poles.'

[34]

On the station platform a well-dressed man stood talking on his mobile phone while a beggar crouched before him, apparently unseen, hand out. I went to my seat and found it free, by the window. God Bless Indian Railways.

We passed through the suburbs of Madras. The eye dances feverishly across the tangled wires, the weeds growing through ballast stones, the decrepit concrete daubed with advertising slogans. The click and rattle of wheels deepens and a filthy river lies below. Once it must have been a sparkling forest stream, not this open sewer slobbered over by hairy grey pigs. 'India is a pile of shit,' an Indian had told me, 'in which are immersed a number of pearls.' The eye flicks onwards with the train, searching for something clean, or beautiful, or well made, like a pearl, but it finds nothing, and so the mind begins to drift away.

I had slowly made my way down India after arriving in Mumbai. Madras was my objective, but I had a need to dip myself in the Indian countryside before starting my task in that huge metropolis. I travelled by country buses, great rattling monsters where no one speaks English and seats are hard-won. All public transport in India is almost always crowded, the entire country constantly on the move.

In Arovli I was blessed by a local deity, and for the price of a banana tree given his protection against bandits; in Bijapur I bought a black doll that warded off the evil eye, and in Old Goa I visited the incomplete cadaver of St Francis Xavier, incomplete because a previous pilgrim had bitten off the man's big toe.

My main contact in Madras had come to me via various people and in confidence. He would speak freely, I was told, as long as his name and identity were concealed. Under the previous state government of Jayalitha, a sort of Tamil Mrs Thatcher, he had suffered imprisonment several times. In her photographs, Jayalitha looked cheerfully self-satisfied, like an Indian mum who had just made the perfect coconut chutney; in fact, she was a career politician with multi-nefarious associates and a conviction for corruption. Most of all Jayalitha hated the Tamil Tigers of Sri Lanka (LTTE) and their connections with extremists who wanted a 'Greater Tamil nation' based on Tamil Nadu state, parts of other Indian states, Jaffna and Mauritius. As Veerappan was now part of that grouping and Jayalitha was poised to return to power, any connection with his sympathizers could be dangerous.

Our first contact had been by email – now I rang him.

'Ah, Boss!' he declared. 'You arrive safely. Now you check email for directions to our meeting.'

'Can't you tell me now?'

'It is so complicated. Better you read and memorize.'

There was a throaty chuckle and a click as he put the phone down. His voice and our conversation reminded me of the film *All the President's Men* and I named him Deep Curry.

The streets of Madras were lined with internet stations, mostly tiny cramped offices, often with an extra mezzanine floor snuggled in at shoulder height so a couple of extra work stations could be set up. Here the male youth of India was downloading pornography, always with a twitching mousy finger to dabble across to that university application form, just in case Uncle Muruswamy should swagger in off the street. The strait-laced constraints of Indian family life had a new subversion. Instead of sloping off to a brothel, the young men would be 'computing'. Some internet places even provide tiny wooden cubicles around the hardware.

I had to wait twenty minutes for a station and then found Deep Curry had indeed sent a message, directing me to a particular suburb. 'When you reach, ask for the main bus stand. Outside is newspaper-seller. Wait for me there at nine p.m. and carry *Times of India* newspaper.'

Although I had two hours to get across the city, it proved insufficient in the snarling traffic. Riding in an open-sided auto-rickshaw in Madras is like placing your lips around the exhaust pipe of a dumper truck and inhaling. The drivers hold their turbans in their teeth and dive for tiny gaps between battered buses; your hair smells of diesel; your clothes are blackened; your lead content rises faster than by firing squad. I arrived exhausted a few minutes after nine, and before I had time to buy a newspaper from the stand I felt a tap on my shoulder. Turning around I found myself looking at a small smiling gentleman in white cotton clothes and metal-rimmed spectacles. He looked cool and collected.

'Come,' he said, 'let us take tea and cakes.'

We walked up the road, past the kiosks selling betel nut and cigarettes to a small tea shop. There were several home-made tables and a black hole in the back wall where three huge kettles were bubbling away on gas burners. One side wall was decorated with lurid Tamil film posters, the other with glass cabinets containing packets of biscuits. The tea when it came was as thick as oil paint and no more tasty.

'Now, Boss,' he began when we had settled in, 'I will tell you directly that I have never met Veerappan and I think it is impossible that you will.' He sipped the tea delicately. 'And let me say, first of all, that you are entering a maze, a dangerous maze, where there is no black and white, only grey.'

I glanced around the tea shop. The other customers were simple working men, all with moustaches and all considerably darker in skin than Deep Curry. He was, I guessed, a Brahmin by birth, revealed by his skin and thinner features. Perhaps he had chosen the tea shop because it was unlikely anyone there would speak sufficient English to understand us. I asked for some background, the Tamil perspective.

'Veerappan is, of course, a Tamil. Actually, he is a Vanniyar, a backward caste.' He held up a hand. 'Do not misunderstand me. I am a Marxist. Although Brahmin by birth I have no time for that Brahmin hegemony. I reject it.'

I nodded, uncharitably recalling the E.F. Benson novel *Queen Lucia* in which the doyenne of the Edwardian English middle classes has an Indian guru to whom caste means nothing, 'just as a Baronet and an Honourable must seem about the same thing to the King.'

'Veerappan was born on the western bank of the Cauvery river in a jungle area,' Deep Curry continued. 'That place was part of Tamil Nadu and was populated by Tamils. But with Independence the border was rationalized to become the river itself, leaving that community of Tamils as part of the Karnataka state. With industrial expansion, the river has now become a major flashpoint as both states claim its waters, for irrigation and hydro-power.'

'Where does Veerappan fit into that?'

'Veerappan saw the corruption of these outsiders destroying his forests. The man who taught Veerappan to smuggle sandalwood himself told me that Veerappan has saved the forests from denudation. And it is quite clear that local people trust him and go to him because they have absolute contempt for the forest officials.'

'Why?'

'They steal sandalwood too. And not only that, they have systematically destroyed all the self-respect of those poor people, the tribals and others, who inhabit the forests. I will say that.'

I tried to sip my tea but it had cooled leaving a thick impermeable membrane on the surface so I put it down and left it.

'Have you been there? To the jungles?'

'To the edges.'

'But Veerappan gets money from selling sandalwood. He must need political connections?'

'It is a grey area. There are so many grey areas, so many games being played. My hunch is that a top politician is holding his money for him.'

'And who is with him? On the ground?'

'He has about thirty LTTE men with him.'

'Where?'

He smiled. 'Beyond the Cauvery river, in the jungles there. They have sealed it off now.'

I took a small atlas of India out of my bag and had him point out the area.

'Here you are having Hogenakkal Falls on Cauvery river. Across the river begins the jungle.'

'Is there a town at Hogenakkal?'

[38]

'I have not visited, but there is something. It is a flashpoint: Veerappan shot five police dead there in 1990. Only to cross is not possible. Beyond the river is only terrible jungles.'

'How to get in?'

He scribbled some telephone numbers on my notebook.

'Try these human rights organizations. You need papers. I am telling you: without those, they will question you, lock you up and maybe beat you. Those police wallahs beat me. The most influential policeman is Devaram and he headed the last Special Task Force.'

'Is he a good man?'

'He is a monster. He used scorched earth tactics. Beatings, burnings, rape. Terrible things happened when his Special Task Force went into that area.'

'And now?'

'No one knows now. Journalists are not free to enter. You need some good papers and good contacts.'

I didn't say, but I had no intention of going in with a police escort. He drained his tea and paid the money.

'And the human rights organizations? Surely they can be trusted?'

He laughed. 'All have their agenda. I myself do not trust anyone. They will never show their cards to you, but will always try and see yours. There are so many issues here: politics, nationalism, caste, racism and, most of all, money.' He stood up. 'It is a maze you are entering, Boss, a huge maze.'

'Can we meet again?'

He thought about it. 'You give me a tinkle, in a few days.'

Deep Curry was right to be wary. As I delved into the maze, I heard how the STF had gone into the jungle area, looting and raping with impunity, how they victimized lower-caste tribal peoples. I heard that Veerappan was the only man standing up for human rights. But I didn't meet anyone who had been in the area, or who did not have a political axe to grind. I could see how the simple idea of Veerappan was useful here: how he could be recreated as an elemental moral force and then used in the urban

[39]

political jungle. There was no need to have much relation to reality – no one would ever go and check it out.

One night I was invited to attend a rally for Nedumaran, a Tamil nationalist who had met Veerappan and helped negotiate the film star Rajkumar's release.

I called Deep Curry.

'Yes, Boss, tell me.'

I told him.

'Nedumaran?' he said with a laugh. 'You are inside the maze.'

'Who is he?'

'He is nothing but he is dangerous. A Tamil nationalist who is using Veerappan and the human rights issues for himself. But he has met the man.'

I arrived at seven p.m. in a rickshaw. In the middle of a street had been constructed a makeshift platform and in front of it were around two hundred chairs mostly filled with young men. Many of them wore only black and had shaven heads. Around this central tableaux were large numbers of policemen in khaki, carrying lathis, the bamboo steel-tipped staves which have been breaking trouble-makers' heads since the days of the Raj. A few carried rifles with bayonets, conveniently fixed. As I sat down in the second row a man came and took some video footage of me.

'Internal security,' said a man behind me, 'don't worry, we are used to it.'

He held out a hand to shake and when we had done so said, 'I am Father Vincent – a Dalit, or untouchable.'

Then I understood the ostentatious handshake. Father Vincent, as he explained, was really at the sharp end in politics, with Christian churches being burned to the ground and Dalits struggling to redress the wrongs of centuries. 'Some say that if you find a snake and a Brahmin in your garden, you must first kill the Brahmin.' He chuckled at the idea. I didn't tell him I'd heard the same ugly joke in Malaysia, except that the Brahmin's role was replaced with a Tamil.

[40]

Several bearded intellectuals and priests were introduced to me and we all shook hands. Cups of tea, cigarettes and betel nut were being sold in the shops. A blind old man was led through the crowd by a tiny girl in a pink party dress and sat down at the front. Vincent told me of wrecked churches and the rape of low-caste women. The wave of resurgent Hinduism released by the arrival of the BJP in power had brought with it violence and extremism.

'Caste-ism,' said Vincent, 'that is the evil. Even in the church we are not being free of it – the priests are usually high-caste.'

The show got under way and there were many speakers, including a human rights lawyer who told a well-known Tamil fable of a crow who grabs a piece of bread from an old woman and flies up in a tree. A passing hungry fox spots the crow and sits under the tree, declaring what a beautiful voice she has, and will she please sing for him as it is so wonderful. The flattered crow opens her beak to sing and drops the bread.

'So we are all taught as children,' said the lawyer, 'to deceive others or be deceived.'

His eloquence was disturbed by the arrival of the main speaker, Nedumaran, a tall thin man with a benevolent smile on his face. Now the meeting had energy and the lathi-wielding policemen began to pace up and down. Speaker after speaker denounced anti-Tamil measures: Tamil lands stolen by Karnataka, Tamil language discriminated against in the English-speaking courts of law, Tamil fishermen deprived of their rightful seas. This was a long way from Delhi: no Hindi spoken, nothing but Tamil lettering on the signs. India here was a dirty word for an outside colonialist dictatorship imposed on Tamil lands. Veerappan was referred to several times. His police oppressors had used the situation to torment innocent Tamils, to steal their goods and rape their women. If they wanted to capture him, they could. How come Nedumaran (cheers) could get to Veerappan and help the release of Rajkumar?

This was rabble-rousing, finger-jabbing talk and I could see how Veerappan, a bandit, had travelled a road from criminal to freedom-fighter without ever having to stop kidnapping people and collecting his tithes. Evil had become good and perhaps the two could never be teased apart anyway. This was a world so sub-divided by caste, race, sex and wealth that common ground on anything was hard to find, least of all morals.

The long speeches soon defied further translation. Father Vincent was called away and so was I. A man at the side of the stage beckoned. I went over and one of the speakers came across and shook hands.

'My name is Kollattur Mani,' he said. 'You telephone me tomorrow. Nedumaran will not see you tonight.' He pressed a slip of paper into my hand.

When I rang the number and asked for Kollattur Mani, I was told he was not there.

'He is gone out-state.'

I tried another number. 'Father Vincent?'

'He took the train for Madurai this morning very early.'

I told them I wanted to meet Nedumaran and left my number.

Deep Curry gave a sharp exclamation when I told him.

'Kollattur Mani? You met him? He spent a year in prison regarding Rajiv Gandhi's assassination but was never convicted. He is an LTTE conduit. These are dangerous men, Boss.'

'I'm trying to arrange to meet Nedumaran.'

'Don't trust him with ten large barge poles.'

There was one particular Madrasi rickshaw man who would not leave me alone. He had fingerless hands, a result of heavy smoking, he said. From the roof of the guesthouse I could see him in the street, watch him snooze while foreign visitors walked past. But when I came out he would jump up and follow me down the road. 'Back to same place like yesterday? You like Tamil people – like Kollattur Mani – I see you meet him. You want we go to those people?'

I don't know what unnerved me more, this improbable interest in my business or his deformed and mutilated hands. I tried to avoid him but he would reach out and touch, with those mottled mucus-covered stumps. 'Nedumaran? He your friend?' I shrank away. He was untouchable; I couldn't bear myself for feeling it.

On my third visit to his house, I found Nedumaran at home. His office was adorned with photographs of Che Guevara, Lenin and various Tamil leaders. His desk was piled high with paperwork and books, behind which he sat, a kindly elderly gentleman in white.

I extended my hand and he took it. I realized that I had forgotten to remove my shoes at the door and this left me feeling uneasy, a little uncouth. After some pleasantries, I explained my purpose and he began to talk.

'Veerappan is the creation of a socio-economic problem,' he said, smiling a lot and stuttering occasionally. 'A problem where police and forest officials are harassing people and committing atrocities. Veerappan came forward to oppose it. He is a smuggler, but he is fighting for local people's causes.

'During the kidnapping of Rajkumar I received a cassette from him requesting help in mediation. At that time racial tension was high between Tamils and Kanaadigas [the people of the Karnatic]. The border between the two states was closed and merchants were saying that thousands of crores of ruppees were being lost. So I went, with Kollattur Mani and two others. We walked into the forest for twelve hours and then rested until Veerappan came down to meet us.'

'What was your impression of him?'

'He is an innocent man, a plain-speaking fellow; whatever he thinks, he will speak.'

The group had been taken to the camp where the film star was held, a simple temporary resting place outdoors. Ironically it was not because of any manhunt that they had kept moving, but because of wild elephant herds passing through on their yearly migration.

[43]

'We all ate together. I am a strict vegetarian but they all became veggie while I was with them.'

'How did negotiations go?'

'It took some days to convince him that kidnapping was not the way forward. Then he had some questions concerning prisoners in Mysore Jail. When those were answered, Rajkumar was released.'

All so easy.

'Those prisoners were released in exchange?'

'No. They are fifty-one persons arrested eight years ago and still without trial under the Terrorism Act – usually charges of giving food and shelter to Veerappan. Then there are four priests from Veerappan's favourite temple. One day he went to pray there and next day the STF arrested them. They are still languishing in Mysore Jail.'

He went on at length, detailing the excesses and outrages of the Special Task Force.

'I don't think they will catch him. Almost all the people inside the zone are Veerappan supporters.'

'What does he want for himself?'

'I asked him that question. Understand that his sister was raped by the STF and later committed suicide. One brother was killed and another is in prison. His wife was arrested. Veerappan said, "My family is ruined, but I am tortured by the innocent people affected."'

'Don't you agree he's a criminal?'

'How can a single man do all those things? I charge that some of our political leaders and officials have collaborated with Veerappan. Now they want to isolate him to get out of this affair.'

At that moment, a Tamil camera crew filed in and filmed me with Nedumaran. It had the air of an orchestrated scene. I was being used too. The human rights violations, Veerappan, me, they were all good material to be used to advantage. I thought longingly of the jungle simplicities of Veerappan's camp and a man who could speak 'whatever he thinks'.

[44]

The trail had gone cold with Kollattur Mani; I sat under the fan in my room in the nawab's palace. You could press a filthy switch and wait ten minutes for a grubby Uriah Heep character to come, then pay him way over the odds to bring a bottle of beer. If it left the shop cold, it was warmed by his paw by the time it reached the room, but the illusion of service was there. I re-read parts of *Reef*, conjuring in my mind the cool clear waters and the narrator's experience as he uses a face mask for the first time and gazes down into another world. Madras was like that for me, except it was an ugly underworld I peered into. The grime and sweat were getting to me, the hammering of children's stones on the shutters of my room, the ubiquitous stench of urine and rotten fruit, the endless phone calls and meetings in distant ugly suburbs, the lecherous male hippies who studied yoga in order to pick up the backpacker girls. I went to the Church of St Thomas where the apostle's bones are laid and prayed to the greatest doubter in history for some firm ground, some evidence, some progress, some scar tissue.

One day, when the bottle of beer came, there was a message too, a slip of paper bearing a telephone number that I recognized as Deep Curry's. I went down and rang him immediately.

'There is a fellow,' he said. 'He met Veerappan several times and he will take tea today at four p.m. with this Tamil fellow who lives near your place. He is a thinker, that fellow, a kind of writer you might say, or revolutionary.'

I wrote down some directions.

'The problem, Boss, is that you must not mention my name. This Tamil fellow and I have had some disagreements, you see.'

'Does he speak English?'

'He may not be friendly, I fear.'

'And this other man?'

'He may speak it, but quite probably he will claim otherwise. He knows Veerappan well, but lately he is sidelined. With Rajkumar and all, he was not involved. His influence is waning perhaps.'

'And how should I explain my arrival?'

[45]

'You are a writer, you will think of something.'

At a few minutes before four I had positioned myself across the road from the alleyway. I bought a copy of *The Times of India* and leafed through it. I smoked a Gold Flake cigarette and it gave me a headache. At ten past four I set off down the alleyway. Almost immediately I realised the impossibility of explaining my presence by some mischance, the story I had hoped to tell. The alleyway was dark, wet and a dead-end. No one came up here unless on some specific purpose. Lines of grimy washing hung out, hoping that sunlight might penetrate down the stained and dilapidated concrete canyon. Waste water ran down one side in a gulch and there were the squeaks of large black rats fighting over bits of detritus. On the left side was a series of doors. This was where bachelor men ended up living, some rejected by their families, others having given away their possessions and retired. Some had bicycles chained up vertically to waterpipes, one had a stack of yellowing newspapers and I assumed this must be the home of the Tamil thinker.

I stood listening outside. There were low voices. I knew I could stand there forever trying to think of a convincing reason why I came to be there, so I knocked.

There was a flurry of activity as people moved, then a voice called out in Tamil. I opened the door and peeped inside. It was a tiny room almost completely filled with tatty books and old manila files of paper. Clothes hung on a rack near the dingy ceiling. Down one side was a bench, clearly used as a bed by night, and on this sat a young man who smiled tentatively at me. In the centre of the room was a desk and behind that sat a more imposing figure, dressed in white cotton with an old bullish face. He did not smile or stand. He frowned.

'Vannakam.' This greeting exhausted my Tamil. 'I'm an English writer and someone told me you lived here.'

He scowled. 'You speak Tamil?'

'No.'

'Go away.' There was a pause. I must have looked rather

amazed at such treatment so he relented slightly. 'Bring a translator.'

'But you speak English.'

He shook his jowls furiously. 'I do not speak English.'

I wondered if I should point out that this, though brief, was delivered in perfectly comprehensible English. But I knew this was not the point. We were in Tamil Nadu, he was a Tamil nationalist. We ought to speak Tamil.

I once bought a book, optimistically entitled *Learn Tamil in 30 Days*. The pinnacle of the month's education was an exchange with a railway porter:

'What luggages have you?'

'Two suitcases and one bed.'

Even if I had been able to recall the vocabulary, it did not offer much help in the circumstances. Undeterred, I turned to the young man who I assumed must be my Veerappan contact.

'English writer,' I said, grinning like a demented doorstep sales-man. 'Sorry to bother you. Do you speak English?'

The older man butted in quickly. 'No, he is not speaking English.'

This was hopeless, all I could think was to state my business. 'I am writing a book,' I said.

'Not now,' bellowed the old man.

'About dacoits and freedom fighters like Veerappan.'

The old man stood up. 'Speak Tamil.'

I acknowledged defeat. 'OK, I'll go. Lovely to meet you.' Only as I turned my head away did I see the foot sticking out behind the door. There was another man there, sitting quietly. The old man saw my gaze and stepped around his desk smartly. I withdrew. The door was closed behind me and locked. This exasperating experience, one of many, marked the beginning of the end of my time in Madras.

A light tap on my shoulder disturbed my reverie. I noted that the train had left the grim suburbs of Madras and entered a land of dry padi fields and stands of areca palms. There was a small European gentleman standing over me smiling, a dapper character dressed in pinstripe shirt, linen trousers, brogues and a trilby. I had never seen him before in my life, but he spoke as if we knew each other, almost as though we were about to continue a conversation that had been interrupted only minutes before.

'You are English? No, don't tell me. The question is ridiculous: you sit there, with a book in your hand, which is,' he peered, '*The Yellow Scarf.*' His words came in little bursts, carefully enunciated. He looked like a parody of an Englishman himself, though he sounded East European or possibly Scandinavian. 'Only an Englishman, it is true, would carry such a book. Not a Pole. For in Poland, I can tell you, no one reads any more.'

'You are Polish?'

He blinked at me with watery pale blue eyes. 'No.'

He smiled at the man next to me and squeezed himself into the space between us. 'So, I always ask Englishmen, when I meet them, this question, "What is furmity?" Do I have the pronounciation – *fur-mity*?'

I hazarded a guess. 'I think it's a drink.'

He laughed genially. 'Thomas Hardy refers to it, if you recall, in *The Mayor of Casterbridge*, and I never knew. The characters drink it, you are right, during the fair, at which he sells his wife by auction. Do they still do this in England? No? A pity. The furmity, in fact, is the cause of it, laced with rum, if I remember. Now tell me why you read of yellow scarves. Oh, I should say, I am Edward. Pleased to meet you.'

We shook hands, then I passed the book to him.

'Is it good?' he asked.

'Interesting,' I said, 'but not good.'

'Ah! You know Francis Bacon? How does it go, "Some books are to be read, others to be perused, and others to be delegated." Yes! True, isn't it? So this is one for perusal, maybe,' he chuckled, 'or delegation. But the scarfs?'

'They were for strangling travellers.'

He dipped his head thoughtfully, reading the title page. 'Yes, of course. Thuggee Sleeman and the stranglers. I think the history of murder is a history of distance. First with hand, then dagger, then sword and gun. By the time of your Queen Elizabeth I, a cannon might reach to a mile. Now we kill from thousands of miles away. We no longer see our killer. But we long for that – ah! – intimacy.'

'But the thugs were not seen either. They strangled from behind.'

He weighed the book in his hand. I could see he liked to hold a book and talk, felt more comfortable like that, could think more clearly that way. Perhaps he was a teacher, more likely a professor.

'There was a deception, yes? But to be deceived is to lose the game. Innocence is a poor defence. I will tell a small story, from my experience.' He stood up and I knew for sure he was a teacher, he so clearly enjoyed standing with a book in his hand and talking, even though he had to sway to keep his balance.

'Have you visited Delhi? Of course you have. I was in Connaught Place, simply walking, when a boy, a very small boy, stopped me and pointed to my shoe, this shoe.' It was a well-made brown brogue, dusty with travel. 'To my surprise I discovered that this shoe was covered in yellow shit.' He mimed his surprise, staring wildly at his foot. The rest of the compartment stared too, two elderly couples, obviously intrigued by this performance.

'How is this possible? This huge and terrible shit on my shoe. The boy offered, very kindly so I thought, to clean for me, and when he finished I was so very pleased that I paid him thirty rupees. I then continued my walk.' He mimed ambling along. I could picture him there, browsing under the colonnades where the men sell books from blankets on the ground.

'Not five minutes passed before a second boy accosts me. "Sahib! Sahib! Your shoe!" And I look down and there is more shit, a huge ball of yellow shit. But I was suspicious. I have seen no shit on the pavement. I go to an old man shoeshine who cleans for five rupees and he tells me that the boys have invented a shit

[49]

gun. Yes, they shoot shit at your foot then they offer to clean! Can you imagine? India is this place where such ingenuity and application of intelligence is used by shoeshine boys. But of course, in a meritocracy we assume that a shoeshine boy is unintelligent, because his mind would help him rise higher, owner of a shoe shop, entrepreneur, founder of a boot polish empire. Yet in a caste society, that assumption is invalid; intelligence, you can say, is spread evenly and nobody can rise, or sink. No movement is possible so the humblest sharp-shooter of shit may be a genius. And likewise the top politician a fool!' He grinned boyishly.

Our fellow passengers were enjoying the story and trying to piece together what it was, nudging each other and whispering. Edward was getting excited by the genius of shit-shooting shoeshines. 'Look at how this place operates and tell me, am I right? The frustrated shoeshine, genius. Do you get a good shoeshine here? No. India is the very worst country I have visited in all the world for a shiny shoe. Why? They are genius shoeshines and spend all their time dreaming of ways to mess my shoe. They invent a gun. Brilliant. They train like special forces – shoeshine commandos, aiming, firing, targets. Imagine such time expended. All to mess my shoe. Now multiply such brilliance, such thwarted genius at every level of society and you have India.'

But it had not finished. 'So I continued my walk around the circle and once more it happened. "Sahib! Your shoe!" And I see really the biggest lump of shit. But now I am very angry. No, truly, I am insane. I am a wild beast. I don't care about the shit, but I want to kill the boy. I chase him through Connaught Place and I am shouting, "I will kill you! I must kill you!" I am hunter! How I wanted my old hunting rifle that we kept for the boars. He is too fast for me. Ah!'

He sat down, exhausted by the memory. 'Shoeshine boys are modern thugs. Do you understand me? It is a society, I will say, of twisted genius and strangling cults make sense – as much as anything.'

There was a silence while we digested this tale, and I looked out the window, chuckling at the pictures he had conjured up in my mind. We were stopping in that slow measured way Indian trains have, as though they will break the news gently. Edward asked what I was doing in India. I told him about Veerappan and something of my experience in Madras, how I had thought to make contact through the jungles of Madras, but was now fleeing. As I told him, I reflected once again that I did not want to go to Salem, and I didn't believe any longer that the people there could really help me.

Edward was taken with the idea of Veerappan's natural lair as a counterbalance to the concrete menace of Madras. It sent him off on a new intellectual tangent. 'In Russia as a boy, I remember the dirt. Yes, you see we hated the inescapable dirt. In summer it was dust. You simply could not escape. All we dreamed of was to be clean. And the rich distanced themselves by their clothes. Embroidery and fashion, you see, as social barriers.'

'You are Russian?'

The interruption irritated him. 'No, no, certainly not Russian.' He paused, getting his thoughts back on track. It didn't take long.

'You see, in India you have a conservative and constrained society where the boys go and watch pornography at internet shops. Edward Said was quite incorrect in his book *Orientalism*: the lasciviousness of the east is not a product of western minds; it is here. The constraint of the high moral code produces lasciviousness. You have one medal and two sides. Now this bandit appears in the jungle, the wild paradise, and he is the mirror image of the city's decay.'

'You mean evil creates good?'

The animation returned. Fellow passengers watched him, fascinated. He *was* fascinating. Dodging and bobbing his head, plucking words from thin air with the tips of his fingers, and the formerly shit-caked shoes restlessly scraping the floor like a horse eager to be galloping. 'You can say, societies create their own balance. The mechanism is subtle and unfathomable. Your bandit has to exist, and his wild untouched jungle must exist, only because the plains are full of terrible people holding shit guns. Now they say to you, the area is sealed off. This is because they must separate themselves, a barrier must exist. Like Brahmins walled off from the rest by threads and rituals and secret chantings. Like rich Russians with clean clothes. No barrier, no mystery; no mystery, no angels or demons. It is that barrier which you must cross.'

The train had eased gently to a halt and so released the cacophony of itinerant hawkers. Trays of snacks were swept along under the window as if on a conveyor belt and men in red jackets with aluminium kettles ran along crying, 'Chaieeeee!!'

Edward jumped up. 'I will bring tea and biscuits for us.'

While he was gone I got out my atlas of India. The line we were following headed west from Madras for a hundred miles, then turned south in a huge curve. Beyond the the apex of that curve, beyond the towns of Dharmapuri and Pennagaram lay the Hogenakkal Falls on the Cauvery river. And there was the barrier, the border between good and evil. I grinned to myself. Fanciful nonsense.

Edward returned with two cups of tea in earthern cups. 'Distance, you see,' he said cryptically. 'Human history is of increasing distance, but in India you could escape that distance. So the sun-baked cup is a tea cup and you taste the earth itself.' We sipped at India.

'Do they still murder with handkerchiefs?' he asked, opening some biscuits.

For me this was a poignant moment. Three years before I had accepted a railway station biscuit, unaware of the embedded drug, and spent the subsequent forty-eight hours unconscious in a monsoon drain. Now I was discussing murder, on a train, with a stranger, and accepting a biscuit.

'I don't know.' I couldn't see Edward as a thug, no matter how hard I tried.

'India throws nothing away,' he said. 'Why discard a perfectly good system of murder?'

He politely took the first biscuit as it had crumbled and dislodged the second for me. I took the third.

'Sleeman did a good job.'

'Aha! Of course he did. He became a thug, did he not? Crossed the barrier in order to understand. Then he destroyed them.'

We were clanking out of the station, soon to rejoin the countryside. I bit into the biscuit and sipped the tea. The earthern cup is a dying phenomenon in India and each time I drank from one I wondered if it might be the last. One day all will be plastic and the railway chai wallah will become a link in a huge industrial chain and there will be no need to feel the mud under his thumb forming the cup. No longer, too, will the passenger have the satisfying experience of hearing the *kerplop* as the cup breaks when chucked out of the window.

'I'm not so sure Sleeman actually did anything like that,' I said. 'The story is that he did. People really want to believe that.'

I might have added that I was one of them. But I had been through all the published works now, searched his thug family trees, his statistics and tables, his reports and transcriptions, and I had found nothing. The story of his epic undercover work, the William Savage version, appeared to have no reliable basis in fact.

Some passengers had got off and Edward had more room. He stretched out. 'Those who cross are revered, of course. In the Jain religion, saints are thirtankars, literally the crossers of rivers. Your English orientalists love that idea, don't they? Westerners passing themselves off as natives: old Etonians equally at home in a dhoti or a dinner jacket.'

I did not answer, staring blankly out of the window at the long flat farmlands. It was the start of the hot season and to a European, India becomes strangely autumnal: the grass yellows, leaves wither and fall, there is a smoky melancholy in the golden light of late afternoon. And yet, flowers begin to bloom, the trees of the country suddenly throw out brilliant splashes of colour and

[53]

the autumn is subverted by spring. There is a poem by Tagore, 'Last Honey'.

> I hear the song of the closing year like a flute in the rustling leaves,
> So smear your wings with pollen's chronicle before its fragrance flees,
>   Take all you can from flowers that summer heat will strew;
>   Cram the old year's honey into the hives of the new.
>   Come, come; do not delay, new year bees –
> Look what a wealth of parting gifts has been laid on the year as she leaves.

Around 1809, when William Henry Sleeman arrived in Calcutta, English attitudes to the Orient were on the move. Where previously Englishmen in India had been largely unconcerned with anything but money-making, they now found some Indian practices intolerable. A certain Dr Buchanan had witnessed ritual suicide of devotees at the Temple of Jagganath in Puri. To his astonishment and the complete unconcern of his high-caste hosts, local men had flung themselves to their death under the gigantic wheels of the original Juggernaut, the cart bearing Lord Krishna's image. Others reported suttee, the ritual burning of widows on their husbands' funeral pyres, and the poet Southey published an impassioned attack on the practice, 'The Curse of Kehama', in which the 'monstrous fables' of Hinduism were laid bare. Little wonder that in 1813 the anti-slavery campaigner William Wilberforce would speak out in the Houses of Parliament, condemning Hinduism's deities as 'absolute monsters of lust, injustice, wickedness and cruelty'. His views were to be picked up and developed by the powerful liberal reformers, Thomas Babington Macaulay and James Mill. The latter, a lifelong employee of the East India Company, wrote that Hinduism was 'the most enormous and tormenting superstition that ever harassed and degraded any portion of mankind'.

In literature the portrayal of orientals as a race of men inherently criminal was well established. From Marlowe's *Tamburlaine the Great* (1590) onwards, the east was as cruel and mendacious as it was exotic and sensual. Translations of *The Thousand and One Nights* hammered home the same message, successive editions heating up the sexual content with tantalizing glimpses of cross-dressing, lesbianism and harem orgies set against the constant clear theme of fraudulence. Many such stories were European inventions, as Robert Irwin shows in his absorbing book *The Arabian Nights: a Companion*, but not all. *The Thousand and One Nights* drew on numerous scholarly Arab collections detailing the misdeeds of bogus holy men and tricksters. *The Book of the Stratagems of Robbers* by Jaahiz of Basra appeared in the ninth century and detailed the many ingenious and occasionally disgusting practices of ne'er-do-wells: beggars who could swallow the tongue and then feign miraculous re-growth, those who could bind and paint limbs to mimic amputation stumps, even those who simulated appalling injuries by dangling animal entrails from their anus. Al-Jaubari, a thirteenth-century traveller, lists various useful recipes for bringing on ailments such as leprosy (boil up indigo-leaf, basil, cubeb and green vitriol) and blindness (apply monkey's blood and gum arabic). More dangerous to others – rather than just themselves – were the various assassins, stranglers included. One eleventh-century group in Persia were known to befriend travellers and then kill. The children of these stranglers were noted for their ability to recite epic poetry and endure police torture. Another gang, in thirteenth-century Cairo, used a beautiful woman to lure victims, then strangled and burned them. When finally caught, the gang were crucified and their house was turned into the Masjid al-Khanaqa, the Mosque of the Strangleress.

No reading between the lines was required in all this literature: the east was a trickster out to get you; the message ran through European perceptions like a blood-red thread. Even the literary greats were not immune. William Thackeray, born in Calcutta in 1811, used his Indian knowledge in *Vanity Fair* (1847) when Scape goes bust with a bad Indian investment. (Thackeray himself lost over £11,000 in the collapse of various Calcutta agencies.) In *The Newcomes* (1853) he has the swindling Indian financier Rummun

Loll cause the downfall of heroically upright Colonel Newcome. Always the racial stereotyping is clear: white and martial equals good; brown and business means bad.

If Thackeray was swept up by the racial stereotyping of the times, he at least ignored the reforming zeal that had gripped many of his fellow countrymen. Not so William Henry Sleeman, arriving in India in 1809, a bookish and ambitious young man who stood aside from the more boorish antics of his contemporaries. His attitude to Indians seems to have been benevolent and fatherly, tinged with regret over the untidiness of administrative life. Crime was an early obsession. India was a corrupted and degenerate society, filled with brigands and thieves, a place where no local was ever as trustworthy as your fellow Englishman. The borderline on that score, at least, was clear.

The train had stopped. I glanced up at the board and saw the name. On my map this was the small wayside halt closest to Hogenakkal Falls and suddenly I knew with startling clarity that I must leap off this train, forget the Salem time-wasters, forget the intrigues of Madras and head for my own particular border, Edward's line between demons and angels.

I jumped up. It was a small town and I had no good idea of how long we had already been standing in that station. Edward was asleep. I slapped his knee, waking him with a start.

'I'm going,' I cried, pulling my bag out from under the seat. 'I have to get off. I'm going to the jungle.'

I don't know if he answered. I dashed out, squeezed down the corridor past the orange-sellers who had climbed aboard and jumped off. The locomotive was hooting. I could see a short platform and building, behind it a few trees and some rooftops. Not much. I prayed for a bus station.

Like rats off a sinking ship, the orange-sellers descended and the wheels squealed. When it had done a few yards, I saw an old khaki rucksack tumble off, then a neat figure in pinstripe shirt and a trilby hat that fell into the dust. Next thing, Edward was standing in front of me, smiling sheepishly, holding something out for me and saying. 'You left your book, you see, and I wondered, shall I accompany you – at least to the river? It's so pleasant to talk. But look at this light and the colour of these walls, it reminds me of Tuscany. Shall we find a bus, do you think?'

# 4

# The River

AN AUTO-RICKSHAW TOOK US ACROSS TOWN to the bus station
where the life of the place was clearly centred. Here in a walled ring
adorned with Tamil film posters were rows of buses, trumpeting
their imminent departures, their drivers as proud and important
as a maharajah's mahouts. We were found seats right at the front
of the Dharmapuri Express next to the Krishna shrine with its
floral offerings and smoking incense sticks. Here we could enjoy
our own driver's masterful control of twelve separate klaxons,
each triggered by a steel lever, as we hammered out of town
and into the countryside. His control and artistry were superb.
Overtaking a bicycle? A trebled crescendo of body shots to loosen
rider from saddle, followed by two short basso profundo thunder-
bolts, blasting elderly gentleman sideways into padi field. Close
friend lounging in doorway? Double-stopped trumpet voluntary
and fruity belch. Village pastoral scene of strolling children and
elderly cripples in pantomime-like state of inattention ('Behind
You!') as behemoth bears down belching diesel death? Klaxon
inappropriate. Accelerate hard.

Edward and I talked little, wrapped up in the performance. The driver grinned gold and wiped his face regularly with a towel. He was popular along the route, children waved, after leaping aside, and he kept up a stream of conversation with the throng of standing passengers. In the countryside the people were preparing for the Pongal festival, bringing out brilliant-coloured powders to plaster their possesssions, mimicking the flowering trees that were bursting with scarlet and yellow. Bulls looked up sheepishly, their sides covered in blue handprints, an image of Krishna between their horns which were all decorated with red pompoms, marigolds and balloons. Outside some houses little ceremonies were going on with offerings of food and camphor lamps flickering. Children bellowed 'Happy Pongal!' and our organist responded with a fulsome concerto of horns.

At Dharmapuri we changed bus, ate sweetmeats and drank tea. Edward drew strength and, for no apparent reason, talked of Vietnamese immigration in Warsaw, theosophy, Tolstoy and Swami Vivekenanda. I gathered that he spoke the languages of Russia, Sweden, Italy, France, Poland and Germany, but not which, if any, claimed his allegiance.

It was late afternoon when we departed and the light came stumbling through the toddy groves in broken pipes of gold. At open shrines men were having their cattle blessed by the Brahmin and entire communities were processing alongside the road. It was wonderful to be out of the city and seeing India at its best, dressed up in brilliant saris. I felt the cares and frustrations of Madras falling away from me. India was full of beauty, grace and humour. I took deep breaths of the fresh air that came blasting in the open windows.

At Pennagaram we changed yet again and set off as the sun set. This bus had few passengers, all men, and I asked one of them why.

'It is because of these Naxalites,' he said, referring to the radical Maoist guerrillas who operate in many remoter parts of India. 'After dark, road closed at nine.'

'They shoot?'

'No, they throw stones.'

This didn't seem too bad.

'What about Veerappan?'

He laughed. 'Sometimes he is spotted, sometimes he kills police-men, but usually he stays across the river. Jungle is there.'

We passed a rusty park gate and descended a valley. The landscape was wild and uninhabited with vast dark areas of forest. There was no moon and soon we could see nothing but the track revealed by the headlamps. At length we passed the bright lights of a large fortress-like police station and came into the town, a much more dimly lit place.

The few hotels were all scruffy four-storey blocks in a row, opposite a few thatched shacks where simple food was cooking over wood fires: idlis and dhosas with a splash of sambal. Most prominent were the bottle shops where you could find all the Indian whiskies, rums and brandies you could want. We purchased by label quality alone: a bottle of Shivas Regal XXX, certainly the most original and imaginative brand name in all India. The rest were stuck in Anglo-Indian Army land with their McDowell's and Sapper's and Royal Ensign's.

The hotel was a shambles, the stairways and corridors full of rubbish, with furniture on its side and ashtrays strewn everywhere. It looked like an army of deranged apes had just sacked it, whereupon an army of deranged apes came bounding along the corridor chased by the receptionist and guard, only to leap out of windows and escape.

'They are very big nuisance,' panted the receptionist. 'Be certain to close all windows when not in residence or they will certainly steal your valuable items.'

The monkeys were actually behaving very much in accordance with local *more majorum*. When we had inflicted some damage on the Shivas Regal, we went back outside. Edward pointed out the large number of chickens on sale, plus the huge parties of drunken youths. 'I would say Hogenakkal is a romper room,' he declared.

'A place where, in fact, the vegetarian peace-loving sober Hindu can go wild. Such a society, of course, requires periodic bouts of unseemly behaviour and where better to site the battleground than this border zone?'

Gangs of wild-eyed youths were shouting at us and every jest met with gales of laughter from their friends. The road was lined with their tour buses, battered and wounded vehicles with temporary torn curtains and a complement of comatose youths sleeping with their feet out of the windows.

We soon tired of the teasing and retired to the Ape Hotel for more Shivas Regal. Edward insisted we use his room. 'I wish to show you my arrangement.'

He had strung up a voluminous mosquito net with a couple of dozen strings at low level, making walking around the room into a commando obstacle course. He had also changed the light bulbs to higher wattage: 'I always carry a small supply of 100-watt bulbs with me – the Indian hotelier is addicted to 30 watts. How do they ever read in such conditions?'

The switches had been cleaned of the usual grime with antiseptic wipes: 'If I am to live here for one night, I must have cleanliness.' As in my own room there was a table whose stains and bacterial infections suggested a life as a sacrificial altar. Edward's had been covered with a fine bolt of damask linen and a neat pile of books. 'Have you read Nehru's letters? Very beautiful.' His hand suddenly flicked out and grabbed a mosquito. He examined the dead creature in his palm. 'I am sorry, but they are my enemies. But look, he wrote so very clearly and wanted his weltanshaaung to be read, though it was muddled, they were letters to Indira – the apple of his – I saw many doctors but they are my enemies and I must kill.' His hand whipped out and destroyed another mosquito.

We drank the remains of Shivas Regal and Edward's talk became as muddled as Nehru's weltanshaaung. I decided it was time to retire to my room, making sure that all windows were closed.

\*     \*     \*

[62]

Hogenakkal was improved by daylight. The surrounding jungle hills came into view and the fresh air was invigorating. We strolled down the main strip to the falls, pestered constantly by gingelly men: lean, well-muscled individuals who promised a full massage with the large bottles of gingelly oil that they carried. The falls themselves are an impressive series of spouts and cascades running through about a half mile of boulders, gorges and islands. In the main gorge you could hire a basket-built coracle and spin gently through the rapids, helping yourself to drinks from floating coracle bottle shops just in case you were insufficiently dizzy. Some lads dived off the higher ledges, others lay in rockpools having gingelly oil hammered into them. The local techniques of massage looked quite robust: all around were obese Indian men grunting in pain while their breasts and bellies were pummelled. We did a boat trip and tried to discover information about 'the other side'. Our boatman made it clear he would not land there. 'Esh Tee Eff!!' he kept shouting. 'Very bad. This place OK. That place, Karnataka, Veerappan and Esh Tee Eff, very bad.' I asked others who came alongside but the lack of knowledge about the far side of the river was incredible. Are there villages? Roads? Buses? Markets? No one appeared to know anything, except that it was bad jungle and going there was not possible.

Edward lay in the coracle, his face hidden under the trilby, musing on the nature of borders. 'Morality ends here. Over there lies a new world where anything may be possible. Veerappan has not done this, it is these people's wish that such a place must exist, an anti-world, a moral opposite, a place without caste systems, taboos, sanctions. Here the norms are broken down, the illicit becomes licit. Veerappan has become a god. You must cross to the Underworld, Kevin. You are Orpheus. We others are content to touch the line only, you see, and withdraw intact, but you must cross the curry curtain.'

This talk, the Regal hangover and the coracle all together were too much: my head was spinning and I insisted on stopping. We made our way back along the concrete walkways, past the gangs of drunken youths and the accompanying sound of gingelly men's hands whacking flesh. In quiet sandy spots there were remains of fires and piles of white feathers and chicken bones. Amidst all the revelry and taboo-breaking, it was hard to remember that only across the river, in the jungles of Karnataka, there was the biggest manhunt in Indian history since the days of thuggee.

Edward had decided to take a bus back to Pennagaram and from there proceed in a big loop south and west to the Nilgeri Hills. He had been an entertaining companion, but I couldn't persuade him to come. 'Email me when you return from the other side,' he said. After he had gone, I realized that I never had learned his nationality, his profession or anything of his family.

I took lunch in the Ape Hotel restaurant and bumped into a policeman in the lobby. I was cautious; I didn't know how my desire to cross over the river might be taken.

'I want to go to Mysore,' I said. 'Can I take the bus on the far side of the river?'

The policeman waggled his head. 'Better you go back to Pennagaram then to Mettur and Coimbatore.'

'Is it closed over there then?'

'There is nothing but jungle.'

I laughed. 'I can walk then.'

A crowd of people gathered around us and when this was translated, they all chortled.

'You cannot. STF are there.'

I played innocent. 'STF?'

'They are hunting Veerappan.'

'Is he a bad man?'

The policeman smiled nervously and glanced at the faces waiting for his answer. 'He is a cunning man.'

'If you saw him now, would you shoot him?'

'No, I would call for others.'

This did not help me much. I needed some information or a guide to help me. I fell asleep that afternoon, listening to the receptionist chase monkeys around the corridors, then woke after dark. A saviour, of sorts, was at hand. I didn't know it but he was here. I got dressed, I stepped out of my door and he grabbed me. Big hairy arms, smelling of gingelly oil enveloped me. I heard a shout: 'Oh, beautiful skin! Oh, English fellow, be my friend!' I saw white teeth and a huge face, a twinkling Indian Little Richard with a coiffed bouffant hair-do, wearing a sarong and flip-flops. 'Oh, proper England! Oh, proper English fellow!'

We danced through the rubbish of the last ape attack, his hairy protruberant belly pressed against me, he giggling excitedly, me wriggling to escape. 'You took your bath already? And your meals? You want oil massage? I am Jayapalani, at your service.'

I managed to spin free of his grasp, feeling rather maidenly. Two friends of his watched from a doorway, grinning.

'Come take oil bath with us! Now it is night and best time!'

There was never any doubt in Jayapalani's mind as to my accompanying his party. While I hesitated, assuring myself that India was a place where an invitation to a nocturnal oil bath plus massage with a Little Richard lookalike meant no more than that, other people were organizing the expedition. Jayapalani had several gingelly men on a retainer and at a booming shout they all came running up the stairs. A green towel was thrust into my hand.

'This for you, my English friend. I made myself in my factory. You have many contacts with English towel merchants? You show them my product.'

Soon all was prepared and we set off. Jayapalani's arm casually over my shoulders, feeling my bicep. 'You are very white,' he purred. 'So very very white.'

Relax, I told myself, it's just occidentalism.

Out in the street Jayapalani had a high status, perhaps reinforced by a method unavailable to Englishmen in India for fear of being termed a neo-imperialist: he simply behaved like a spoiled aristocrat and loudly ordered everyone around, then paid them.

Our gingelly men took us among the rocks and the roaring river, then sat us down. Everyone stripped to their underpants, including the gingelly men. First of all, a litre of oil was poured gently over the scalp. This was then slammed into one's cranium with repeated skull-cracking blows to the fontanelle.

'I – tell – him – gen – tle – for – you,' said Jayapalani, his huge shiny tits being tackled by a wiry middleweight.

I was thankful for this as a knee went in my lumbar region and the vertebrae cracked like walnuts. Jayapalani's breasts were now being chased around his chest like runaway blancmanges.

'Why – you – come – here?'

I waited until my shoulder had been forcefully rotated through 360 degrees then yanked till it cracked. 'I came to see the jungle – the jungle where Veerappan lives.'

The name had an instant effect. All the gingelly men stopped their work and said, 'VEERAPPAN! Ah!' Reinvigorated by the invocation of a bloodthirsty bandit, they resumed their belabours. My arm was held out and a nerve in the bicep pinched. An electric shock zipped down my arm, straightening my fingers and making my ears itch.

'My friend – was kidnapped – by him,' said Jayapalani. 'I will tell you – later.'

For a further hour, I took my beating without complaint, then thoroughly marinaded and tenderized, I hobbled after the others toward the *pièce de resistance*: the waterfall.

This was why men come from far and near: to grab hold of safety bars and edge into position under hundreds of tons of falling water. The effect was incredible, like being a human nail under God's silver hammer. The water set up a thrumming noise inside my brain, the sound of thoughts, feelings, memories, electrical circuitry, synapses, all being pulverized into grey jelly. I was breathing water without drowning; I could see only shimmering darkness.

Supreme self-control. The management of cortical impulses until none appear unbidden. The final filling with emptiness. Samadhi. Nirvana. Hammering your head with large amounts of water is one way, like the head in the bass bin at a rave. Meditation on mountain tops (Shiva did 69,000 years of it), yogic alchemy with

[66]

breathing exercises, sensory deprivation by self-interment inside a Tibetan cave (the only western woman to have done this for the requisite seven weeks told me it works), intense prayer; these are all ways to achieve states of bliss. Breathing and oxygen are often a major part of the mystical road to earthly paradise. Strangulation is an interesting method of interrupting respiration, either permanently or temporarily. Sexual deviancy is often associated and several notable people, usually with right-wing political ideals, have been found dead in suspicious circumstances after applying a tourniquet to the neck. Hypoxyphilia, it's called. Other motives may be adduced to the obsession of western culture for restricting passage of blood to the cranium, especially in men, through ties. Women might argue this is scarcely cause for concern in many cases. All items of western male clothing – think suit, shoe, hat, waistcoat, overcoat – all have found favour with women, except the tie (excluding Dietrich). A tie signals manhood and virility because any tie-wearer is open to immediate and painful death by asphyxiation. The tie draws attention to the vulnerable point like a boxer dropping his guard and taunting an opponent: go on, try it, see if you can. Ties restrict breathing. Loosen your tie, get high. Hurricane Higgins had a doctor's letter saying he couldn't play snooker in a tie. Captain Sleeman's judicial disposal of thugs always employed hanging. Stand under a shower and breathe. Less oxygen. As close to a fish as you ever will. You enter another world. The water drums on the shoulders and relaxes the muscles. Stop breathing for more than three minutes and, if you are an average person, your body ceases to tell you to breathe. You are alive but no longer know how to prevent death. You die because your body simply forgets to tell you to remember to breathe.

Jayapalani pulled me clear.

'Tis Vil Bastard Furlong,' he said. Or that is what I heard.

We all went back to the Ape Hotel and lay on Jayapalani's double bed drinking Guru beer and playing gin rummy. The rules were strange and they played with four decks, one of which was 'original' and the others 'duplicate'. I could not see the difference

[67]

and every failure was met with roars of exasperation: 'No, no, no. That one is original, this one is duplicate.'

Supper arrived to save my embarrassment. A tray containing several bony river fish and some uttapams. Then I asked about Veerappan.

'He was born only fifteen kilometres from here,' said Jayapalani, lolling on the pillows in a silk sarong and looking for all the world like a debauched potentate. 'In a village downriver.'

I made a mental note of this. 'You said a friend was kidnapped?'

'Yes, he is a quarry-owner and Veerappan snatched him there.'

'What happened?'

'He made my friend walk many miles in the jungle and sleep out in the forest – he didn't like that.'

'Was a ransom paid?'

'Yes, the family paid one crore rupees [about £25,000] and swore never to tell anyone.'

'So the case was not publicized?'

'Oh no! Veerappan said he would come back and kill my friend if the police were told.'

'Did he say what Veerappan was like?'

'He said he could talk to the birds and animals – like Tarzan.'

I wanted to talk more on this but Jayapalani and friends had other, more pressing, concerns.

'How many cows do you own?'

'None.'

They were rather surprised at this. 'But lands, you must have lands?'

'No.'

They looked distinctly unimpressed. 'And your property? Is it large enough to accommodate us when we visit?'

'Well, I'm sure I can arrange something.'

'And towels. How many towel merchants do you know?'

I had to shake my head.

\*　　\*　　\*

Next morning I went back to Jayapalani's room. The three men were already awake and into their first round of gin rummy. I explained my plan to Jayapalani and he nodded. There was a distinct impression that interest in me had faded after the discovery that I was not a cattle-herding gin-rummy-playing landowner with towel trade connections, but he called one of the youths hanging around the corridor.

There was some quick explanations in Tamil.

'This youth has a boat,' said Jayapalani. 'If you pay him well I think he might take you to a place downriver. From there you will have to walk – and you must go now as he must return by sun-setting time.'

'How much do you think?'

He traced a number on the pillow where the youth could not see. I nodded. 'OK.'

Twenty minutes later I was at the riverbank with my bag, having said goodbye to my friends. The coracle was lifted into the water and I boarded. All around the morning's revelries were getting started with youths, already drunk, flinging themselves into the water from high cliffs and tinny Bollywood music rattling off the boulders. It felt like setting out from Disneyland to find the Hole-in-the-Wall gang.

The noises soon faded. Rangnaut, my boatman, paddled us out and the current sent us swiftly downstream. The forest thickened on either side and kingfishers darted across. I had been told that elephants crossed the river in places and it was certainly not deep or too strong a current in this, the dry season. On the Tamil shore there were occasional villages, thatched huts surrounded by a thick brush fence. In the narrow strip of mud at the water's edge, the people had planted rice but we did not see anyone. Ahead were impressive jungled mountains and as the hours passed, we moved in among them, paddling and drifting on and on down the river: spin to starboard, spin to port, spin to starboard, spin to port.

\*     \*     \*

It was some time after midday when we stopped. Rangnaut helped me ashore, then dragged his coracle up out of the water. I had now crossed the river and stood for a few moments enjoying a rather spurious sense of achievement. At least there were no burly policemen ordering me back into the coracle. We set off across some small fields and came to a shack where two women were sitting, watching a naked child play in the dust. They stared at me in astonishment, but when Rangnaut spoke to them they pointed towards the forest.

After fifteen minutes we hit a distinct dirt trail heading south-west into a steep-sided valley. Rangnaut made gestures to show this was the way, then waved goodbye and set off back to the river. Within a few seconds the forest had swallowed him up and I was alone.

I hitched my bag over my shoulder and set off. It was hot and dusty work, the track covered prettily in fallen yellow flowers. There were no birds, no sounds at all, in fact. The mountains ahead promised luxuriant jungle, but I wasn't there yet; this was scrubby forest, tinder dry, too slender to offer shade.

Until then I had had little time to think about this enterprise. In the light of what I had been told in Madras it was foolhardy, but then I did not believe much of what I had been told in Madras. There was a border here, it was true; a border between two states that Veerappan and any other bandit could exploit, according to how the separate state governments were disposed. But if this was truly an exclusion zone, I had entered with remarkable ease. No one had yet leaped out on me and demanded paperwork; there were no shouted commands to go back. By all appearances this was a tranquil slice of forgotten India.

I came to a small shrine and stopped for a while. There was a tiny pagoda and facing it a black stone cobra. Inside were some broken shaivite tridents. So much in Indian iconology is superficially devilish to a western perspective: Shiva's tridents akin to Old Nick's pitchfork, Kali's bloody maw like a vampiress. Images writhe with serpents and extra limbs; violence and death are ever present. No wonder that Macaulay, Wilberforce and others were so vehement in their condemnations, conveniently forgetting that the symbol of Christianity was a crucifiction.

As I sat there a man in a grubby loincloth came strolling past, his wife five paces behind him in a tattered sari. They stared, heads turning as they walked. I smiled, waved, shouted 'Namaste', but there was no response, simply those heads turning until they could turn no more.

I walked on myself, coming after a mile or so to the brim of a natural bowl. It was a lovely spot: a fertile valley about a mile across with jungled mountains rising up for about three thousand feet all around. Stands of mature toddy palms gave shade to emerald green padi fields where a few villagers were working. Beyond them were the houses, easily visible with their new pantile roofs. In all my Indian travels I had never seen roofs like this, so neat and well made. I wondered how these had been paid for.

No one appeared to notice my approach. The country lanes, broad enough for a tractor, were deep and shady with toddy palms and thickets, like the old roads of India where travellers feared bandit attack and turned, fatally, to their fellow wayfarers for security. I certainly did not expect any bandits here, only STF. Veerappan's family had lived in this area but they were not here now: his sister was dead, one brother too and the other in prison; his wife had fled across the river Cauvery to Tamil Nadu and his parents were most probably dead.

Two women, whiplash thin, were persuading a calf to drink water when I passed barely twenty feet away. Neither appeared to notice me. This was not a community on red alert. As I got among the first houses, men appeared and came alongside me. One smiled.

'Angrez?'

'Yes.'

'Reporter?'

I smiled. 'What is this village?'

He waggled his head. 'It is Gopinattam – home village of Veerappan!'

We both laughed and I looked around with interest. The birthplace of India's greatest living bandit was impressive in its well-swept simplicity. Each one-storey house had blue distempered walls and a deep shady veranda, the front pillars set in a low wall where the people could sit. This wall also held a notch where a fire burned, more often than not heating a large blackened kettle. The hard mud yards were clean and decorated with rice powder mandalas and brilliant marigolds grew in pots.

There was an atmosphere of gentle industry, of people busy about their tasks, but not so much as to ignore the unusual visitor. As I walked up the street and examined the plinth where the village gods were displayed, my welcoming party swelled to several dozen people. One man spoke some English and I asked why the houses all had new roofs.

'The temple committee paid,' he said, pointing over towards a large brightly painted temple. 'Sri Mariaman.'

'And Veerappan – does he give money?'

The question in translation elicited laughter from the crowd. 'Veerappan does not come here now.' I nodded though I was not convinced. The man continued: 'The STF destroyed his family house and they all ran away.'

We strolled to the village tea shop and in the broad shady porch, drank several small glasses of Boost, a malted drink. Then they showed me their temple on the outskirts of the village. The jungle was quite close here: frothy stands of bamboo edging the fields, then forest rising up on the mountainside. Inside the temple on either side of the deity house were garlanded portraits of a young man and I asked who he was.

'Srinavasan – wildlife officer.'

The story came out with some prompting. Srinavasan had been assigned to Gopinattam as a wildlife ranger. Very quickly he had won over the locals with his generosity and incorruptible nature. But this had aroused Veerappan's jealousy. There was gossip too, tales had circulated about Srinavasan and the bandit's sister, tales that had travelled through the jungle and reached the ears of Veerappan.

Srinavasan had persuaded Veerappan to talks in the village one night in 1991. But as the bandit approached, something changed his mind, or perhaps he always intended to renege on the deal. Instead of arriving unarmed, as agreed, Veerappan crept up to the meeting point and shot Srinavasan dead. Press reports say he beheaded his victim, but my informant hadn't heard of that.

'You see across there,' he said. 'That was the place. The Veerappan house was there. His family were woodcutters and went to the forest to collect firewood.'

'Have you seen him recently?'

'I knew him before he ran to the forest – twenty-five years ago. They were living over there when I was a boy, not inside the village, but close to the jungle.'

I formed the impression that the family were not part of the complex interwoven core of the village, outsiders already perhaps. Cutting wood and familiar with the jungle, they were unlike the majority who were farmers, planting their padi and fearing the tiger's attack. For them the jungle was a menacing shadow at their backs, but for the woodcutter it was the source of a livelihood. The family were very poor, even by local standards, and Veerappan had not mingled much. At the age of seven or eight, his grandfather taught him to hunt, using a gun that he had got from the British.

When Veerappan first came to the authorities' notice, it was for illegally felling sandalwood trees. His dependency on the village was purely emotional after that, visiting his family. But Srinavasan had upset that relationship. He was a wildlife ranger, a man dedicated to bringing the jungle under government control, taking out the human element from its savagery, tidying things up ready for exploitation by tourists or loggers. To someone like Veerappan the ranger with integrity was probably a bigger threat than the corrupted official who could at least be subverted. Perhaps Srinavasan had deliberately used the sister. I could well imagine

[73]

the powerful forces of male rivalry and doorstep gossip leading to such a tragic killing. I asked if there were no distant relatives remaining.

'They are all gone. The house is destroyed and no one goes there. They say there is a she-elephant who comes to drink water in that place.'

'And what is your opinion of Veerappan?'

There was much discussion about this among the crowd but the man was swift to answer. 'He is fifty per cent original and fifty per cent duplicate.'

'You like gin rummy?'

'I like it too much.'

The people were keen for me to appreciate the temple from the outside. The figures on the roof in particular had been carefully painted with brilliant realism.

'By a Muslim,' they told me proudly. 'A graduate of Bangalore University.'

I liked that they told me this, and their obvious pleasure that a Muslim had done a good job. The gentle friendliness of the comment reminded me that I had yet to see a uniform.

'Are there police here? STF?'

'The police are having their duty, and we too have our duty.'

What did that mean, I wondered aloud.

'It means the STF do not come here.'

We returned to the tea shop for yet another glass of the village favourite drink, made with great panache by pouring rapidly at arm's length from one glass to another until it was both foaming and cool. It was now late afternoon and the light turning golden. I asked if there was anywhere to sleep in the village.

'Better you go to Yum Yum Hills,' said my friend. 'A bus will come here before sunset and you get down at Palar Gate, then take any vehicle to Yum Yum Hills.'

Rather to my disappointment Yum Yum was only a Tamil mispronounciation of MM, which itself stood for Mahedeshwara

Malai. This was the site of Veerappan's favourite temple, so the prospect of spending a night there was interesting.

Half an hour later a battered old State Transport bus came thundering up in a cloud of dust. I squeezed on board and we departed.

I suppose I was relieved to discover that the STF and the no-go zone scarcely existed. Nor had I seen any signs of tension. We rolled and bounced through the jungle for a couple of hours and I was just relaxing, forgetting the way the men of Madras had built up the myth of jungle, when we stopped. Everyone was shouting at me, 'Palar Gate! Get down!' I hauled my bag through the passengers and stepped down into the road, straight into a gun barrel.

To be fair, it was not pointing at me with any intent. I had stepped into its line of fire. But I couldn't hide my surprise and the policeman noticed. As the bus growled away, he marched me across the road to a group of men sitting under a tree. Palar Gate was a bridge, I observed, and heavily guarded. I said hello and sat down, conscious of the impression that I had been marched at gunpoint across the road. There were two young officers in uniforms and an obese sweaty man in stained civvies, reeking of cheap booze; they smiled, he scowled. Sadly, he was the senior man. He began interrogating me.

'Your name?'

I told him. He took out a notebook and handed it to me. 'Write your full name and address.' I gave my correct name and address. Why worry? I hadn't done anything wrong.

'Your bag?'

Obviously it was my bag, but I didn't take the cue to open it. I was very aware that sitting right on top, just under the zip, was a fat file of cuttings on Veerappan.

'Where did you come from?'

'Hogenakkal.'

There was a rapid discussion with the others in which I heard Gopinattam mentioned forcefully. I began prattling on about the wonders of Hogenakkal gingelly massage.

[75]

'How did you come that way?' asked Scowler. 'Did you visit Gopinattam?'

'It's quicker,' I said. 'I'm going to Yum Yum Hills, then Mysore.'

It was very difficult to say Yum Yum Hills without grinning.

Scowler spoke sharply to one of the young constables and I guessed, rightly, that the top man was being called.

'Passport,' said Scowler, and I showed him. He weighed the maroon book in his hand, reading each entry carefully.

The top man now appeared, a kindly faced gentleman with a large white moustache. He smiled genially, shook my hand and enquired, 'And what is your sweet name?'

I knew I was all right. Scowler tried to arouse suspicions, explaining that I had come via Gopinattam and looked like a foreign journalist, but he failed. The top man simply waved them away. 'There's only one Englishman we fear,' he laughed. 'Nasser Hussain, the cricket captain.'

It was a joke all India was enjoying – Hussain having been born in Madras. The display of amiability completely stumped Scowler who was made to return my passport. We chatted about cricket for a while until a bus appeared on the bridge. Top Man despatched a constable to stop it. 'Take your enjoyment,' he said. 'The views are most splendid.'

He was correct. The road from Palar Gate up to Yum Yum Hills is a wonderful switchback ride, rising up and up through dense virgin jungle with endless vistas of misty ridges and deep dark canyons swinging past the windows. I sat on the gearbox housing next to the driver who was keen to talk. He broke the ice by passing me a small card that he took from his shirt pocket. I read: 'Emergency. I am a Catholic. Please call a priest.'

'Are you a reporter?' he asked. He politely insisted on eye contact while chatting. I told him I was a writer, not a reporter, and he was interested to know how I came to be waiting at Palar Gate.

'Very terrible place,' he said. 'Veerappan likes killing so much in that place. Ten years ago I was driving this route when he killed a ranger on the bridge.'

'Actually on the bridge?'

He waggled his head while hauling the wheel round and round. The bus seemed to be spinning on itself as first vegetation flashed past behind him, then suddenly open sky. 'Veerappan was hiding himself in a jungle place, then when ranger came across the bridge on the back of a police motorcycle, Veerappan shot him. He is a very wonderful marksman. Another time he exploded a land mine near there – it was 1993 – that explosion killed twenty-two commandos. That is why they guard it so much, always they are expecting him to attack.'

'Aren't you afraid he may attack the bus?'

'No, Veerappan loves the temple at Yum Yum Hills. He will never attack this road because his temple is on it. Additionally, he does not hurt the poor man.'

'Is it true then, that Veerappan is a champion of the poor?'

'It is true! People are hating STF because so many false arrests, beatings and even rapes last time.'

'And now?'

'Now is not so bad, but false arrests are there. If they find a letter from Veerappan you may get ten years imprisonment. The Chief Minister gets letters from Veerappan, but is he in prison?' Once again we span around, the engine digging deep. When we straightened he wiped his face with a towel. 'Veerappan loves this jungle. He has all that a man desires: a small television, newspapers, plenty of food. They will never catch him because he also is having a small bottle of magical water. With one drop of that water, he is rendered immediately invisible.'

It was a gorgeous late afternoon now, the sunlight stumbling across the seried ridges. Somewhere in there was the bandit and it was obvious that finding him would be well nigh impossible, the magical water was superfluous.

Tom Harrison, who fought in the Borneo jungles during World War II, once recalled how impossible it could be to find a man who wanted to be found, never mind fugitives. In one instance a man stepped from the path for a second and was lost. His companions searched and searched, but failed to locate him; some weeks later his skeleton was found by chance a few yards from the path, stripped clean by the ants.

Veerappan's ability to slip away has been a great contributor to tales of his magic powers, though cynics have suggested deep pockets have also been involved. There can be no doubt that he knows his territory and is alert to all the signals nature sends.

After much grinding of gears and steady climbing we had emerged on the top of the mountain, a hilly plain where the forest was interspersed with cultivated patches. Soon we reached Yum Yum Hills, a small rather ramshackle town grouped around a huge temple complex. The bus dodged several donkeys, then drew up in a dusty square next to the market. Saying goodbye to the driver, I got down and strolled into the market which was almost completely devoted to the temple. Most of the products on display were devotion-related: brass bells, lamps, rosewater sprinklers, incense burners, incense, sandalwood sticks, anodized pots for carrying milk to the gods and soap. I stopped then, looking at the blocks of soap piled up in elegant spirals and towers, big rectangular soaps in various colours. The seller smiled. 'You like to buy ghoor? Take to temple and make offering?'

Only then did I gather that this was not soap at all, but sugar. More particularly it was jaggery, or ghoor: the crystallized product of sugar cane juice. And this ghoor had been the holy sacrament of thugs, a substance considered so powerful that when eaten during a thuggee ritual, the consumer would have no choice but to become a thug for eternity. In *The Deceivers*, William Savage finds himself doing just that and, sure enough, within a few days the stiff upper lip and public school backbone have been dissolved, as easily as a sugar lump in hot water, by the seductive appeal of Kali. Then he strangles his first victim.

I went up and admired the display. 'Try!' said the man, holding out a piece the size of a man's Adam's apple. I did so. It was

[78]

delicious, both sweet, crunchy and with a slightly caramelized coconut tang.

'Very good,' I said. 'Do many people buy ghoor to offer to Shiva?'

He shrugged. 'Really I cannot say because it is not my shop. I only watch for my friend.' He stepped out around the counter and stood next to me weighing a few crumbs of ghoor in his hand.

I told him about the thugs and their sacrament and he nodded as though this was common knowledge.

'There are so many thugs these days.'

He did not mean stranglers. Thug is a commonly used name for con-men, cheats and general villains.

'Are you a merchant?'

He laughed. 'No, I am a policeman. Actually I work with the Special Task Force. Have you heard of them?'

I touched his hand. 'Let me have some more ghoor.' I just couldn't resist the thought that I had first tried the thug sacrament from the hand of Veerappan's pursuer.

The owner of the stall had returned while we were talking and the STF man offered to take me down to the temple. We left my bag there and set off.

He was quite ready to talk about the hunt for Veerappan. He had been assigned to it ten years ago and drew 3,500 rupees a month extra as danger money, quite an incentive not to end the drama I reflected. When I mentioned that I had not seen much sign of activity from the STF, he waggled his head in assent.

'We are not trying to catch him. You wait: in three months there will be a political settlement.'

This seemed barely credible, but others I spoke to confirmed that the STF were only going through the motions of searching. They knew Veerappan was unassailable and were waiting for the politicians to sort it out. Meanwhile, generous allowances were being enjoyed. There are two takes on this financial angle: one is that the allowances are too good to lose, the other that the STF men lose out in big city bribes and are worse off. This man was adamant that he didn't want Veerappan caught.

It was dusk when we reached the temple and there was plenty of activity. On the path that surrounded the high perimeter wall, naked devotees were rolling full-length and a painted elephant was doing a good business blessing penitents. For the less pious there was a pavilion where, on payment of a small charge, you could see yourself in several distorting mirrors.

We left our shoes with a boy and went to the front entrance of the temple. Here a sprinkler system built into the lintel washed our feet before the press of pilgrims carried us in through the turnstiles past a Brahmin holding a camphor lamp on a tray. I dropped a coin there and wafted the smoke into my face with my right hand while a brahminical thumb daubed the holy spot between my eyebrows.

It was a lovely temple inside: an inner sanctum was surrounded by a stone-flagged yard where there was plenty to keep the pilgrims amused. Monkeys scampered over the temple carvings; there was a holy phallus where couples could rest their hands and hope; there was even a chariot holding a deity that could be hired for circumambulations – the wailing horns were extra but a definite plus point.

In legend, the holy man who founded the place, Mahedeshwar, had come here eight hundred years ago riding on a tiger. The local people, seeing this, had petitioned him to help rid them of a terrible demon who was making the area uninhabitable. The saint then devised a cunning plan, fashioning some sandals from his own skin and taking them as an offering to the demon. Flattered, the demon put them on, only to burst into flames and die. Brogues booby-trapped with virtue.

It was appropriate that Veerappan should have chosen this temple. He was said to leave no prints, or he hopped backwards, or left animal tracks. Often in Indian folklore, the feet leave signs by which we may know the invisible powers, just as the Buddha was known by his five signs, including his footprints (the other four being the wheel of life, stupa, five pillars and lotus flower). Veerappan's weapon is the land mine, a foot-destroying booby-trap and something which has terrified local police as they do not have the equipment to counter the threat. The parallels with the legend are clear, but was Veerappan deliberately manipulating them? I have no doubt that, after his death, some will declare he was the reincarnation of Mahedeshwar, sent to rid the jungle of demons – the STF variety that is.

I slipped away from my STF man while he did his pooja and sought out the temple superintendent in the office. The walls around him were covered in large lurid posters featuring scenes from Mahedeshwar's life.

'Did Veerappan pray here?' I asked first.

The superintendent, a large middle-aged man, smiled paternally. He was clearly used to questions about the bandit. 'The one time I personally saw Veerappan here was in 1970. He was a young man then, and he came to borrow money from the bank.'

'He must have been a memorable man – that's thirty years ago.'

He either did not understand me, or feigned not to. 'He was just a woodcutter.'

'Did he come here three years ago and afterwards some Brahmins were arrested?'

'I have heard that rumour, but it is not true.'

'Has anyone ever been arrested?'

He didn't answer directly. 'The police never bother us here in the temple.'

'Is it Veerappan's favourite temple?'

'The newspapers say so but who can say for sure – except Veerappan?'

He turned away from me and spoke to one of the old men sitting around the room. I felt I had been dismissed.

Back in the courtyard the STF man was more forthcoming. 'It is certainly Veerappan's favourite temple, but he will not come while the STF are in town. It is too dangerous. Unless he came disguised. That is possible. Who knows what that man will do?'

[81]

We collected my bag and went to the guesthouse, a simple concrete box with, I was pleased to see, blankets on the bed. It was cold now the sun had gone down.

'Come and see headquarters,' said my STF man.

So it was that the same day I visited Veerappan's home village I found myself sitting on a sack of rice in the mess of the STF, the cooks fussing around me, offering dollops of sambal and rice. 'Another chappati, kind sir?'

There was a sense of camaraderie here, and busy orderliness. There was a very definite sense of this as separate from the outside, of not being at one with the temple and village. Men were introduced to me by rank and, as they came in, I progressed to more senior men, their English improving almost with each advancement up the heirarchy. The inspectors were a boyish group, affable and bright-eyed, each with a batman, a moustachioed Gunga Din character, hard men with forage caps pulled low.

'In one month we'll catch him,' one inspector assured me. 'We have men trained in jungle warfare and we are giving affection to the villagers.'

'I heard that the STF gave them beatings and torture?'

I could have added that it was the level of inspector most often accused. The man did not miss a beat. 'No, no, such things never happened. But before when we offered a man a hundred rupees for information, Veerappan would give a thousand.'

'And do you intend to capture him alive?'

'We want him alive, but he has cyanide pills – from his LTTE comrades. Don't you worry, sir,' he added, keen to assure me of their good intentions. 'I guarantee that within one month, the police will assassinate Veerappan.'

But later, when my sweet-shop friend took me back to the guesthouse, I heard a different story, whispered to me in the shadows of the gateway. 'They do not try too much,' he said, casting anxious looks around. 'When they go ten kilometres into the jungle, it is because they have information that Veerappan has gone twenty.'

[82]

I spent a couple more days in Yum Yum Hills, but nothing unusual was happening. The STF were busy cooking their curries and guarding their HQ, the pilgrims kept arriving, the jungle remained resolutely quiet. A walk into its green envelope was a marvellous experience, but an easy reminder of how impossible the STF's task was. They had realized that Veerappan would be caught by political rather than military manoeuvres.

There seemed little more I could do, but I wanted to meet someone who had suffered at Veerappan's hands, a hostage. There was no answer on Jayapalani's number in Coimbatore, but another enquiry brought me an alternative. His name was Senani, a wildlife photographer who had been held by Veerappan for several days before being released unharmed. I managed to get through to him in Mysore and arranged a meeting.

Mysore appeared an orderly but idiosyncratic place. Policemen in slouch hats and white galoshes were directing traffic while cows painted brilliant yellow with red horns strolled across. In the main bookshop I found essential reading like *Etiquette for Northern Italy* and *Critical Judo*. There was also a useful letter-writing crib book with all the usual job applications, family problems and 'decent' love letters ('I know you are a dutiful plus beautiful lady and can manage household affairs quite nicely'), but there was one surprise: 'A father reports to a police officer about the kidnapping of his little son'. The suggestion that a parent might alert the police by sending a letter seemed plausibly Dickensian – 'Drop this in the post, would you, darling? Shrikant is missing, you know.' The specimen letter detailed his son's appearance in touching detail: 'He is wheat-coloured, but stunted for his age. He wears silk half shirt and chocolate coloured half pant and polished black shoes. He will answer by the name Shrikant.'

Senani and his photographer colleague and fellow ex-hostage, Krapakur, met me in the car park of a restaurant. We sat in their jeep and had tea brought out to us.

'We were at school together,' said Krapakur, from the back of

[83]

the jeep. 'And even then, we were both interested in the jungle and animals.'

He was a few years older than his friend, in his early forties I would have guessed. It was Senani, however, who sat in the driver's seat and somehow appeared the senior partner.

'What were you working on at the time of the kidnap?'

'A film about wild dogs.'

'When was it, and where?'

'October 1997. We have a bungalow in Bandipur National Park, deep in the forest, a very isolated place. It's a base for us.'

I took out a map and got them to point it out. Bandipur is about fifty miles due south of Mysore on the northern slopes of the Nilgiri Hills. Its position made me realize the extent of Veerappan's territory: Hogenakkal was over a hundred miles north-east.

As their story came out, the two men became animated, competing to tell bits of the tale.

One evening, shortly after sunset, they told me, they had arrived back at the bungalow and were moving around, getting ready to start cooking some food.

'I was walking around the side of the house,' said Senani. 'I can't remember why, but it was a cloudy night and very dark. I think there was some rain: anyway the sound of my footsteps was disguised. As I came around the corner, I saw a figure at the window, trying to look in the house. I shouted at him, asking who he was. Next thing a gun was on my cheek.'

He had told the story many times but I could see he enjoyed reliving the moment.

'When I saw his face, I recognized him and said, "Oh, Veerappan!" He was very happy to be recognized and asked how I knew him. I said, "You are Veerappan. The whole world knows you!" That pleased him.

'Then I saw armed men running in the house, and I was made to follow them. Veerappan asked me how many people we were and where the gun was. They could not believe we did not keep a gun. That was impossible for them to understand. I knocked

[84]

on the bathroom door and said to Krapakur, "Don't worry, it's Veerappan."'

'I was actually in the shower,' said Krapakur, leaning forward now and grinning. 'I didn't know anything was happening.'

I had the impression that he was the tougher of the two; his actions in the hours that followed certainly showed he was capable of handling himself in a crisis. 'I put on some shorts and opened the door. There were three torches and three guns pointing at me. I hadn't heard what Senani said and when I saw them – they were wearing STF uniforms – I was furious that they had come in without a warrant. Then I saw the famous moustache.'

'Krapakur was cool,' said Senani. 'He wanted them to sit down and discuss things. Veerappan, though, he behaved like a top investigator, asking clever questions. He was convinced we were wildlife officers and had guns hidden.'

Senani had had a harder time in those first few hours. He was taller, somehow more commanding, but fresher in the face. There was the possibility that Veerappan had spotted that Senani might be the one to work on.

'He asked about the local rangers and, when we told him that the men had all gone to Mysore, he became angry. He said, "You are going to take us there to the ranger's house and call him out." I was sweating then. We told him the ranger's place was next to the police station and that he had gone to Mysore, but that did not bother him. He said I would lead them through the forest. When I said I couldn't do it, he ordered the boys with him to chain me up. He said he would shoot me if I didn't do it.'

Krapakur had shown his worth at that moment. Some of the boys had spotted a book about African wildlife and he offered to show them the pictures. They were very impressed with the elephants' tusks and also the guns of the African wildlife rangers, earnestly discussing types of self-loading rifles.

'I wanted a glass of tea and food,' said Krapakur. 'At first Veerappan completely refused – I think he feared poison – but then I persuaded him. The boys were fascinated by the gas lighter torch; they spent a long time inspecting it. Then we put on the lights, solar-powered, and that fascinated them. Veerappan too. He was a very curious fellow.'

The rain, however, caused a problem. Thousands of beetles had flown and were blundering in through the open door.

'Veerappan would not allow the door to be closed. It didn't matter about the beetles, I would say he cannot be comfortable inside a room.'

When nine glasses of tea were ready, Veerappan chose the one Krapakur should drink. Only then did he relax his fear of poisoning. At midnight, without warning, Veerappan declared that they were leaving. Still chained, Senani was made to lead the way, but instead of taking the path to the ranger's house, they walked deeper into the forest. At dawn they came to a lake where they stopped among a clutch of large boulders next to a dirt track.

'We discovered then that his plan was to stop a tourist bus full of VIPs,' said Senani. 'This lake was on the route into Bandipur from Park HQ.'

They watched while Veerappan cleverly deployed his men, taking a keen interest in the methods of ambushes. I could see that they had enjoyed it, even felt a part of the team, and Veerappan's psychology was acute: having treated Senani harshly, he now was friendly towards him and the man responded. 'He told us to wait by some rocks and he would bring the people from the bus to me for questioning. I was holding my chain and Veerappan asked me to let one of the boys do it, "So my men take it seriously."'

Senani's translation skills would be necessary, they explained, because Veerappan only speaks Tamil; the VIPs were expected to be Hindi speakers. When I expressed some surprise, they were quick to point out that the man was uneducated, barely literate. If there is something of the Robin Hood in Veerappan's story, it does not extend to him being a noble slumming it with the peasants. He is a working-caste hero, no doubt an immense plus point for those who support him.

A roadblock of rocks was prepared around a corner, then men

posted as lookouts. They watched as a bus came slowly up the track, then stopped at the barrier. Suddenly Veerappan was there, by the driver, with a gun, and he led him out very gently and pointed towards Senani and Krapakur, asking if they were wildlife rangers.

At all times, the two told the story as if they had been quite easily the masters of Veerappan. They were middle-class, high-caste; he was a common criminal, low-caste. There was an arrogance about them: they understood Veerappan, they had manipulated him, even tricked him. The rangers had been at the ranger's house all along; they knew very well how to find it in the dark; they knew the tracks and paths far better than even Veerappan. They had the upper hand, they had had the upper hand by birthright. But this little moment revealed Veerappan's masterful control. He knew the driver would know their faces and identify them.

'He brought the first passenger across to us then,' Senani said. 'He was a huge guy, six feet tall and overweight.'

Krapakur was laughing at the memory. 'He gave Veerappan a comical salute – and us! He didn't want to rub anyone the wrong way. But he was perfect kidnap material: well dressed and healthy, good skin.'

'I asked where he was from,' said Senani. 'And he had this tiny squeaky voice, "Delhi." Veerappan was not interested in him – maybe he thought he could not walk far.'

Slowly the men were interviewed and a scientist from Bangalore selected as a hostage. The bus had been carrying only a few tourists, most were menial workers, cleaners and suchlike. Loudly announcing that they had two hundred kilometres to walk and no more time, he ordered the party of hostages to set off, leaving the unwanted people behind with a cassette tape demanding fifty crore rupees ransom.

In fact they went only two kilometres but the message soon got back and the STF, once galvanized, spent several days scouring far and wide, but never on the park HQ doorstep.

Now the kidnappers and hostages settled in a routine with

[87]

little to do but talk, something Veerappan liked to do. He told stories about the animals, imitating their calls with uncanny precision.

'Each sound that a monkey makes,' said Krapakur, 'the baby's cries, warning signals, safety signals, food signals – he did each one so well, I could not tell the difference between him and the real thing.'

One day the bandit described how he had sat in a tree watching a leopard hunt langur monkeys. The movements of the leopard and the monkey calls were mimicked so well that they became entranced with the story. I could see that even the memory enthralled them as they recalled how Veerappan had become the leopard, sliding with infinite patience towards the feeding langurs. The guile of the leopard was what interested Veerappan, however. How it spotted a weakness and exploited it, eventually pouncing and killing.

There were limits to his knowledge, however: all snakes were treated as deadly. 'I had to show them which ones were harmless,' said Senani. His tone was contemptuous.

As the days passed, the two became friendly with Veerappan's men – boys really. Many had committed several murders and knew there was no alternative to them but a life on the run.

'We spoke to the boys about turning themselves in; we felt we could convince them of anything!'

There had clearly been an attempt to subvert Veerappan's authority and I wondered at the sway of human politics, the morality of it. The two educated men, symbols of an elite that none of Veerappan's band could ever hope to join, gently re-establishing the authority that was theirs by tradition. They were different to normal captives: capable of walking in the jungle, unafraid, even useful. Veerappan had responded in straightforward and guileless manner; he liked them. After some time, they told him they must go, that they could no longer be captives, and the bandit begged them to stay a little more, a few days, as he enjoyed their company. The feeling, however, was not mutual.

'He was a big bore,' said Krapakur. 'Veerappan is a third-rate criminal.'

In this way the civilized men had the advantage: with their ability to feign friendliness and tell lies. It struck me that, in all their story, Veerappan never once dissembled; he had deprived them of their liberty, of course, made them suffer a little, even put their lives in jeopardy, but he had not lied to them.

Eventually they helped their captor make a cassette tape for them to give to the Chief Minister of Karnataka.

'But he was shouting and there was no respect. We told him to be quieter, more humble.'

Veerappan did as they suggested, only insisting that there must be nine demands, not eight, as eight was his unlucky number. (The respectful civilized tape was delivered eventually and the Chief Minister's reaction was, 'Listen to him, he is weak. We'll kill him within a month!' The bandit, perhaps, had more of an instinct for politicians' thinking than the educated men.)

The more they spoke, the more I felt for Veerappan. He was a wounded tiger, lashing out. His tricks were learned from contact with civilization: like the hostage-taking which a policeman had suggested to him. His money box was small, his possessions limited to six aluminium plates, a pot for rice, five gunny sacks to sleep on, a kettle, a radio, a cassette recorder and a few ageing weapons. In money he was constantly tricked, his lack of education made him confused over big numbers. The amounts bandied in the press never reached him, siphoned away by mediators and negotiators. His family had been killed, poisoned, harassed and dispersed.

'He gets sentimental over his brother,' said Krapakur, referring to Arjunan who died in police custody.

And all because, long long ago, some city man from Salem, taught a young woodcutter to chop down sandalwood trees. Veerappan's story was that of the Delhi shoeshine boy writ large: a man with some genius, a spark of life, who finds a way to push the glass ceilings of low caste and illiteracy up and up until they

[89]

burst open. His crime was to kill the men who came to stop him and he called this dharma yuddha. A holy war, a jehad. It was his jungle.

But what of Veerappan's worst crime, the killing of the unarmed and much-loved Gandhian, Srinivasan? Had he spoken of it to the two photographers?

'He said Srinivasan had tied his weapons in a tree and called him to talk. Then Veerappan got a tip-off that it was a trap and he should look in Srinivasan's neighbour's hut. That night Veerappan came down and found two rifles in the neighbour's hut. That was why he killed Srinivasan.'

I had something to add here, an extra Machiavellian dimension: a police informant, one that must remain anonymous, revealed to me that it was a jealous policeman who had betrayed Srinivasan.

As to the reasons for the release of Senani, Krapakur and the others, there was, according to their account, nothing more than the fact that Veerappan liked them and gave up on a ransom. On the face of it, this seems wholly improbable. One would tend to assume that the price of continuing to work in Veerappan's fiefdom was a high one.

I had been interested in the phenomenon of Veerappan, seeing the foundations of a myth laid down. The bandit's own story continues to the time of writing. In some ways the kidnapping of Senani and Krapakur marked a turning point. Three of Veerappan's younger and less experienced boys turned themselves in. Another, Madesh, could not, having too serious a criminal record. He had particularly liked Senani and Krapakur and cried when they left. 'If I come to your house one night,' he said, 'will you give me tea?'

One year later he died, possibly poisoned.

Gradually the old brigand saw his merry men become a tattered and tired bunch of fugitives and at some point he fell in with the Tamil separatists. These were a very different type of fighters, politically motivated and accustomed to using modern contrivances

[90]

like cars and mobile phones. Despite their claims to be fighting for all low castes, their numbers were mostly made up of Vanniyars, the same as Veerappan. Probably that fact eased the birth of an alliance.

The separatists were not in good shape at that time. Campaigns of bank robbery and assaults on police stations throughout the eighties had brought neither followers nor funds. They were perpetually riven by disputes and any gains soon dissipated. Some resorted to legal methods, forming a myriad of minor political parties, but one diehard advocate of violence, Maran, made contact with Veerappan.

Maran had been on the run for almost a decade, building a collection of arms and ammunition by raids on police stations. Now he needed a jungle base and Veerappan could provide the necessary knowledge, plus some added notoriety. In 1998 Veerappan was spotted during an attack on a police post, soon he was making overtly political statements and broadening his vision.

Then in July 2000 came the thunderbolt: Rajkumar's abduction, reportedly instigated by Maran. With it came a list of demands that revealed the bandit's reincarnation as rebel leader: money was wanted, of course, but also the release of political detainees. Most astonishing was the demand for the erection in Bangalore of a statue to a Tamil poet.

Robin Hoods rarely emerge as social reformers. If they have any agenda, it is usually that the good old ways should be restored – in Veerappan's case, to the times when the woodcutter was the link between jungle and village. When wedded to social revolutionaries, however, the picture changes.

The furore resulting from the film star's kidnap was immense, the negotiations tortuous, and initially at least Veerappan emerged intact. Soon however, the stranglehold of the STF on his territory began to tell. In February 2001 his group were spotted on the Kerala border, far from their normal stamping grounds. After a shoot-out, the gang escaped, but two weeks later Maran was captured along with a mobile phone, radio equipment and two bombs.

Veerappan disappeared again. One last sighting has him clutching a home-made double-barrelled shotgun, hardly the vast armoury with which he is credited, and hardly a match for the vast resources of the state ranged against him. He had made the mistake of paying a villager way over the odds to fetch ten kilos of rice for him, then another eight hundred rupees to repair a bicycle puncture – that's about twenty dollars. Perhaps he has forgotten what the real prices are, or was still flush with Rajkumar's money; either way, he paid well for the help and sent the man into the town, trusting him to return. However, the villager was more scared of the police than of Veerappan. If they found out, he would be in trouble so he went and told them. An operation was mounted but the bandit escaped.

Still that same old trusting nature. Once, early in his career, Veerappan took his first ever hostage, a policeman. One night on the radio they heard that the man's wife was ill and so Veerappan allowed him to send a note out of the camp. It was a trick: the note was discovered and the police attacked. Veerappan, however, narrowly escaped. Time and time again, Veerappan has trusted other people – his life forces that upon him and one day, probably quite soon, it will kill him. In this he is a classic hero, a good man driven to bad deeds. But his appeal was always limited while he did nothing to right wrongs, an essential Robin Hood action. Now he has started down that path, his danger to authority increases and history shows that the closer a bandit gets to the noble ideal, the closer he gets to his death.

# PART TWO

# DARKNESS DOUBLED

... [for] these Hindus there was no conflict between God, who is all-powerful, and Satan, who yet flouts and perverts His intentions. Here, creation and destruction were opposite faces of the same medal, equal energies of the same universal spirit.

John Masters, *The Deceivers*

Breath is the bridge between body and mind and between mind and spirit. To the Yogis it is the life force and vitality of all beings. To the Romans the word for breath was *spiritus* which also meant spirit, and it is the common root found in respiration, inspiration and aspiration. To the ancient Greeks breath, wind and soul were all said to be the same.

Swami Ambikananda Saraswati

# 5

# North to Jabalpur

A FEW MILES NORTH OF MYSORE lies Sri Rangapatnam, a sleepy place that appears not to have recovered from some devastating calamity. Piles of rubble and ruined walls dominate the town; there are large areas of waste land and few signs of economic activity. That calamity, so palpable even today, was the arrival of the British in 1799.

It was often said that the British took India in a fit of absent-mindedness. The great orientalist Sir William Jones declared that Bengal fell in their lap 'like a ripe mango'. This, however, is misleading: certainly the East India Company policies were often muddled and contradictory, but India came to them through decades of all-out war, not a few random skirmishes. If some of these battles were genuine attempts to secure the hinterlands of major trading posts like Calcutta and Madras, others were straighforward land-grabbing offensives, none more so than the seizure of Mysore state and its capital at Sri Rangapatnam.

Tipu Sultan of Mysore was a Muslim autocrat with a taste for European-style development tempered by a positive hatred for the British. One of Tipu's favourite desk ornaments was a mechanical toy that featured a tiger mauling a British officer and the ruler's summer palace at Sri Rangapatnam, still intact, is beautifully painted with scenes of British military humiliations.

Unfortunately for the Mysore potentate he could find no military allies in his anglophobia. The French Revolution scuppered his hopes for a pact with Paris (his ambassadors reached Versailles only months before the Bastille was stormed, coming away with gardeners, seeds and glass-blowers, but no regiments) and the British general Cornwallis was determined to have an Indian triumph after losing the American colonies to George Washington. After a vicious battle Tipu's body was discovered among nine thousand others on the walls of Sri Rangapatnam. Arthur Wellesley, the future Duke of Wellington, was appointed governor and took up residence in the summer palace.

Those years around the turn of the nineteenth century were pivotal in the development of British India. In addition to vanquishing Tipu, they defeated the Rohillas of Bareilly and the Marathas in Poona, Nagpur and Gwalior. Huge swathes of territory were seized and, to pay for the operations, taxation of the peasantry was ruthlessly increased: Pax Britannica, as the historian John Keay has pointed out, was also Tax Britannica. Marginal land was brought into use in order to increase revenues and one side effect of this was an extensive wave of deforestation throughout the subcontinent.

In return the people got law and order, certainly more than they had been used to. But spinning away from the defeated armies were dozens of clans, groups and mercenary gangs who knew no way to earn a living other than plunder. They took to the hills, the dwindling forests and the badlands, places such as the Chambol Ravines fifty miles south-east of Agra. For the British, these men were now the enemy, standing in the path of development and progress. Veerappan, the strangely anachronistic modern day bandit, is in many ways the child of those times, a man created by the encroachment of civilized society on his jungled world.

[96]

It was in Arthur Wellesley's southern fiefdom that the most terrible threat was uncovered. One hundred men were arrested at Bangalore and accused of strangling travellers. Further evidence began to appear in the following decade. As the British gained control, it was noticed that significant numbers of sepoys returning home on leave failed to report back for duty. At first these disappearances were put down to desertion, but then a series of murders was uncovered. On 28 April 1810, Major-General St Leger issued an order from HQ Cawnpore stating: 'Several Sepoys proceeding to visit their families on leave of absence from their Corps have been robbed and murdered by a description of persons denominated *Thugs* . . . these murderers contrive to fall in with him [the traveller] on the road or in the Sarais . . . they first use some deleterious substance, commonly the seeds of the plant Duttora, which they contrive to administer in tobacco, pawn, the hookah, food or drink of the Traveller. As soon as the poison begins to take effect, by inducing a stupor or languor, they strangle him.' The general went on to warn all sepoys to take great care and avoid hospitality from strangers.

I spent a day in Sri Rangapatnam, touring the ruins and finally reaching the summer palace towards evening. The British had been magnaminous in victory, honouring Tipu with a proper burial, preserving his bellicose murals, and caring for his many children; Thomas Hickey's large and delicate portraits of them were on display. Tipu himself appeared in the murals, riding into battle while imperturbably smelling a rose.

At dusk I hailed a bus on the road to Bangalore and began the journey north. For an hour I had to stand, then got a seat next to a well-dressed young man who struck up a conversation. He was a contractor, he said, working on a project to lay fibre-optic cable all across India. There were many problems, the corruption was terrible and the gains not so high. He gestured through the bars over the open window. 'See this trench by the road?'

I had seen it earlier, noticing the gangs of men and women

working on it, a snaking narrow ditch, a yard deep, worming its way alongside the tarmac in a rather wayward manner. If a large tree or a stone came in its way, it simply veered around it, not at all the behaviour one would expect of an advanced scientific communications system. And then there were the workers: slender women in saris, bearing battered metal trays laden with soil, and men in dhotis down in the trench, hacking away with a short pick. The thugs had used just such a tool for quickly excavating graves and William Sleeman's grandson James had put a similar item into production for World War I. The result was that millions of Allied soldiers dug out their trenches in Flanders with a tool first used by Indian murderers.

My companion had little interest in his workers. He thought they might have come from Orissa; he was sure they came as families and were happy to live under plastic sheets by the road.

'Do they ever find anything?' I asked. 'Treasure? Bodies?'

I was thinking of the thug bhils, the extensive system of burial grounds that Sleeman discovered and plotted on maps, a supposed two million skeletons. All those secret burial grounds had been beside roads and roads have a habit of enduring. Yesterday's old trails and lanes become tomorrow's motorways, so why not bodies?

The young man laughed. 'We have dug hundreds of miles now and not a single body has appeared – as for treasure, I'm sure I would never hear of it.'

At Bangalore I rested in a hotel near the railway station, spent the next morning in the Botanical Gardens, then boarded the train north to Hyderabad. I much preferred to be on the rails than the buses: I could read, walk around, meet people – the buses were too often merely an endurance test.

But this train was no bed of roses: large numbers of passengers had crowded on board, including a battalion of soldiers going on leave, all burdened with heavy trunks and bedrolls. Next to me in the second-class sleeper was a Gurkha, smiling exuberantly and sharing his chappatis with anyone who looked hungry.

The landscape in the dying sun was stark and beautiful, strewn with vast smooth boulders, glowing with russet and pink. We rattled over iron bridges and saw green waters below where boys swam. Two young girls, both blind, walked through the carriage singing songs that ached with melancholy. The tough soldiers shoved small change at them and stared away into the countryside. I watched a family opposite, the elder daughter perhaps seven years old, constantly harried by her mother while the baby son was pampered. And yet the girl behaved with such quiet patience and sprawled gracefully on the pile of luggage, her big eyes, kohl-rimmed and watchful. I gave her a cheap chocolate bar that I had in my pocket and she stared at it, uncertain, then handed it to her mother who promptly fed it to her son.

The shadow of the carriage flickered on the ballast piles and the bushes covered in pink flowers. Across a field a group of men in orange turbans squatted under a tree, elbows on knees and hands on cheeks, listening to one of their number speak.

In 1810, the same year as Major-General St Leger issued his warning to sepoys, a case occurred on the road north from Nagpur to the Nerbudda, the most dangerous and thug-infested territory. A group of forty travellers, including several wealthy Brahmins, were befriended by a huge party of 360 thugs, all feigning, ironically, to be sepoys going on leave. Days passed and any suspicions the group might have entertained were forgotten. One night the travellers camped in an isolated stretch of countryside, comforted no doubt by the safety of such a large gathering.

Thug attacks were recorded meticulously by Sleeman twenty years later so we know what would have happened next. The party, having eaten, would relax – the thugs were expert at telling stories or singing and dancing, anything to distract their prey. By the time the stranglers began to casually move into position behind their victims, the graves would have already been dug, with the little pick-axes. At a signal, the rumals would whip around the throats and within a few seconds, the windpipes broken, all would be still again.

In this instance, however, two girls were spared, kept by the thugs for their beauty. In a deposition, taken by Sleeman in 1834, a thug present at the time recalled what happened next.

> The daughter of Gunga Tewarree was a very handsome woman; and Punchum, one of our Jemadars, wished to preserve her, as a wife to his son, Bukholee. But when she saw her mother and father strangled, she screamed, and beat her head against the stony ground, and tried to kill herself. Punchum tried in vain to quiet her, and promised to take great care of her, and marry her to his own son, who would be a great Chief; but all was in vain. She continued to scream; and at last Punchum put the roomal around her neck, and strangled her.

The other girl was younger, only three years old, and was brought up by a thug, then married to his son by whom she had two sons. But it was the vast riches secured that made the case infamous: 17,000 rupees, a huge sum of money. The case would become a *cause célèbre*, exactly the sort of criminal mystery that an aspiring young English officer might hope to solve.

William Henry Sleeman had not arrived in India as an administrator but as a soldier. Born on the eighth day of the eighth month in 1788, he was the son of a military man who had finished his career as superintendent of excise and duty in Cornwall. In this the family were something of poachers turned gamekeepers as they were said to have once been renowned smugglers themselves. William's boyhood ambition was to join the army, but family fortunes fell after his father died young and he was forced to sign up for the army of the Honourable East India Company, a rather different prospect to His Majesty's regular forces. Typically Sleeman set about his career with determination and thoroughness, equipping himself with a fine sword from Wilkinson's, a pair of Manson's guns and several useful books. He read the latest economic theories of Ricardo alongside his military primers and was well ahead in Hindustani and Arabic by the time he boarded the East Indiaman *Devonshire* at Gravesend in March 1809. The excitement must have been almost as intense as the dread: heading east could spell fortune for a lucky few, but the majority would find only an early grave. Sleeman himself would survive many years, and a couple of assassination attempts, but he would never see England again.

Arriving in Calcutta, Sleeman was posted to the 12th Native Infantry and sent up country to Awadh (Oudh to the British – its capital was at Lucknow), a turbulent kingdom whose ill-judged annexation by the British in 1856 was a crucial factor in the Great Mutiny of 1857. He was not at all similar to his colleagues, being well read, earnest and hard-working, qualities that were almost entirely superfluous in a society that valued hard-drinking, humour and laziness. In this he was a new kind of Englishman in India, one not affiliated by long-standing family ties with the country, nor wrapped up in customs and traditions of the Orient, a man familiar with the latest trends in European thought and not much impressed by what he found of his dissolute fellow officers in the east.

With the Company now consolidating its grip on India, an uneasy peace had come to great swathes of Indian countryside, though battles still occurred. Sleeman saw active service in the 1815 war against the Gurkhas, surviving only to regret that the British were too lenient on their enemy. At some point, probably early on, he must have realized that satisfying his interests and ambitious nature would not be possible in the army – he would have to win a political appointment. He was not to be disappointed: not only did he have some powerful patrons, he had his language skills (now augmented by Gurkhali, Persian and Urdu) and his modern outlook on India's problems. In 1819 he was appointed junior assistant to the government agent in the Saugor and Nerbudda Territories, arriving in Jubbulpore for a short apprenticeship before posting to Narsinghpur in 1822.

Quite where Sleeman got his fascination with crime from is not clear, unless it was with the bootleggers and rum smugglers of his childhood. There was certainly plenty to absorb him in India. One of the most widely read books on India at the time was John Fryer's *A New Account of East India and Persia* (1698) which mentions gangs of stranglers. There were other mentions in Thevenot's *Voyages* of 1727 and James Forbes's *Oriental Memoirs*, first published in 1813, both popular works in their day. Information, however, remained patchy and uncollated without any indication of human sacrifice, nor the invoking of Kali. Indeed the earlier accounts suggest a simple act of highway assault. The word phansigar is used, meaning strangler, but not thug, meaning deceiver.

It took a medical man, Dr Richard Sherwood of Madras, to finally gather all the pieces together and suggest there was a significant and violent menace out there on the highways of India. Sleeman appears to have read the doctor's monograph while in Allahabad in late 1816 and it made a lasting impression on him. Underneath the surface of Indian society was an evil secret. Just as in Cornwall, where the magistrate could turn out to be in cahoots with the rum smugglers, the outside appearances of law-abiding and respectable Indians could be a façade, but in this case for something far more sinister. The stage was being set for a momentous change in Sleeman's life.

The Gurkha soldier had been away talking to his colleagues, now he came back and squeezed down beside me. The Indian Army, like the British, maintains its fine tradition of using mercenaries. His journey, he told me, was an epic he repeated every six months: train to Hyderabad, then Varanasi, change again in Patna, then bus to the Nepali border, another three buses after that, then hitch his kit bag over his shoulder and walk fifteen miles into the mountains. I thought of Major-General St Leger and his missing sepoys, the first clue.

'Your woman is a cultivator?' he asked. 'My wife is growing

wheat, rice, maize, onions and potatoes. How many cows do you keep?'

He was full of questions about me.

'Does rice grow well in London? Are you in service? Do you stay in hotels in India?' He never had. 'Do they provide ladies for sex?'

I said I thought some might be able to, but I'd never asked. He snuggled up even closer. 'You think maximum sex is good for health?'

'What is maximum sex?'

He ignored this. 'How many times you are having sex?'

'Oh, every day,' I said casually.

He looked disappointed. 'So, you do not have maximum sex?'

That was an irritating thing for him to have said after I had been so obviously honest with him. I demanded to know what maximum sex might be.

'Two or three times per day.'

Reasonable, I thought. He was clearly bursting with sexual energy after six months and I hoped his wife was too. But I had completely misjudged him; in fact, he was building up to a confession. 'Brother, I take one peg of whisky and I cannot do maximum sex. My wife likes sex too much. She wake me up for maximum sex every night for two months. What can I do? How to make good sex?'

I became very wise and knowledgeable. 'Well, obviously you should not hurry. Better to do it once a day, and do it well, than rush through and do three bad ones.' I suppose a sharper listener might have detected some nettled pride in that. I continued, 'Let your wife enjoy it. Go slow.'

He shook his head. 'My wife enjoy too much already. She want more and more sex. Maximum sex, she says, give me maximum sex and I am tired. Long journey – five days! I am very tired and take one peg. Ah!'

His face was full of woe and I wanted to help. I didn't like to think of this warrior running out of ammunition so quickly in the Himalayas.

[103]

'There's no big secret . . .'

He grabbed my arm. 'Big Secret. What is that? Big Secret? Is it pill or powder?'

'No, I said there is no big secret.'

'You don't have Big Secret? In your bag, maybe a little for me? Give me one piece Big Secret.'

His face pleaded and I couldn't think what to do.

'I don't have any big secret. Sorry.'

'I will pay you money,' he said, reaching into the breast pocket of his fatigues. 'I will pay Indian rupees not Nepali. How much for one piece Big Secret?' He pulled out a wad of ten-rupee notes and began counting them. The man was desperate.

I'm not proud of what I did next. It was probably, on the strictest criteria, unethical. Afterwards, I wondered about the risk of damage to the poor man's psyche. Or perhaps there was success and a subsequent rising demand for a product that did not exist. If the latter is true, I would like to call on entrepreneurs to pull out all stops, to do what is necessary, to get out to eastern Nepal and market Big Secret.

I told him to put away his money, then reached in my bag and got hold of a packet of paracetamol. Concealing the label with my hand, I pressed out four of them into his shaking palm.

'One a day,' I said seriously. 'Never two. An overdose could be, er, dangerous. I mean really dangerous – do you understand me? For your wife.'

He nodded furiously, tearing a corner from a newspaper and folding the pills into it. 'Thank you,' he said. 'Thank you, brother.' He stuffed them into his pocket and buttoned it up. Major-General St Leger must have been turning in his grave. I felt like a thug who had just successfully administered a dangerous drug to an over-trusting travelling companion.

In Hyderabad I crossed the river and walked up to Char Minar, the huge central monument built by the city's founder, Muhammed Quli Qutb Shah in 1591. The structure is a sort of mosque on top of four stone arches with a 186-foot-tall clocktower combined. Certainly it's imposing, if not quite lovely, especially now that it's become a traffic island.

The prince chose the site of his city because it had romantic associations with the woman he loved, and the romantic associations have continued ever since. Philip Meadows Taylor knew these streets well and used them to good effect in *Confessions of a Thug*, building the sense of exotic orientalism with descriptions of night-time assignations with beautiful women and deadly encounters with victims in the traditional lodging houses, or serais. Nowadays the old town remains exotic, but also filthy and impoverished. The meat market was overrun with brown rats, packs of them boldly grabbing tidbits from the butcher's block, others strolling down the alleyways which were soft underfoot with the accumulated blood and feathers. The stench sent me reeling to the perfumery shops where I sat with an old merchant as he recalled the visits of the Prince of Berar, the debauched son of the seventh Nizam. Back in the 1930s the Prince had a reputation as a serious womanizer.

'He came by car and never got down,' said the merchant. 'Everything was taken to him.'

There was a display of glass vials bearing strange and wonderful scents: of jasmine, rose and mogra, then ambergris. 'You Europeans don't like it, except to put in a cigarette at the casino.' I nodded in agreement.

He pulled out weird roots and splinters of rare woods: 'Agar from Assam, smells like pigshit but is popular with Arabs.' There were syrups of spices, collations and infusions of flowers. 'Agal or gula. Trade was better when I was young. Then men had four wives and ten concubines.'

He showed how he had once twizzled pompoms of cotton wool around a bamboo cocktail stick, then dabbed it in the perfumes and proffered it to the prince's footman. As a merchant he was too lowly to pass the stick directly through the car window.

[105]

'This time is becoming like that time,' he added gloomily. 'With a few rich and many poor. They spend all the money trying to make this a high technology city, but outside in the countryside it is chaos.'

I walked on, passing pearl dealers, purveyors of exotic gilded slippers and glass bangle merchants, heading down the street that leads away from Char Minar to Karwan and Golconda Fort. This road was once full of diamond merchants, back in the seventeenth century when India was the only source of the stones. I was hoping to find caravanserais from that time, the sorts of places where thugs came to assay their prey, chatting to merchants while casually eyeing up their goods.

I found shops selling charms, shops selling spices, painted doorways and mysterious archways leading to ruined palaces; there were chestnut horses living in ornamental domes, people living in stables; there were tombs of saints covered in green cloth and garlanded with glittering tinsel; there were old men sucking on hookah pipes and children at the breast. But there were no caravanserais.

I knew exactly what I wanted to find: I had seen such galleried courtyards surrounded by rooms on the Incense Road in Yemen and the Silk Road in Turkey. Places where straw was thrown down for the animals in the yard while merchants stored their merchandise and took rooms above. I even had a memory of seeing such a place five years before on my first visit to Hyderabad, but the best I could do was a Mughal mansion house, half in ruins, with a family who had taken it over when the Muslim occupants fled to Pakistan in 1948. After a whole day scouring the entire length of road from Char Minar to Golconda Fort, I had to admit that what I wanted was not there. It no longer existed.

Exhausted, I reached the tomb of Muhammad Quli Qutb Shah, founder of Hyderabad, and sat listening to three Muslim youths singing, their voices rising and entwining, echoing through the passageways below the tomb.

Since travelling up from Madras I had gone through all of

Sleeman's writings and all the photocopied reports, searching for evidence of an undercover operation. My frustration at failing to find caravanserais was matched by a frustration with the thuggee legend. There was now no avoiding the fact that the fabulous agent of *The Deceivers* was totally fictitious, a deception in itself. I'd known it when Edward had recalled the story, but I'd still hoped to find some clue, some possibility that Sleeman had disguised himself and penetrated the cult. There was none. The myth was unreal – just as Veerappan cast as Robin Hood was unreal.

The history of thugs, I could now see, had various levels. There were the romantic and imaginative accounts started by *Confessions of a Thug*, a tradition that had allowed the legend of Sleeman the undercover agent to develop. This was entirely untrue, but fired by exotic orientalist ideas had persisted with a tenacious disregard for the facts right down to John Masters's *The Deceivers* and the Merchant Ivory film based upon it. This was the history I had come out to India believing, wanting to believe. Here you have it, Confessions of a Writer, I had come hoping to discover that thuggee, the glamorous sacrificial cult, still existed. I wanted to write about Sleeman's undercover exploits, how he had learned the language, disguised himself, travelled the roads, handled the scarf, piecing together the full and horrible truth. And I wanted anxious policemen still battling against a tide of evil.

Underneath the romantic stratum of history was the official story: British officers in newly conquered territory uncover a longstanding criminal sect, then defeat it by the first example of steady policework, plus some robust retribution. So efficiently do they manage this that thuggee, a centuries-old fanatical cult, disappears completely and is almost forgotten. Sleeman gets much accolade and the plum post of Resident in Lucknow.

This is the history told in his grandson James Sleeman's book and in Francis Tuker's biography. It is a history that allows Sleeman to be a hero, but a less flamboyant one. Without Sleeman and his colleagues, wrote James Sleeman with unselfconscious pomposity in 1932, 'millions of Indians alive to-day would never have been born, including possibly those who now agitate for a restoration of the conditions under which Thuggee thrived and battened'. (By which we guess he means the horrors of self-rule.)

I much preferred the romantic tale, but the facts were unavoidable. What Meadows Taylor had done, so perceptively, was satisfy his audience's desire for sensual eastern romance. Once that aura was established, other writers had rushed off with it, making Feringhea a demon-lover-killer and Sleeman an Orpheus in the Underworld. The east, as usual, played its traditional role of lascivious lying beast.

I must have sat for two hours listening to those boys sing their hearts out. Songs of religious fervour and love's longing that went on and on until darkness was falling and the caretaker was shouting that he would lock the gate on us. Then it was time to go and leave the tombs to the ghosts. I felt I had taken off an outer skin, like a snake, eased myself away from the old coverings. The romance and the fictions of thuggee were seductive, but they were not part of the truth, only serving a European desire for India to be exotic, mysterious and dangerous. It was orientalism, the myth of the east, and surely should have died long ago.

From Hyderabad I travelled north again, through the badlands of Andhra Pradesh then into Nagpur, a huge sprawling textile town. Several hours later we rattled across the Narmada river at sundown. This strange river, revered by Hindus as sacred, flows west across the Deccan when all others go east. 'As wood is cut by the saw,' goes a local proverb, 'so at the sight of the Narmada do a man's sins fall away.' Traditionally it was the border between south and north, the gateway to a lawless country of isolated towns and small princely states.

I watched men walking home through a fine land of dark mango trees and dusty roads. Each field was guarded by a watchman's grass hut, an oil lamp flickering by the door.

Jabalpur is one of those cities that rarely scrapes into any guidebook, lacking any great architectural treasures or museums, but in the 1830s it was famed as a centre for Sleeman's anti-thug operations. It was also notorious for the dangers of its roads; thug gangs roamed at will in the countryside, often destroying large parties of travellers. At the start of their hunting season they would all go to pray at the Kali temple in Brindachul on the banks of the Ganges, then come south towards Jabalpur. The countryside was often fertile but interspersed with barren patches of uncultivated land and forest, dangerously isolated and lacking in safe havens, perfect for the quiet and uninterrupted pursuit of strangulation.

I jumped down from the train and, throwing my bag in the back of a cycle-rickshaw, asked for a decent hotel. My intention was to stay a good while here.

It was mid-February and there was the sharp chill of winter in the air, a chill that brings an autumnal glow to the dry trees and a thirst for strong drink – Shivas Regal preferably – by log fires. We swept through broad time-worn streets of fine Raj-era buildings, past the busy cinema and bus station, and the rickshaw wallah wrapped his shawl tighter around himself. In the dark streets beyond we came to a halt outside a large concrete building: the rickshaw wallah hotel of choice: 'Deluxe! Yes, recommended! Luxury!'

I went inside and saw that the rickshaw man set great store by space and concrete. Fortunately most of the concrete was bare and so more easily appreciated. I was shown a premier room on the third floor by the manager himself, a man in his late fifties with hair boot-blacked and a mouth stained scarlet with betel, plus one greenish tooth and one gold. His smile was like a broken traffic light, warning me to be careful.

It was a room, so typical of backwoods India, a room that would be unimaginable in most countries of the world, a room totally devoid of personality, comfort, cleanliness, or the basic necessities of human existence. It was a room of cheap laminate furniture, scabbed and smelly, a room in which opening the wardrobe was an act of courage, a room of ragged stained curtains, a room without a single redeeming feature, a bed without rest, a window without views, a shower without soap. It required force of character to survive in such a room; it required a stoical indifference and yogic inner strength that I did not possess. I sat on the blanket that had all the luxurious softness of a doormat. I would have hung myself from the light fitting had I not been absolutely sure it would bring the ceiling down on me killing those unfortunate guests in the room above, except that the appalling stench seeping from the open bathroom door signalled that any other guests were already dead.

'It's fine,' I said to the manager, too tired to believe that anywhere else could be better. 'I'll take it.'

When he had gone, I lay on the bed and fished out the newspapers that I had yet to read. They would cheer me up. The newspapers always cheered me up. There was, however, no time. Before I even finished the first article, I was stopped by an ear-piercing scream.

It was a scream one could not ignore: it had an edge of madness in it, not really fear but danger. It demanded a response. I jumped up and went out into the corridor. At the same time I saw a youth run across the landing and set off down the stairs at breakneck speed. Then a woman appeared from the room next to mine, a European woman, tall, slim and sunburned with a large white towel wrapped around her hair and another around her body. I remember the towels, they were so clean, and my surprise at seeing another foreigner.

'Peeping Tom,' she yelled in English. 'He saw me naked! Stop him!'

There is a certain Victorian prudishness about India, matched by lasciviousness, as Edward had pointed out, and in that environment, where a woman's modesty may be outraged, where men may be Peeping Toms, you find yourself drawn into the thing. I reacted pretty fast.

I went down the first flight far too fast for my flip-flops, swerved hard, over-corrected, hit the balustrade, recovered. I got one glimpse of the youth and it remains imprinted on my mind. He appeared like a racehorse in those prints that were painted before photography could reveal that horses do not stretch forelegs forwards and hind legs hindwards, simultaneously. He was full stretch, defying the laws of photography, taking the bend rather well.

When I got to the ground floor, he was gone. I stopped to listen but all I heard was my breathing. In an armchair, set for no discernible reason in the middle of the concrete wasteland that was the lobby, sat an old Sikh gentleman. I stood in front of him gasping and said, 'Did a man . . . young man . . . come running . . . fast? Peeping Tom. Lady upstairs.'

The Sikh gentleman regarded me with rheumy ancient eyes. 'Eve teasers,' he said. 'Shabby lot.' Then he looked away.

I went back up to the first floor and searched along a bit, did the same on the second without luck, then went to the third. The woman was standing at her door waiting, now dressed.

'My God,' she declared loudly, smiling. 'You really did chase him! Were you going to punch him? I think I wanted you to.'

She was English.

'I'm afraid he got away.'

There was a silence, then she realized an explanation of some sort was needed and pointed to a narrow door between the two doors to our rooms. 'Look in here. I think I found out what's going on.'

It was actually an access panel for maintenance work. Inside were the plumbing guts of the building, black pipes, dripping and algal. There was also a narrow concrete platform on which someone had stood a bedside cabinet. The woman pointed to a hole at eye level. 'He was looking through there into my bathroom.'

She was rather beautiful and, I reflected, probably got the room that all beautiful female foreigners were allocated. We went in her bathroom and examined the small hole that had been carefully drilled in the wall.

'Someone had put a little piece of tissue paper in the hole,' she said. 'And I was standing here in the shower, wondering why, when it began to move. Can you believe it? When it fell out I looked through and saw an eye!'

We debated what should be done. 'Maybe I'll go to another hotel,' she said. 'I know it's only some pathetic creep, but it is unnerving.'

Her room was certainly no improvement on mine and we inspected it together, beginning to laugh at the sheer magnificent squalor of it.

'We mustn't,' she said, after a while, straightening her face. 'I love India. It's a wonderful place. Focus on the good things, not the bad.'

I looked around the room with an eager face and she began to laugh. 'Yes, OK, I'm not going to stay. I'm going to pack my bag and complain to the manager.'

A few minutes later we both entered his office. I sat down but Maddy refused and remained standing. The manager was sitting chewing betel, his mouth brimming with scarlet saliva as though he had just devoured a guest. His smile was truly horrible.

'Pleesh,' he said obsequiously, pointing to Maddy's bag. 'Pleesh, put your luggagish.'

He leaned sideways and delicately spat a long spurt of liquified flesh into the waste bin. An ancient man in an approximation of a porter's outfit now scuttled in the door and tried to take Maddy's bag from her hand. She resisted.

'One of your workers,' she said angrily. 'Maybe many of them, are looking at women secretly in the shower. Peeping Toms. Shall I tell the whole town about it? What are you going to do?'

The grim visage of the manager rose up. I could see the craquelure of his skin, powdered like a panto dame, and the untreated grey hairs sprouting from his ears next to the fake black of his scalp hair. 'Madame! Madame!' he cried. 'We will catch this rascal. The police will be informed.' As he spoke, the betel made his salivary glands work and his mouth was filling again. This caused him to tip his head back more and more, revealing the yellows of his eyes. 'Pleesh! Put your luggagish baa' ina womb!'

He made a sign and the ancient porter made a lunge. Maddy, I was noticing with increasing respect, was almost six foot tall and not to be messed with. She pulled the bag away with ease, then fixed the porter with a withering green-eyed glare worthy of the most fearful Kali image, and hissed, 'Stop that – immediately.'

He did.

The manager turned to me. 'Shuuh. You are not involved. Pleesh.'

This was too much. I stood up. 'I am leaving too and I do not expect a bill.'

Half an hour later we were sitting in the bar of another hotel, not a great improvement, but the two adjoining rooms were definitely without peepholes.

'I'm studying yoga,' she explained. 'To be exact, I came to study breathing.'

This was not as simple as it sounded. A month at the Iyengar Institute in Poona, followed by a course in the hills of Goa. This had involved rising at dawn, cold showers, then two hours of sitting in the lotus position and breathing before breakfast.

'I gave up drinking – temporarily – and smoking permanently.'

I was toying with my Wills cigarette. 'Why?'

'The first thing I noticed was that during a good meal I would be thinking of the cigarette to come, not the food. Then I realized that I used to roll a cigarette every time anything happened to me. If I was angry, I'd roll one; if I was sad, or relaxed, or hungry, or bored, I'd roll up a cigarette – Golden Virginia.' A wistful look crossed her face. 'I do miss it sometimes, but you see it was like a substitute for feeling anything properly.'

'Not health then?'

'Mental health. I didn't want to experience my pleasures and my emotions via cigarettes.'

It was a strangely convincing theory, though it didn't apply to me, surely? I reflected back over the previous year. I had gone from one a day to a packet, setting fire to angers and resentments outside various back doors. I had felt my chest tighten up, breathing

[113]

compromised. Then I had set off to investigate a cult who helped stop breathing all together.

'If a person can get control of breathing, then they begin to control their mind,' said Maddy. 'You see prana is circulated, bad chi expelled.'

'Hold on, I need some jargon-free explanation.'

'Don't you have mental ruts and whirlpools? Thoughts that drag you down. You know they do no good, but they are compulsive. Mine is that I'm not intelligent enough. If anyone says don't be stupid or something, down I go. I'm not bright; I never succeed; I always give up; I've achieved nothing. Like that. But with breath control, you wrestle away your mind from the ruts. You're in a quiet place, with nothing to do, just the situation when you might go down the same old rut. But instead, you steady your breathing and steady your mind. Prana is vitality, but it's more than that, it's the force of life. Yama is cultivation, extension. Pranayama charges up your batteries: it's a fitness regime based on alchemy. That's what I'm practising.'

There have long been reports of yogic breathing feats. In fact, I had read of one in the newspaper a couple of days before. At the Kumbh Mela festival on the Ganges, a Japanese woman had been buried alive in the mud for three days, emerging unscathed and alive. Unfortunately, a few weeks later I saw video coverage of the stunt, showing the woman in a hole that her acolytes simply covered with corrugated iron sheets.

'I'm heading up that way,' said Maddy when I told her. 'After I finish my course in Hindi, I'm going to catch the Shivaratri, the night of Shiva at the Kumbh.' She was studying Hindi with a local teacher: three hours a day every day, after her three hours of pranayama. I felt positively decadent beside her, but it spurred me. The next day, I told myself, I would be out on the track of Sleeman and his thugs.

The reason given in the legends for thug strangulation has less to do with breathing than blood. Once you accept the basic tenets of belief (that Kali exists) then the story is quite logical. The goddess is not the devil, though her appearance is awesome and horrible. In times past she encountered a terrible demon that was eating humans as fast as they were created. She attempted to destroy the monster, but as she hacked pieces off with her sword, the drops of blood became new demons. To counter this threat Kali wiped her brow of sweat and created two men. These she supplied with scarves to strangle the demons, a task they did so well that all the monsters were destroyed. Their reward was to roam the earth strangling any who did not acknowledge the goddess.

Throughout human history strangulation has been associated with notions of ritualistic killing, often allied with the idea of necessary or licit murder. Strangling of princes and unwanted royals was common in many cultures, presumably because spilling blue blood was not desirable. In Burma they solved that problem by beating spare princelings to death in a purple sack, but elsewhere strangling was favoured.

The first recorded hanging in England was in AD 695 and thereafter slowly increased in frequency. Alfred the Great hanged forty-four judges for over-zealous hanging of others, further indication perhaps of his sagacity. Henry VIII was particularly brutal, over-seeing an estimated 72,000 executions. Not all were hanged, however. Under Henry's imaginative rule, cooks who poisoned their masters were boiled alive,

Hanging was very much the poor man's punishment: until 1695 the ability to read Psalm 51, 'the neck verse', was sufficient to reprieve a man, though not a woman. After 1700, however, the so-called Bloody Code was progressively introduced, allowing hanging for every offence except petty theft and 'mayhem'. Chosen for the pain and ugliness of the death, it sent all the right signals to the sinners watching. Children were not excluded: ninety per cent of those hanged were under twenty-one. A few did cheat the hangman: in 1833 a nine-year-old was sentenced to hang for poking a stick through a crack in a London shop window and stealing tuppence-worth of paint. He was reprieved, but in another case of theft a fourteen-year-old went to the gallows.

In all this the Church stood square behind the forces of law and order. Vengeance was an attribute of God and the civil magistrate was his instrument on earth. It was rarely questioned that execution was the correct expression of that vengeance; some went on to suggest that justice for the individual was not the main objective. Archdeacon William Paley, guardian of public morality in the late eighteenth century, was clear that 'the proper end of human punishment is not the satisfaction of justice, but the prevention of crimes.' This conveniently did away with any need for rigour in proof – the hanged man became a sacrificial lamb to the public good. If he was guilty, it was a bonus and the innocent received scant consolation: 'he who falls by mistaken sentence may be considered as falling for his country.'

The involvement of the church was so pervasive in the business of execution that a good hanging was merely a type of service. It started long before the appointed day with priests working to win the confessions of the condemned. Samuel Johnson wrote, 'when a man knows he is to be hanged in a fortnight, it concentrates his mind wonderfully.' For the evangelist movement, the death sentence was an opportunity to gather sinners back into the fold. It became quite fashionable among the religiously enthusiastic to enter the condemned cell and take up the prisoner's last few hours with homilies and tracts. And they were determined: Richard Faulkner, a fifteen-year-old child murderer, had spurned all the do-gooders, even threatening to kill two clergymen who came to him in Norwich Prison in 1810. The pair were not to be discouraged: they dressed a small girl in the murdered child's clothes and had her parade past his cell in the dead of night. The ghostly sight quickly quelled Faulkner's spirit and he was soon begging for divine forgiveness. Two days later, he was taken out to the gallows by a priest and assisted up on to the 'altar' of the gallows. There was a clear attempt to symbolize the act with a sacrifice. If the priests had done their work well, the condemned

[116]

prisoner would confess publicly, then ask God's forgiveness and warn the crowd against following such a life. Their words were often clearly scripted, if not scripture. James Tilley, hanged for burglary in 1822, told the crowd at Horsham, 'I hope you will take warning by my unhappy situation: don't break the Sabbath, always go to Church, and beware of bad company for that brought me to the gallows.'

No matter how fulsome the repentance, however, it did not mean a reprieve. That would be missing the point. The prisoner was now ready, cleansed and fit to be sacrificed. Little wonder that Sleeman and his fellow officers displayed an obsessional interest in the religious connections between thugs and their victims. Transcripts of interviews with thugs show their British captors returning again and again to the notions of sacrifice and ritual. In one typical instance, as Sleeman mentions Kali and her evil ways yet again, the prisoner protests that, 'All men worship at her temple.' No matter, religion, murder and sacrifice were inextricably intertwined and hanging was a fitting punishment for the strangler – a chance to awe society through the means of Divine Vengeance, in India as it is in Horsham.

Jabalpur by day. I rode along in a cyclo, through the old Anglo-Indian suburb of Wright Town, past the zoo with its collection of pigeons, a goat and a large ballistic missile. The rickshaw wallah wore a string of pearls, nail varnish and plenty of coconut oil – not transvestism (common enough in India) but the ideal of beauty preserved in old lithographs of moustachioed rajahs and thakurs. Small children squatted by the road stringing beads under black umbrellas, hawkers with barrows laden with fruit called to the houses with their old-fashioned cooler boxes stuffed with grass. Jabalpur seemed to be of an India that is fast disappearing elsewhere.

I had the driver stop at a bookshop where I asked about a local historian. One of the customers, a man in a rather strange Parsee hat, immediately offered an answer. 'You want Dr Choubey.'

[117]

He gave directions to what proved to be Jabalpur's high street, a constant jam of people, honking vehicles and cycle-rickshaws. Choubey's clinic was one room on the ground floor of an ornate old building, its gay pink façade just visible beneath the grime. There was a man in a scarlet turban selling baby pineapples from a barrow outside the door and a bench for patients to wait. Choubey's assistant heard my story then disappeared behind a flowery curtain. After a short wait I was shown in.

Dr Choubey, a stout genial man in a white coat, was sitting inside his tiny consulting room. His stethoscope was hung on a coat peg and one wall had a shelf of ageing Tupperware containers neatly marked: diarrhoea, constipation, anti-diabetes and vertigo.

'You are a writer?' he asked brightly. 'Oxford or Cambridge?'

The doctor had a rather traditional view of Britain. I told him what I was researching and the mention of Sleeman's name clearly interested him.

'Now I have my clinic,' he said. 'And tonight I have dictation between five and six.' He gave no explanation of this, simply handed me a card with his home address on.

'Could I come at six-thirty then?'

'That will be most appropriate.'

I was shown out by the assistant.

It took some time to find Choubey's house in the dark, a large gloomy villa with creaking doors and dim lights. An old woman let me in and showed me through a heavy curtained door into the doctor's study. This was a high-ceilinged dingy room lined with books and yellowing papers. Choubey, by contrast with his surroundings, was full of zip, laughing heartily at his own witticisms, his conversation dashing in all directions.

'Look at my study. Only a fool lends books and only a greater fool returns them! Are you Irish? I'm a great lover of the Irish. There's no snakes in Ireland you know, they have the English instead! Ha! Here have a notepad, have five notepads.' A handful of medical notebooks landed in my lap. 'Tea and biscuits?' He shouted a command at a curtain and I heard someone move. 'People said I rescued Sleeman from the grave around here, but we are just a few fools interested in the past now. What is education in India? If I teach you that this is beautiful,' he lifted a small figurine off his crowded desk, 'do I teach anything? No. If I ask you why is it beautiful? Ah! Beauty is not a skin disease, it goes deeper. Marx died in penury and materialism triumphed: "force is the midwife of history" but midwives produce abortions too. Ha!'

I made occasional attempts to nudge this flood towards thuggee, gleaning from a torrent of aphorisms, quotations and asides that the only monument left in Jabalpur that was associated with Sleeman was the School of Industry for Thugs. 'If you go up to Sleemanabad,' he said, 'ask for the police thana – the police post – that building was Sleeman's residence when in that area. They have a photograph of him and a plaque. They'll tell you that the thugs were hung from the tree in the yard but there is no evidence of that.'

The tea was brought, with rich tea biscuits. Choubey delved through his correspondence files, recalling a human sacrifice that had occurred on the Narmada ten years before. 'If you go to Narsinghpur, you ask for the white cliffs on the river – that is the place where human sacrifices occurred.'

There were snippets of useful information here, but I felt he had learned all he knew from the same English texts that I had read. There was no sense that he had benefited from local contacts or memories. I had to get even closer, down on the earth where Sleeman had been, in the places where he had lived. And Narsinghpur was the first posting he had come to after joining the political service.

I stayed for over an hour, then a friend of his arrived and the conversation became even less comprehensible, spinning away through the literary reference points of pre-Independence schooling. I was trapped in a human museum, the Anglo-India section, where pre-television English was like some ornamental gee-gaw on an Edwardian mantelpiece, a shiny sharp glittering thing of no discernible utility but endlessly entertaining over the tea tray and biscuits.

Maddy had persuaded me to come to her Hindi class, proving her progress to me as we rode out there by reading the shop signs that were in devanagari script (lit: 'city of god' – a grand name for an alphabet).

Her teacher was Regina, an ex-politician who had become a recluse, her only contact with the world outside the students she found through the local newspaper. She was a stout woman with short black hair and a cheerful face. We were made a great fuss of and the inevitable tea with biscuits was brought from the kitchen. On the wall was a picture of the Last Supper and a little homily about home. Books were put out, but we never really got them opened; Regina was so starved of company that she regularly forgot to teach and chatted instead.

'I don't go out much,' she told me. 'My fourth auntie's daughter is in town but I don't like to go there – they are very showy with money. Mummy came at Christmas, of course, and there were so many callers – 103. Maddy, I wish you could have seen. They all came to wish me. All cakes and biscuits for everyone and we sat together – Muslims, Hindus and Christians – and sang some songs. There was nothing like you see in the newspapers.'

I was reminded of the pride shown by the villagers of Gopinattam about the Hindu temple that a Muslim artist had painted. Sad to say, India's politicians more often exploit the suspicion between communities, rather than such good will. Maddy mentioned that Regina's first husband had been a Hindu and that had led to problems.

'It was a love match,' she smiled. 'And my family said, OK, you are now dead to us. But I wanted to reform him, I don't know why.'

'Was he a bad man?'

'Somewhat. He was a goonda. What do you say? Gangster? I saw him beat people; he beat me too. I even saw him use shooters.' She laughed again, at our faces. 'He was chote mote – brawns no brains – but I loved him and he was not all bad. Like this bin Laden, my Arab students tell me he is not all bad, and I understand that. No one is all bad.' She handed around the biscuits. 'Those goondas look after their wives well. In a cinema once, a man said something to me and my hubby punched out two of his teeth. And he always prayed – he was very regular with that.'

Her words reminded me that several thugs had been caught after their families were taken into custody. The menfolk soon meekly followed, belying the supposed reputation for toughness.

Despite such good deeds by Regina's ex-husband, however, the marriage failed after seven years. 'I had nothing: I had to walk to the bank to borrow money.'

Walking out on a husband is no easy matter in India. Maddy asked if men treated her differently as a divorcee.

'In Marathi they have a proverb,' she said. 'When a woman needs a helping hand, a man will come along and grope her.'

It was in Maharashtra that she had become a politician for the BJP, the ruling party. Her husband's goonda connections had helped. Were all politicians corrupt then?

'Not all. But to do good you must be a little corrupt. A good man will achieve nothing; politicians must have brains, but dirty brains. People give you money to get something passed – building permission or something – then another one comes to say their village has no water. Then you must use that corrupt money to pay officials to do something. It works like that: you collect money and give out money.'

This made corruption sound like a benign financial distribution service and she admitted it did not always work so well. 'Some keep so much for themselves.'

And does the line between goonda and politician become blurred?

'Those goondas work in the same way: they collect money from some and give it to others. Then the poor people love them and give hideouts and protect them. It is the same with politicians except the poor give votes for money.'

This then was the symbiosis of crime and power: the would-be politician needed to buy votes, dishing out saris and cooking utensils by the hundred.

'Many women will not vote for you unless they get a sari.'

Once in power the politician needed to recoup investments and that need brought alliances with criminals. In this way everyone was corrupted to greater or lesser degrees. As Mahesh Bhatt, the Mumbai film producer, had told me: 'We are all rotten, Kevin, this whole country is rotten to the core.'

'In England most people would not know who was their local goonda,' I said to Regina. 'Many wouldn't know their local politicians either.'

'In India it is different,' she declared. 'Everyone knows the local goondas and the politicians, and sometimes they are the same person.'

I asked if it would be possible to meet her ex-husband, but she shuddered. 'Oh, now he has started with this drinking, I never go there. So many bad words.'

She became coy as to what those words might be, holding her face as though it was burning hot at the thought of such profanities. 'Why do you want to meet a man like that? He is no good. Better you meet Dr Dikshit, my ayurvedic consultant, or Omar, my Arab lodger. He is a good boy.'

I told her why I was interested and my plan to get to Narsinghpur.

'Narsinghpur is nothing,' she protested. 'Why don't you visit the marble cliffs, or the park? Take a nice picnic.' She went to the telephone. 'I will contact my friend Anthony. He will drive you. Maddy, you go too. Take a picnic. Anthony is a good boy too, not showy at all.'

# 6

# Narsinghpur

ON APPEARANCES ALONE ANTHONY LOOKED JUST the man: middle-aged, slightly greying, a thoughtful nod, good English and string-backed driving gloves. When he came at seven next morning, however, my hopes of an Ambassador, the old Morris Oxford with flag fluttering on the wing, were dashed. Anthony drove a van and had brought a friend to talk to about the biscuit industry. This was their fascination, both having once been travelling biscuit salesmen.

Maddy had decided to take up Regina's suggestion and come along. We motored out of Jabalpur southwards and Anthony reminisced about the biscuit world. 'I had a huge patch to cover,' he said. 'I went everywhere by train, carrying samples of products in suitcases: milk biscuits, Reading biscuits, custard creams, rich teas – I was the man who introduced ginger snaps to Madhya Pradesh and now look.'

We looked out, unsure whether he meant ginger snaps had brought civilization to this region, or perhaps that those fine times were gone, despite his pioneering work in snacks.

After passing some boulder-strewn crags populated by naked sadhus, we took a long straight road lined with mango and jamun trees, many of them planted by Sleeman himself during his tenure here.

After taking control of the Saugor and Nerbudda Territories, the British imposed as cheap and efficient a system of governance as they could. In the words of Francis Tuker it was 'based on undivided authority from bottom to top', which is a fine way of saying the handful of British officers had dictatorial powers. What saved it from tyranny was that those men appear to have had a genuine concern for the country and people, albeit one refracted through their own prejudices and interests. Narsinghpur district was a region busy with people crossing the Narmada (also known as the Nerbudda), many heading north towards the Ganges and the holy places. There was plenty for Sleeman to do.

Soon after arriving he received a taste of the violence and danger that lay under the surface. It was February 1822, and a group of thirty men came through town, claiming to be heading for a wedding ceremony. One was even dressed up as a bridegroom. With the police post only twenty yards away, they set fire to a house, murdered the owner, stabbed several others and made off with as much booty as they could carry. When Sleeman was alerted, he rode immediately into the bazaar but no one could, or would, tell him anything. The event left a deep impression on him. 'This was not all of which I was only half aware at Narsingpore: there were other more fatal and secret activities about us and very close to us.'

The sense of danger and the flimsy power with which he controlled a large population was always there with him. Roads were poor, communications slow, and there was the growing and uneasy feeling that there were very few who could be trusted.

I tried to explain to Anthony what I was looking for, but he waved his string-backed glove airily. 'I have a friend, a biscuit wholesaler, in Narsinghpur. He will help you with these tugs. This friend is going there.'

[124]

'I am taking samples of a new line in garibaldis,' said the friend.

This drew a sad shake of the head from Anthony. 'Narsinghpur is a milk biscuit market,' he said, with the air of man who has seen his world go crazy. 'Fancy Jabalpur items will not work there.'

We stopped for an hour at Bheraghat, a place where the Narmada river dives through a beautiful canyon of white marble. In Sleeman's day the British had begun to go there for day trips despite its reputation for suttee, the burning of widows, and for human sacrifice, of the voluntary kind. Religious devotees would leap to their deaths in the swirling waters, a tradition that is kept alive, so to speak, in modern times, though most are now what one local described as 'college failures and love problem people'. Along with thuggee, these traditions helped convince the Englishman, and many of his evangelical contemporaries, that England's mission in India was to reform and civilize. Out with stranglers, suttee and self-sacrifice, in with picnics and public parks.

We motored onwards through fields of chickpeas and padi, reaching Narsinghpur at lunchtime. Anthony chose a restaurant just past the prison, itself a relic of Sleeman's day and still in use. Whether my stated intention of attempting to gain entry annoyed him or not, I don't know, but he studiously refused to eat with us. 'It will not be proper.' He sat with his friend on the far side of the room. As occasionally happens in India, I could not decide if this was because he regarded us as above or below him in the social pecking order.

The waiter distracted us by having thirteen toes, something Maddy noticed: she was very observant of human bodies, noticing how they sat or moved, how they altered with age. 'It's yoga,' she explained. 'It teaches you to see those things.'

Prison visiting was not her idea of India, unless ashrams could be considered so, but the sound of Anthony's voice convinced her. 'The milk biscuit is your foundation in the marketplace – build on that and you will not go wrong.'

We paid the bill and made our excuses. 'When you come out,'

said Anthony, 'walk down the main street and look out for the van. We will be in the wholesaler's shop.'

The prison had a grim aspect. A huge curtain wall hid everything from view and there was a single arched entrance guarded with iron bars leading to a dark Dickensian tunnel. A big-bellied jailer stared at us through the bars, a fistful of keys in his paw.

'Visit?' He turned the word over in his mouth like a lump in his porridge.

'Is that all right?' cried Maddy gaily. 'We love prisons.'

She was wearing brilliant lilac harem trousers, a purple blouson shirt and a tight white tee-shirt. Her navel glinted with ruby in the gap and a tattooed snake came sliding up between her first and second toes. The jailer wore olive.

'Governor can decide,' he said, not in an unfriendly way. 'I will ask for you.'

We waited.

'I'll bet it's horrible,' I said. 'Men chained to walls. Filth. My God, when you think of Indian hotels, the prisons must be so much worse.'

But Maddy's eternal optimism was not to be dampened, even by the sight of ten glum detainees arriving, all dressed in long white shirts and Nehru caps. We watched as they were signed in by a guard sitting at a high desk, slowly writing in a huge old ledger. The young men kept their eyes down, clearly scared stiff.

The governor sent word that he was agreeable to a visit and the gate was unlocked by the baffled warder. We were shown up to his office above the entrance, a roomy space decorated with paintings by prisoners and a statue of Gandhi carved in carbolic soap. The governor was a man in his late thirties, rather proud of the plaque dedicated to a prisoner from British times who had later become a minister in the state government.

'We are a young offenders borstal,' he told us in halting English. 'Ages sixteen to twenty-one.'

A prisoner in white shirt and cap laid tea and biscuits before us. His eyes, carefully cast down, never met ours and I remembered how I'd seen the serial killer in Wakefield; he in contrast had appeared openly truculent.

'This trusty is here for rape,' said the governor.

'My God,' said Maddy. 'He's only a boy. Can we speak to him?'

'Not possible.'

We sipped the tea.

'All biscuits, cakes and bread we make in the kitchen,' said the governor. 'Other criminals are dacoits, thieves and murderers.'

I asked about Sleeman and the governor recognized the name. 'The thugs were moved here from Jabalpur after some years,' he said. 'But that is all finished now. We have only young offenders.'

The reason that the thug prison was kept going so long was, of course, because many were sentenced for life. The School for Industry, however, was also aimed at their families. Sleeman was convinced that the sons of thugs would become as dangerous as their fathers if left alone; they too, then, had to be incarcerated until they were 'reformed' by learning a trade. Legally, this was achieved by recognizing the hereditary nature of the thugs, a recognition that would have serious and enduring consequences for all India.

After tea we toured the prison and were surprised to find it immaculately well kept. There was a yard with trees and neat flowerbeds, then the simple blocks where the inmates lived. We looked inside one, no more than a large cage really, with concrete benches for beds, each with a neatly rolled blanket on it. As we passed through, the youths stood to attention and none dared raise an eye.

In the workshop were some long handlooms where youths were making carpets.

'Thugs were also using these carpet looms,' said the governor.

The murderers had actually managed to do quite well with their simple equipment, producing at one time a carpet that was one hundred and sixty-seven feet by twenty-four and weighing over two tons. This, however, was a special offering for their new Empress, Victoria, who replaced their old mistress, Kali,

[127]

as the recipient of their handiwork. No doubt the monarch was fascinated to receive such a thing after reading *Confessions of a Thug* with such interest. The carpet, a floral design on red background, was laid in the Waterloo Chamber at Windsor Castle in 1894 and remains there today, reputedly the largest single carpet ever hand-woven.

The prison had metalwork and carpentry buildings too, plus a school and hospital, all run with the same well-scrubbed and rigorous simplicity that Sleeman installed. When we left, I had to admit I had been wrong: although it was severe and stark, it was certainly well kept with a hopeful atmosphere, better in fact than many Indian hotels.

Back in the main street of Narsinghpur we discovered a beautiful old dharmshala, a kind of travellers' resthouse-cum-temple, and many people in the crowd wanted to talk. At one shop there was a commotion about a bull that had been brought to bless the establishment. Covered in cowrie shells and pompoms, it was not immediately obvious why this animal had the power to bless until Maddy noticed the extra legs. There were two of them dangling from its hump.

'This beast is able to read the human mind,' said the shopkeeper. He pointed towards the crowd of faces. 'If you ask it, "Which one is Ravi?" it will go to that person.'

The bull shook his head and frowned.

'Which one is Ravi?' Maddy shouted.

The bull immediately set off up the street at a canter, people jumping out of its way, the owner chasing. Clearly Ravi was somewhere else.

The traffic here was mainly ox carts, creaking along with mountains of sugar cane in the back. Wandering fakirs and naked babus begged from the shops and there was a magician turning marbles into snooker balls. A crowd gathered and he began to turn their ten-rupee notes into one-rupee coins. He'd done about five of these before anyone refused him. I felt

Maddy's hand on my shoulder. 'Look at the man next to you. His hands.'

He was a farmer, a grubby turban around his head and thrown over his shoulder a bundle that he gripped tightly. I could see one hand, but two thumbs.

As a rational man I had never considered omens important but the coincidences were building up. Thugs themselves were said to be extremely superstitious, particularly when it came to bird calls. An owl, for example, was a terrible omen if it screeched or was seen in daytime. Two owls were so bad, you turned around and went home. A partridge or a crow were deemed favourable, as was the appearance of a tiger. There were also taboos about strangling certain people: the castes of oil seed carriers and metalworkers were exempt, as were women (though this rarely appeared to save them). Polydactylism was a life-saving attribute too: a man with four thumbs or thirteen toes would not be a suitable sacrifice to Kali.

Narsinghpur was particularly busy that day. The Muslim community were seeing off a group of pilgrims on the haj and a huge procession could be heard in the distance, firecrackers and drums over the chanting. When we found Anthony in his wholesaler's shop, the vanguard were just appearing, wild-eyed youths dancing and whooping. The pilgrims themselves, half-a-dozen elderly people dressed in white, were sitting in a pick-up truck looking completely terrified.

'They are poor farmers,' explained Anthony. 'If they have visited Jabalpur twice in their lives I will be surprised.'

In the old days a popular proverb was 'If you reach Nagpur from Jabalpur safely, your mother will kiss you', on the grounds that it was so dangerous. Thankfully these travellers would probably be safe, but the tradition of a huge send-off survives.

We sat on small stools and drank the inevitable tea, ate the even more inevitable biscuits, and Anthony fetched a friend of his, VK, who 'knows history'.

He was a handsome man, a tax collector by profession and

suitably grave in manner, dressed in shot silk kurta and trousers. I read a passage of Sleeman to him.

> While I was in charge of the district of Nursingpore in the years 1822, 1823 and 1824, no ordinary robbery or theft could be committed without my being acquainted with it; nor was there a robber or thief of the ordinary kind in the district with whose character I had not become acquainted in the discharge of my duty as magistrate; and if any man had then told me that a gang of assassins by profession resided in the village of Kundelee – not four hundred yards from my court – and that the extensive groves of Mundesur – only one stage from me – was one of the greatest beles or places of murder in all India . . . I should have thought him a fool or a madman.

When I had finished he leaned back and sent a jet of blood-red betel juice out of the door. He chewed betel and tobacco at the same time, a powerful concoction that gave him an intense troubled expression.

'You say Kundelee?'

'Yes.'

'My friend, this is Kundelee.'

That stopped me. It crossed my mind that asking about thugs here might be like asking if your great-grandfather was a serial killer. The faces of yelling youths were pressed against the window. A firecracker went off in a great rip of explosions, leaving a pall of smoke over the procession.

'Have you heard of thugs?'

He nodded slowly. 'They are here.'

'Living in Kundelee?'

'They are everywhere – in modern form with pant and shirt. Or sometimes they come on the train as holy men and offer you prasad [blessed temple food] that contains drugs. When you fall to sleep, they can rob you.'

'Do they kill?'

[130]

He nodded. 'Sometimes.'

'How do they kill?'

He did not answer and I repeated the question.

'We are thinking,' he said, spitting thoughtfully. Betel gave a man dignity in this older India, a measured thoughtful face and long slow scarlet exclamation marks to lay in the dirt.

When he spoke, it was not to answer my original question. 'In former times they did not live here. The thugs and pindarees came and made a camp by the forest. In those British times the forest was close to Kundelee.'

I wondered why he had avoided the enquiry. Was it a loss of face to say I don't know? Was it shameful? I repeated the question.

He frowned. I was pressing too hard. 'The thugs and pindarees used many methods to kill. If there was a rich man with some valuables, they would use any means to kill him.'

Here then were two niggling worries for me. First, Sleeman had explicitly stated that Kundelee was a village inhabited by thugs; second, the accepted history is that thugs murdered for Kali not for riches and they did it by strangulation. Was VK a reliable man then? Or a misinformed one? Anthony's friend, the biscuit wholesaler, then interrupted with a story that added to my problems.

'Those thugs are so clever fellows,' he said, smiling broadly. 'They say that one time a man bought a horse from the market and began to ride it home. On the way he met a stranger by the road – of course he did not know but this man was a thug. The thug said, "What a beautiful donkey – how much did you pay?" The owner protested, of course, "This is not a donkey, it is a fine horse." And he rode further until he came across a second stranger – he did not know that this man was a thug also, and of that very same gang!' He paused while a firecracker exploded outside the shop blasting red paper shrapnel through the open door. I wondered where Maddy had gone, it was looking rather boisterous out there and she was sure to be attracting plenty of attention. When the racket stopped, the biscuit wholesaler continued.

[131]

'So the second thug says, "How much did you pay for the donkey – it seems quite old." Again the man protested saying it was a horse and all that. Well, eventually he comes to a third thug, of the gang, and this one is laughing so much and pointing at the horse. "Why are you laughing?" He was angry now. And the thug says, "I am sorry but you look so comical riding on that old donkey!" At this the man jumped off the horse and gave it a furious kick. "Be gone, you filthy old donkey! I don't know why I paid good money for such an animal." Then the horse ran away and the thugs captured it!' He roared with laughter. 'That is what these thugs are like.'

But it was not what I had assumed they should be like. VK had remained impassively unsmiling. I began to ask him about Sleeman.

'He lived in the old deputy collector's house,' he said. 'It is still here but not used. Later he went to Jubbulpore and Saugor, hanging the thugs and dacoits.'

'Was he a good man?'

More thought and a bloody exclamation mark. 'He made the roads safe to travellers.'

As if on cue, Maddy came in the little shop looking flustered. 'Sorry, I'm disturbing your conversation,' she said. 'But it's getting a bit rowdy out there.'

I suggested we try and get out to the old deputy collector's house and VK agreed to come with us. It took some time to squeeze out the door, through the mob and into Anthony's van but, once we were clear of the procession, we sped along. After a few hundred yards on a dirt track, we pulled up at a fine porticoed building, its sturdy Tuscan columns in good condition but the windows behind long since broken. Inside I could see old furniture piled up and a place where someone, a watchman perhaps, had made camp.

'Sleeman lived here before he was married,' said VK. He pointed to the capital of one column. 'Look there.'

There was a movement and I saw two baby owls staring down at us. It seemed perfectly appropriate that the owl, the thugs' most

[132]

dreaded omen, should make an appearance on Sleeman's house. A pair of them too – the worst omen.

The Englishman had kept up his interest in crime, but the thug problem receded into the background as his life was taken up with complex land revenue settlements. Tax Britannica drove its collectors hard. It was not until 1826 that Sleeman was given his chance.

One morning a gang of men were brought to the courthouse, suspected of carrying stolen goods. They certainly had large quantities of merchandise, but there was no evidence it was loot. Sleeman was forced to release them. That lunchtime, returning to his house, he was accosted in the street by a man Sleeman recognized as Kalyan Singh, a petty thief who had been with the gang earlier in the day. Sleeman quickly realised something was afoot and drew the man aside. A dispute had blown up among the gang and Kalyan Singh was disgruntled: the gang were thugs, he told Sleeman.

The Englishman's response was swift. Kalyan Singh was locked up for his own safety and Sleeman set off in pursuit of the gang with a troop of mounted sepoys. After a few miles the posse came upon the unsuspecting thugs and surrounded them. Lacking any evidence, Sleeman accused them of setting fire to a house in Narsinghpore and murdering the owner, an accusation that they laughed off. It had the effect of buying time, however, as the thugs believed they could easily talk themselves out of trouble.

Lying down near them to wait for reinforcements, Sleeman heard a few words that sent a shiver through him: he recognized them as the thug dialect. Sherwood had made a list of their vocabulary, words Sleeman had memorized several years before.

It was when the gang were safely locked up that Sleeman showed his true mettle as a detective: a man called Moti, 'Pearl', was separated from the others and interrogated. Playing him off against the group and Kalyan Singh, the Englishman soon had a confession. That same night Moti led Sleeman and his men to an isolated grove of mango trees. In one particular spot he told them to dig.

There were four bodies, three men and a boy, each with his neck broken, buried in shallow graves, their sides pierced with knives to prevent any bloating of the corpse. Next day more bodies came to light and relatives came forward to identify the dead. Among the accused Sleeman was appalled to discover a government messenger and a police inspector. Suddenly, the nature of this evil seemed horribly clear: no Indian could now be trusted and the thugs were everywhere. The floodgates were about to open.

Moti later gave a detailed deposition of his own crimes and those of others. In 1823 his gang had been on the Nagpur road when they came across a munshi – a native clerk of high rank. The man was travelling with his wife, two children and six well-armed servants. In typical style, however, the thugs managed to wheedle their way into the man's confidence. The roads were known to be dangerous and even a stout group of wary men would welcome more numbers.

Once accepted into the confidence of the group, the thugs waited until a suitable evening before attacking. Two played music to the unsuspecting munshi, while a third stole his sword. The wife and children were in a tent behind, hidden by a curtain, the servants were drowsing or asleep. At the thug signal, 'Bring tobacco!', they went to throw the rumal, but the munshi saw and shouted, 'Murder!' It was too late. Once the rumal was around a victim's throat they stood little chance. As he died, his wife ran screaming from the tent but was captured and strangled before she had gone twenty paces. One servant made it to the horses before he fell. The other five were strangled. Then the thugs went in the tent and killed the eldest child. The younger was only a baby and for a few minutes, while the rest were buried, one thug debated whether to adopt her.

Unfortunately for the child, however, he changed his mind and threw her, still alive, into the parents' grave.

Inspecting the building where Sleeman had lived and worked proved problematic. No one had a key and entry was complicated

[134]

by strands of barbed wire. It was now late afternoon and I wanted to find the village of Mundesur before sunset. I explained to my plan to VK and, after some discussion with Anthony, it was decided that the village did exist, a few miles west. This fitted with Sleeman's own description of the notorious thug burial ground.

Out of town the roads became increasingly potholed. The land was flat and fertile with vast stands of sugar cane being harvested. Everywhere we looked there were groups of cutters gathering the canes and loading them on to carts. Nearby would be a whirring mangle, crushing the juice out and then a fire with an iron skillet bubbling away.

'Ghoor,' said VK. 'They make the ghoor – in English it is jaggery.'

A flock of plovers wheeled above us and a man came wobbling along on a bicycle, his rack stacked with clothes.

'Travelling salesman,' said Anthony with a hint of professional superiority. 'Biscuit representatives use the train – second-class sleeper.'

We stopped the man to ask the way and he redirected us down a long avenue of jamun trees. At a corner next to some mangoes we found a group of Lohars, a caste of travelling blacksmiths and their simple homes, wooden wheeled carts with hooped shelters over them. Their children came around us, filthy and fly-ridden. VK translated.

'Every year we go up to Bihar, then Nepal, then back through Maharashtra. We make and mend.'

'Schools?'

He laughed. 'How can our children go to school? We are all illiterates.'

This was a life unchanged in its relentless poverty. The men and their dogs were aggressive and mangy, the women shy and undernourished. Only the children had some vitality, dancing around excitedly. The scene was very much one that Sleeman would have recognized, certainly the travelling people were often thought to be criminals, supposedly using their children as light-fingered pickpockets while the women danced or prostituted themselves. Their insularity is born of centuries of prejudice against them.

The road they directed us along deteriorated further and the reddened sun was sinking behind the dusty trees when we reached a village. A group of men were standing at a paan stall.

VK stepped out of the van, eased his back with a sigh, then dusted off his kurta. He was the collector of taxes, Sleeman's successor, and his dignity was paramount. Only when sufficient time had passed for the men to take heed of this, did he turn and notice their existence.

'What place is this?'

From among the group a leader emerged.

'Mundesur.'

VK translated my enquiry about Sleeman and the thugs, but I noted that the word thug had become pindaree.

The leader, a bright-eyed man of about fifty years, thought carefully. 'This place is called Mundesur,' he said, then loosed a stream of betel juice before continuing.

'What is the history, as told by your fathers and forefathers?'

'We know very little: this place is new Mundesur. Our people came here 150 years ago.'

'Why?'

'We do not know. Our forefathers did not tell us. Here there was jungle in those days. They cleared it for farming.'

It was hard to imagine jungle in such an agricultural setting, deforestation has so completely altered the scenery.

And the graves? Had they heard stories of bodies being dug up by the British?

'That we have never heard.'

'What about thugs?'

'We know they exist.'

'It is said they were a group who worshipped Kali and killed for her.'

They laughed. 'We never heard of that.'

VK spent some time talking to them, but no translations were forthcoming. I struggled to follow the conversation: it was still on the subject of thuggee and yet he waved away my requests for clarification.

A flight of egrets came over and settled in a reed bed. It was twilight now. They told us how to find old Mundesur by the Narmada river and we set off again.

In the van, VK began to talk about the meaning of place names: Narsinghpur is 'man-lion-city'; Jabalpur is after a rishi or holy man. He was talking as if no one was listening, his eyes glazed with all the tobacco powder consumed.

'Mundesur though,' he said. 'Sur is good. Rishetka is evil things done for the sake of gods. They threw the rumal, the handkerchief, with an iron washer tied in the corner so it would not slip.' His hands made the movements.

Maddy and I exchanged a look. It was an unsettling moment; his manner was strange and distant. When his hands reached out and showed how the strangling was done, I could almost believe he was a thug. It was the particular word, washer, that did it. In history books it is mentioned that the thugs would tie a coin in the corner of the rumal, but never a washer, that seemed more modern, a bicycle-era innovation.

'Do the thugs strangle victims today?'

He touched my knee with his fingertips. 'They use so many ways.'

'And do they follow Kali?'

'All criminals in India follow Kali, housewives follow Kali, businessmen, even tax collectors, anyone can follow Kali.'

We were out on the main road now, heading north-west to the river with the windows down, breathing the dampness of the night air. Anthony had withdrawn from all conversation; VK had taken on the project completely. I could feel my suspicions moving. Was this how Sleeman got started? Coming to this peculiar place with its thirteen-fingered and four-thumbed population of cloudy-eyed drifters, imagining all kinds of plots and subterfuges below the surface, reading omens into insignificant coincidences, being drawn down towards an underworld of shadows and suspicions? Why was VK hijacking my project, his translations becoming sparser and more oblique? Why had he not said right away that the thugs were stranglers and that he knew their methods? When Sleeman came here, he was new to public administration, a man more used to the rules and regulations of army life than the twists and turns of native farmers and landowners. And the hold of the Company must have seemed so tenuous on the vast and complex beast it had captured, a beast of many faces and superstitions, held by a few stout characters who needed all the stiff upper lips they could muster. Had he begun to mistrust those around him? Even to the point where a nebulous evil organization of killers seemed likely? His words that I had read to VK suggest as much, words that convey the sense of what the British most feared: evil within, on their doorstep, among the servants and sepoys, an evil of gigantic proportions and yet invisible to all. They had conquered the land and now found that an enemy faced across a battlefield was far preferable to this, the enemy within.

We reached the bridge long after dark. There were a few shacks lit by Tilly lamps where trucks could stop for tea. There were pots on wood fires and trays of parathas and wadas, and biscuits of course. On either side of the road lay small hills and the big damp shade of old mango trees. One of the tea-sellers, short on trade, agreed to show us to the ancient tombs on the hill.

'This place was where the ferry came until they opened the bridge in 1964.'

In former times then there would have been the boatmen and they were always held in great suspicion, men who had knowledge of water and floods and river creatures besides the people who had passed and the cargoes that came with them. Several boatmen were hanged as thugs.

Our guide, however, had come with the bridge. 'No one is left from old times. Those people all went away.'

'To where?'

'We do not know.'

'And where did you come from, and your father?'

'I myself came as a small child. I do not know where I was born as my parents died when I was still small. Some say my father was from Indore, but the truth is long dead.'

I walked up through the bushes with those words in my head: the truth is long dead. It was dark under the trees and sounds were diminished by the dust underfoot. From huts we could not see came the sound of voices and the soft strong breathing of cows in byres.

When we emerged it was beside a ghostly white temple and below shone the river, a great silver sickle cutting west. From the temple door large bats appeared, one every few seconds, heading away to the river with a leathery crack of wings.

VK was conversing with the man in Hindi, but my requests for translation went unheeded or were brushed away with 'His mind is confused' or 'No new information.' I was frustrated and angry, but if I concentrated hard I could follow a little: they talked of caves under the hill, a system that once led to the river but was now blocked off for fear of cobras. The words thug and pindaree were clear, and I understood that graves were in those tunnels, but VK was lost to me. For some strange reason, fuelled by nicotine and betel, he had slowly and surely strangled my quest. I stared out towards that thin crescent of river, now fading to burnished blue. He had attached himself so easily to the party; his clothes and manners were educated and trustworthy. And now he had choked the life from the day. I should have heeded the owls.

Anthony had stayed at the roadside but Maddy had followed. Now she came forward. 'I don't like this. Let's go. It's weird what he's doing; it's as though he has become you, taken on the project.'

We set off back down and VK came too. When we got going again, back towards Narsinghpur, we had not travelled more than a mile before we saw an electric torch waving in the road ahead. Anthony slowed and we passed an accident. A cyclist had been hit in the centre of the road and his lifeless body lay mangled in the twisted remains of his machine. A crowd had gathered and they moved aside to let us pass. We were right over on the far side, close to the edge of the levee on which the road ran, yet our tyres went through the pool of blood.

# 7

## People of Cain

IN SOMERSET MAUGHAM'S SHORT STORY 'Flotsam and Jetsam', the main character, lying in a stranger's bed somewhere upriver in Malaya, reflects that when he had complimented himself a few days before on his great good health and survival while travelling through the jungles of Borneo, it was perhaps only because he felt the first chill of impending fever. Within days he was unconscious and near death. Now his awakening comes in the spare bed of a strange and uncommunicative planter whose wife seems half-deranged.

Likewise, it seemed to me that the first chill of doubt about Sleeman and his mission to defeat the thugs, arriving just as I successfully discovered his original house and offices, was a prelude to an increasingly troubled phase of the journey.

In truth the feeling had been growing for a long time. First had come the realization that the myth of William Savage, a.k.a. Sleeman, was exactly that, a myth, one created by a desire for the dangerous and exotic. That had left me with the supposed facts: a fanatical cult of stranglers brought to justice by less colourful means than previously assumed but, nevertheless, still a good story. Sleeman had simply locked up his suspects, then played them off against each other, encouraging informers and betrayals by promising them an escape from the hangman's noose and transportation.

Events in Narsinghpur now cast doubt on that more conservative version of history. What most disturbed me was the mismatch of perceptions. For the Indians I had spoken to, thugs were deceivers and con-men – not a hereditary religious cult of human sacrificers. And there was precious little memory of them at all. Narsinghpur was a place, in Sleeman's time, so infested with the brutes that no journey was safe, and yet no one remembered much about them. At first I thought that too much time had passed and perhaps a thug ancestry was not to be advertised. But Sleeman was remembered, at least a little. Hardly surprising that in the darkness and with VK's strange behaviour, I had begun to believe in conspiracies, but now I embarked on something a little less fanciful: I began to read the thug literature more critically.

I took out my battered photocopy of Sleeman's *Ramaseeana*, the language of the thugs. The book, he declares in the preface, is a collation of all information available relevant to the thug, the purpose being to educate British officers so as to better recognize and prosecute thug crimes.

This was Sleeman's major work and it is astonishing in its detail. His thug family trees set out to show how the hereditary organization worked: fathers passing thug lore and knowledge on to their sons. His elegant handwriting is linked with curling lines of association and kinship. Comments on characters are colourful and informative:

> Dead in the Hatta Jail after the Lucknadown Murders.
> Allahdad, executed at Saugor before our rule. He was buried up to his breast in the Ground and shot at with arrows. His tomb near Saugor is still visited by Thugs.
> Nidhan. Died of the bite of a snake.
> Kunholee. Cut his throat as a Sacrifice before the image of Davey

[142]

[Kali] at Brindachul 32 Years ago but recovered in three days by
a Miracle as all Thugs believe. He died 1824.
Name forgotten. He cut open his Belly before the image of Davey
at the time his Brother cut his throat, but he died as it is supposed
from the want of the same faith.

Before, when looking at these snippets, I had tended to skip over
the repetitions and short entries, but now I saw how important they
were. 'Adopted' was repeated again and again, so too was the 'dead
in jail'. But surely the thug trade was a hereditary crime? Sleeman
had specifically and repeatedly said that the thugs were a set of
families united in an evil enterprise. In 1916 the ethnologist Robert
Russell included thugs in his *Tribes and Castes of the Central
Provinces of India*, placing them between Teli (oil men) and Turi
(a cultivating caste). They were a social stratum of murderers, the
devil's own breed of killers. One entry on the family trees caught
my eye: 'Ruheen Khan. At home a mere Boy but he will follow
his father's trade of Murder if he lives and is left to his choice.'
So the boy was to be convicted before he committed a crime?
And many entries were briefly curtailed with 'died with no issue'
– hardly the stuff of great lineages.
The supposed thug language, Ramasee, did not fill me with
confidence either. It was a list of words, nothing more. A language
needs grammar, a dialect has a separate vocabulary. But this did
not even look like a dialect, more a set of jargon terms that might
be used by any group of people on a common business. Thieves are
well known for devising such slang, but by terming it a language,
the notion of a separate people was further implied.
The word thug itself provided ample ambiguities. In eighteenth-
century Hindi, as now, it meant cheat or deceiver. There was no
necessary connotation even of robbery. The blank faces I'd met
with in Narsinghpur were indicative, not of a conspiracy of silence
on some embarrassing history, but a mismatch of terms. Phansigar
did mean strangler, but that was taken to mean men who used a
noose, in the manner of a lassoo, to snare their prey. In Indian

minds the word thug did not mean a murderous sect peculiarly devoted to Kali, it meant a con-man, nothing more. That was why the stories people came up with were so innocuous: the thug was a man who would convince you the horse bought from market was a donkey, he would certainly deceive, but not necessarily strangle.

Now I began to read more critically. And I found plenty to worry me about William Sleeman and his crusade. In their depositions, so many thugs informers, or 'approvers' as they were called at the time, had said they had only followed the profession for a year or two. Even some of the first ever approvers, caught by Captain Borthwick in Malwa, had claimed only a couple of seasons of thugging. Naturally, these men tended to be overshadowed by the big time confessors, men like Buhram who claimed to have murdered 931 people over a period of forty years. Of those who were younger, many had been adopted after their real parents were murdered by thugs. Few, in fact, had been born into the profession, as James Sleeman puts it, 'brought up in a faith which regarded the killing of men as a legitimate sport'. There were several cases where sons of thugs were found to be quite harmless men going about the business of farming or even holy men.

On the issue of plunder, Sleeman's theory of a murderous sacrificing cult would suggest loot to be a secondary matter. But almost every account from a thug spoke of searching for good prey: treasure-carriers, bankers' agents, wealthy men of all kinds. It was common for such men to travel disguised as impoverished ruffians, and when the thugs mistook a genuine impoverished ruffian for a camouflaged rich man, their anger was plain. No great play was ever made of Kali and as for the supposed taboos – of which the British made great play – they were constantly flouted.

There was no doubt that many murders had been committed, that was not in question, but who by? Sleeman's evidence did not add up to a criminal caste working away at their infernal profession for centuries. His attempts at genealogy were weak: the Sagartii horsemen following Alexander into India marrying their strangling skills to Kali worship and founding a dynasty? In fact, the thugs were drawn from all backgrounds and castes: there were Muslims and Hindus, Brahmins and untouchables, warriors and farmers, as disparate a bunch as one could hope to gather. Perhaps most suprising of all, the clinching anomaly, was that one thug was found to be British: a renegade soldier named Creagh who started a gang in Cawnpore in 1802.

Now I began to compare the thug legend as started by Sleeman and propagated by fellow Victorians, Philip Meadows Taylor, Edward Thornton and Caleb Wright, with the actual verbatim accounts given by thugs in prison. They did not match up. In almost every case they came across as normal peasant farmers, traders, officials, even police officers who went out to murder occasionally. Their loot was divided up and a tithe paid to a local landowner or prince in much the same manner as the gentlemen adventurers who set off from England in Elizabethan times, hoping to grab a Spanish galleon and some jewels for the monarch, before returning to the business of farming.

When I set down my books after a steady bout of careful reading I was filled with unease: Sleeman and his supporters had ruthlessly exterminated a menace, but was the nature of that menace their own invention? And if they had twisted the truth into something new, then why?

That same night, after we had returned from Narsinghpur, the hotel was taken over by a noisy and drunken bachelor party who hammered on the walls, barged into the rooms and caused general mayhem. They were staying several days too and the management of the hotel suggested that Maddy and I, the only other guests, should leave. So when we arrived at the coffee house that morning, it was with luggage and without accommodation. Too late we had discovered there was a big conference in town, plus several weddings. There was tension in the air too, a palpable sense of impending violence, and the reason was simple: St Valentine.

Some days previously Hindu extremists had declared the saint an evil interloper, bringing unwanted foreign traditions to Mother

India. In Mumbai, the leader of the Shiv Sena, Bal Thackeray, called for Valentine's Day to be banned and promised that celebrations would be disrupted by his men. Thackeray, model for Salman Rushdie's hoodlum-cum-politician, Raman Fielding, in *The Moor's Last Sigh*, is the man who steered communal politics back to the forefront in the 1980s. The patron of love was an outlaw and they began to burn him. All across northern India bookshops that stocked Valentine cards were torched and lovers who bought red roses (clearly anti-Hindu agitators) were threatened.

When we gave up searching for rooms and decided on breakfast, we found ourselves in our rickshaw, bags under feet, rattling along past the Young Ladies Domestic Science College – in other words, a flashpoint.

I wasn't paying much attention. I had Lieutenant-General Francis Tuker open on my knee and was reading out loud about a shrine at Sleemanabad that had given Sleeman and his wife Amélie a son after four barren years. 'From that day on the village prospered and expanded so that the inhabitants renamed it Sleemanabad and ordained that at the shrine a lamp was to be kept burning for ever to commemorate Sleeman's association with the village and its holy place. The lamp burned in 1937: perhaps it burns today.'

'Let's go and see,' said Maddy who was at a loose end because Regina's mother's stay in Jabalpur had been extended.

At that moment there was a shout, a tremendous thwack and our rickshaw stopped dead. We could see a commotion around us: several burly policemen were struggling with a group of young men, dragging them to a prison van. Then a large handlebar moustache came bristling into the rickshaw attached to a large head and a uniform. 'You are most welcome in Jabalpur,' he said. 'Heartiest congratulations on Valentine's Day.'

There was no way forward so I got down and asked what was happening. The police far outnumbered any protesters and were belabouring a motor scooter with iron-tipped lathi canes. Through it all, serene young ladies in delicately colourful shalwar kameez sailed through the crowd towards the main gate, hugging textbooks to their chests.

'We are here to prevent any unpleasantness,' said the moustachioed officer. 'Those fellows were nabbed when attempting to prevent the delivery of gift items to young ladies.'

'What gift items?'

'Romantical greetings cards.'

Once clear of the Valentine's Day flashpoints, we sped around seeking accommodation but to no avail. At nine o'clock we found ourselves sitting with our luggage in the coffee house, contemplating our future.

Maddy regarded the map. 'Sleemanabad is north of here,' she said. 'And you've got nothing left to do here – why don't you set off?'

It seemed only appropriate that a visit to Sleemanabad should happen on V-Day, as the press had begun to refer to it; after all, the town was named in honour of a successful impregnation.

I pointed out my projected route: ride up to Sleemanabad, across country to isolated Sagar, then north to Jhansi and the Bundelkund. From there I planned to work my way east along the Ganges to Varanasi.

She tapped the map. 'I'll come with you to Sleemanabad, then carry on direct to Varanasi. Maybe we could hook up there in a month?'

'What about Regina and your Hindi classes?'

She sighed. 'To tell the truth I'm not making much progress. I think I've become a psychotherapist that pays her client. All we do is gossip. I want to hang out on the ghats and watch the sadhus do pranayama.'

I put the map away. 'OK, we'll have breakfast and set off.'

She stood up. 'I'll skip breakfast: I'll have to go to Regina's to explain. I won't be long.'

The door closed behind her and I picked up the English newspaper that the proprietor had thoughtfully placed on the table. A minute later the door opened and a middle-aged Indian gent came

[147]

in and sat opposite me. He had barely got himself in his chair before he leaned forward and waved at me.

'Hey! Give me the newspaper.'

For a second I thought there must be a second paper lying there, but no, there was just the one in the whole café.

'I'm reading it.'

He scowled. 'I need the paper. Give it to me.'

I felt the ire rising. 'You'll have to wait.'

The man leaned over to two men sitting at another table and said loudly, 'We are independent India now. They are no longer in charge but they still come here and behave like this.'

I shook the paper angrily and ostentatiously turned the page. Suddenly every story needed to be read in detail. It's true that in India there is a stratum of society, old men mostly, who either love or loathe the British: one group tells you that things would be better if the nation of pipe-smoking, tweed-jacketed, cricket-playing Old Etonians came back and lorded it over the cartographic pink bits; the other tells you that the nation of pig-sticking, native-baiting Old Etonians is still lording it over the ethnographic brown bits. In either version 'The British' have become a kind of 'Aryans', a highly suspect but politically useful tribe who probably never existed.

The man continued venting his frustration to his neighbours. 'I ask give me the paper but no, he considers himself the boss.'

I ignored him for a while, assuming the tirade would subside but instead it got worse. 'Give me paper. Give me now. Give me that newspaper immediately!'

It should not happen, I admit, that such petty things should flare into serious things. But I was tired: the hotel business, the trip to Narsinghpur business, the death of St Valentine. Then there were conflicts back home, money, all those things I had pushed back down and closed the lid. My emotional life was an overstuffed suitcase with a dodgy lock. In a flash of insight, I understood that I hated this man more than any other beast on earth. I could strangle him and enjoy the experience.

[148]

*Thugs Strangling a Traveller on Horseback.*

Watercolour by Captain James Paton of thugs strangling a victim. Paton's frame of mind during the anti–thug campaigns of the mid–1830s is revealed in the marginal notes of his reports: 'Brutal as wolves and jackals are, they are surpassed in brutality by fallen man. The wolves follow their nature, man follows his, both are evil … All must be born again ere they can see the Kingdom of heaven.'

Man Khan
hung at Indore 1830.

Hunholee

Soobhance
transported
1833

Behra at
large and on
Thuggee alias
Kishuna adopt-
-ed

Baha...
in the S...

Hunholee cut his Throat as a Sacrifice
before the image of Davey at Bindachul
32 Years ago. but recovered in three days by
a Miracle as all Thugs believe. He died 1824

Hurlee Khan
alias Futteh Khan
hung at Jubbulpoor
1831.

Laadut died
at Mahoba
without issue
Male —

Gesa

Musulman
name forgotten

Moneem alias
Eedul

Pulha

Puharee adopted,
and from a Brah-
mun and Musulman
dead.

Deendar

Sehtoo alias Laadut
executed for Murder
at Muttra. no Male
issue —

Sheikh

Hinga Junr.

Jafirolla
alias Chuppara died
without issue. on a Thug
expedition in the Duckun

Noor Khan
11 or 12.

Sheikh Imaet Junr.
approver arrested 10th Novr
1839

Chund Khan
hung at Saugor
1832.

Dulele hung
at Saugor 1832

Dhurrum
Khan sentenced
to Death 1832, but
reprieved

Mungul Khan
a river on a Thug
Saugor District

Nijabut at
Mithoo appro...

At large of this family
Yalim Jemadar
Khoda Buksh Jemadar
Atae Khan
Puchora alias Man Khan
Sawun his Brother
Ashraf Son of Iktear
Paun Khan Son of Do.
Hunwer Son of Ditto supposed to be dead
    Relationship to the family forgotten.

Relationship to the
family forgotten.

Bhujjoo died at Lahore

Name forgotten He cut open his Belly before the image of Davey at the time his Brother cut his throat, but he died as it is supposed from the want of the same faith.

Fail

Names forgotten dead

Zubur Khan at Jubbulpoor Sentenced to 14 Years imprisonment in the Bhilsa Case.

Noor Khan sentenced to 14 Years imprisonment in the Bhilsa case.

Ghazee in Saugor Jail.

Buksha adopted. hung at Indore 1829.

Posee

Durab

Zalim Jemadar adopted at large on Thuggee.

Hutka died without issue

Durroo Shot at Sonwarra by Mr Halhed's party

Choteya adopted. at large.

Ghussa transported 1832 adopted.

Bagha

Rampanee adopted

Horkon, alias Zulfukar transported 1832

in

Imamee approver

Bukhtawur

Dulele

Blank Sain Khan

at large and on Thuggee. arrested 1835

Samlee in the Saugor Jail 18 years of Age.

Adopted Khoda Buksh Jemadar at large on Thuggee. arrested 1834.

Sd/ W. H. Sleeman

William Sleeman's thug family tree drawn up in the 1830s and 40s to establish links between the thug groups of central India.

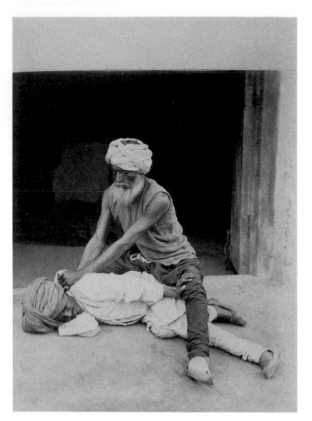

Rare photograph of convicted thugs demonstrating their techniques. To avoid the death penalty or transportation these men must have been informers. Taken in the 1870s at Jubbulpore Prison by an unknown photographer.

Thug prisoners drawn by Captain James Paton in the 1830s. Probably these were part of a group who were tattooed below the eyes with the word thug, then transported to Port Blair in the Andaman Islands.

Major-General Sir William Henry Sleeman. The portrait was probably painted in 1851 at Lucknow by George Duncan Beechey with the medals added later. During the siege of 1857 the picture was rescued from the residency in Lucknow.

Koose Muniswamy Veerappan, India's most wanted bandit. His career started with smuggling sandalwood and ivory but has recently branched out into kidnapping. He is reputedly responsible for more than 120 murders.

Paddling down the Cauvery River in a basket coracle. The jungled hills on the horizon form one of India's largest surviving wildernesses. Forming the border between Tamil Nadu and Karnataka, the river and its resources are a politically sensitive issue – one that the bandit Veerappan has exploited.

Men bathing in the Hogenakkal Falls on the Cauvery River.

The School for Industry in Jubbulpore set up by Sleeman. Here, thug families and informers were incarcerated for life – those convicted thugs who did not become informers were either hanged or transported. The building now houses the Indian Home Guard.

(*Left*) A follower of Hanuman the monkey god, living as a monkey in the grounds of the Kali temple in Brindachul (also Vrindyachul) near Mirzapur. The temple, sited where Kali's breast is said to have fallen to earth, was also the holiest place for the thugs.

(*Below*) Kali worshippers at Brindachul during the Navaratri festival – the nine nights dedicated to the goddesses.

In that moment I lost control to a demon. I leaped to my feet. I barrelled across the room, shaking the paper in my fist. 'I-WILL-GIVE-IT-TO-YOU-WHEN-I-FINISH-YOU-IGNORANT-POMPOUS-PRAT.'

The man's face fell. With an adroit manoeuvre he swung his table around between us. It took the wind out of me and it was comical. The murderous fury disappeared.

I stalked back. The demon went back in his box and I now regretted what I'd done. Out of the corner of my eye I could see the man, silent but his face black with anger. After a minute for my pride, I got up and placed the paper in front of him. He ignored it, drank his coffee and left.

The coffee house-owner was a pleasant man who hurried over; he was full of apologies and disbelief. 'He is not a regular customer, but I know he is a big man in the town, a professor I think.'

My breathing returned to normal. Wry looks were exchanged with other customers. A feeling of quiet support came from them, or was it commiseration that I had lost face so badly by flaring up? I tried to read Tuker.

In the months immediately following the birth of Sleeman's son, famine gripped the region and the roads were strewn with bodies. Everyone, including his wife, begged Sleeman to requisition grain from the merchants but he refused. His reasoning was that there was sufficient grain but requisitioning would send the merchants scurrying off to hide it. The famine worsened.

I left off reading when Maddy returned, arriving, as ever, with great panache. No one could ignore this woman; somehow all eyes were gathered towards her by the colourful clothes and sheer vitality. 'Regina wasn't there,' she said. 'I had to leave a note.'

The coffee shop proprietor, his hair and teeth attractively blackened, pulled out her chair with a flourish. 'Madame,' he said, 'you have missed a most amusing episode.'

But before explanations could be made, the amusing episode took another turn. The door was flung open and the angry professor was there with two burly policeman brandishing lathis.

[149]

'There he is,' he cried loudly, 'arrest him, the miscreant!' He bounded forward, full of courage and wagged a finger in my face. 'Aha! You, sir, are going to prison! Ha ha!'

The two policemen strode in valiantly. Their boots and bellies were big and heavy, their lathis stout and ready: they had come to break skulls. But then they saw Maddy. She kind of rose from a half-crouch – she had never actually sat down – and towered over them. Half a head taller than both, she was dressed in reds and oranges, something akin to a fireball, and she was like nothing ever seen before in the Jabalpur coffee shop.

'What is the meaning of this?' she demanded.

One of the policeman crumpled instantly; he went to the counter and slouched against it, ignoring everyone, and everyone was now talking excitedly and simultaneously at them. The second policeman, older and moustachioed, cocked his head on one side, nonplussed. I think they had expected to find a bar-room brawl, not this angry angel. Even the professor had retreated a little, still waggling a finger, but his shouts had become squeaky, 'Arrest him! Arrest that man!' The proprietor was between the policemen, his hands wringing, face pleading and voice wheedling with explanations. The policeman turned to the professor and told him to be quiet, then listened to the proprietor. Finally he turned to me.

'It is better that you apologize.'

I bridled, but then remembered with a twinge of shame how the demon had made me stamp across the room. Plus I wanted to get off to Sleemanabad. 'I apologize,' I said reluctantly.

There was an instantaneous transformation. The professor straightened himself up, smiled. Maddy sat down. The proprietor offered tea. 'No hard cheddar,' said the professor to me, shaking my hand sportingly, as if I'd just been dismissed with the last ball of the match and only one run for victory. Then out he went with the policemen, who were whistling and twirling their lathis like cricket bats.

*     *     *

There was a last stop for me on the way out to the bus station. At Christ Church School I stopped the rickshaw and asked a man the way. I could hear the distant sound of chanted responses from a classroom and girls in green cardigans with neatly plaited hair were cycling sedately past. The man proved to be a teacher and quite familiar with thuggee. 'Look at that tree,' he said, pointing out a fine specimen by the school gates. 'Sleeman Sahib hanged thugs from there – and innocent men too.'

I'd heard such accusations of injustice before and never really heeded them, but now my thinking had changed. I remembered a section in the confession of Feringhea, the dark-eyed panther who inspired Eugène Sue and John Masters. But this genuine Feringhea did not behave like a cruel oriental killer should: he gave himself up after Sleeman incarcerated his family. Then, when questioned one day about his young nephew, Jharhu, he burst into tears. 'You ought not to have hanged him,' he said to Sleeman. 'He never strangled or assisted in strangling any man.' The outburst had the ring of truth, but Sleeman ignored it, observing only that Feringhea did not weep for any of his victims.

The School of Industry, the original building set up by Sleeman for holding thugs and their families, is now the offices of the Home Guard. It is well kept and freshly painted with neat borders marked out with white stones. Nobody challenged me as I wandered in through the gate and around the three barrack blocks with their cool whitewashed rooms, a few filled with the tin trunks of the Home Guard men. On a wall to the left of the gate a plaque had been raised: 'The Jubbulpore School of Industry was founded in 1836, by the late Major-General Sir W.H. Sleeman, K.C.B., then General Superintendent of operations for the suppression of Thuggee and Dacoity.'

Initially I had been pleased to find the buildings had survived, but walking around I wondered if I really felt that way. What kind of a monument was this to be better kept than many fine temples or mosques?

[151]

In the commandant's office I said hello to the senior officers and had a rather stilted conversation that went: 'You are from?'

'England.'

'Itself?'

'Yes.'

'Take tea?'

'No thank you.'

This exhausted the commandant's English so we did something similar in Hindi until my stock was exhausted, then to save further embarrassment, he simply returned to his previous task, a chat with his other visitor. I glanced around the spartan room, the place Sleeman would have used to write up his reports and notes.

He was a prodigious writer: for him, like most British in India, letter-writing was a daily activity, a means of keeping in touch with your own kind. These letters and documents are the raw material of the thuggee history, along with the contemporary drawings and sketches, the original confessions of thugs, as handwritten by their accusers at the time, and the official correspondence and reports made during the thug trials. With my doubts about the published history, these sources were crucial. Only in these could there be any hope of finding the true facts.

The commandant was writing something in a huge leather-bound ledger, finishing with a flourish, then calling out of the open window for his sergeant. There was birdsong in the trees and the murmur of voices. Nothing much had altered here in 150 years. The sergeant arrived with a stamp of his heels and was detailed to show me around the compound. I didn't like to say that I had already done the tour so, like the conversation, I did it all again before escaping to meet Maddy at the bus station.

Reading the handwriting of previous eras is usually tricky. One wonders how well human beings will manage the task in a few generations, when computers and printed text have taken over completely. Perhaps there will be bookish men in shabby suits sitting under umbrellas at the door of the British Library offering

[152]

letter-reading services, just as they now do for letter-writing outside Indian courthouses.

William Sleeman's letters to his friend and colleague Charles Fraser are a good example. Written on pale blue notepaper in faded sepia ink, with the orange sealing wax still affixed, they start in 1821, reasonably legibly. He discusses a cholera epidemic and the causes, asks for certain books and comments on others; the words of an intelligent and interested man. One letter survives that was sent to Fraser from Mauritius where Sleeman found sugar cane varieties that he would later introduce to Indian farmers. Compared to Fraser's replies, there is a certain pressure of thought, an intensity, that speaks of a man who drives himself hard. Fraser seems cooler, laid back at times. Their relationship suffered later on because Fraser gets passed over in the choice of a leader for anti-thug operations, a role that goes to Sleeman.

Now the work of thug-hunting takes over and Sleeman's handwriting deteriorates remarkably. By 1835 his hand is a crazed scrawl that is in many places completely indecipherable. 'I avail myself of what little power I have in my eyes,' he begins on one occasion, and then proves what little that power was. He was often in camp, using candles, tired, sometimes sickened by what he had seen and heard, always on the march, an implacable nemesis hunting down the demons.

The papers of another officer, James Paton, provide a startling example of what the times were like. There were watercolour pictures that he had done, depicting the thugs in the act of gouging out eyes, of dismembering and disposing of bodies, strangling innocent travellers. So vivid and horrible are the images that it is difficult to remind oneself that Paton could not have seen such things, only imagined them, prompted by thug confessions. (Many of Mrs Fanny Parks's thuggee sketches, the ones that caused so much horror in England, appear to be straight copies of Paton's works.)

The depositions in Paton's notes were often macabre and the weight of numbers was horrible as each thug expedition was

[153]

recounted. The vile litany of murder and loot interspersed with Paton's own almost despairing comments: 'like demons, set at utter defiance the dictates of conscience, and the Laws of God and man'. The mood was of asphyxiating madness, a terrible darkness of human depravity, and in this moral nightmare the British turned to God: 'All have sinned,' wrote Paton in a marginal note, 'and all must be born again ere they can see the Kingdom of Heaven.' These were the remarks that never made it to the final reports or Sleeman's own exhaustively statistical papers, but they gave the true flavour of the anti-thug operation, and that flavour, I realized, was that of the witch hunt.

There were glaring inconsistencies and doubts. In the testimony of one Rumzan, I read: 'I may have seen as many as 80 or 90 men strangled yearly. This would give in *his* 22 years of thuggee 1,700 victims.' The mistake I have italicised, of using 'his', did not make it to the official record as the whole testimony was marked 'omit' and Rumzan is later recorded as saying, 'I have strangled about 300 men with my own hands for I was a great strangler.' There was even a pencilled note at the bottom: 'The statements of this miscreant seem incredible . . . it seems unlikely they should be true.'

The accused thug was fighting for his life, turning queen's evidence to save his own neck and condemning his former associates to the gallows, knowing full well that it was his word against theirs. Though many bodies were exhumed, the confessions far outstripped them in numbers; the accused desperate to gain sufficient importance to be accepted as an informant, an approver, the only way to save his neck. A deluge of macabre and fulsome depositions resulted. Sleeman's friend Charles Fraser acknowledged the problem in a letter dated 22 September 1842. 'We find great difficulty in getting evidence,' he wrote, 'and are dependent for information chiefly on the disclosures of accomplices.'

Not all English officers agreed with Sleeman's methods, believing the opportunity for malpractice too great, and it is thanks to one such man that we see Sleeman's campaign in a different perspective. G.T. Lushington, political agent to the Rajah of Bharatpur, a princely state near Agra, does not warrant a mention in the various biographies of Sleeman. He only makes it to the selected records of the Thuggee Campaign as an example of how difficult Sleeman's work was made by a handful of Englishmen who were blind to the evil menace and the steps required to destroy it.

In early 1832 a company of Sleeman's sepoys, with a munshi, a local clerk, and guided by three thug 'approvers', rode into Bharatpur and began arresting suspects. Uproar ensued. For a start the legal position was that the raiding party needed to inform the rajah and Mr Lushington. Added to this were the arrests themselves: a bodyguard of the rajah himself and a much-respected Brahmin named Kuloo, both of whom were put in chains.

Sleeman regarded the position and respectability of suspects as yet more fiendish thug disguises. Had not Feringhea himself, the infamous thug leader, once been a valued servant of Sir David Ochterlony? The fact that these particular men hid themselves in the princely state of Bharatpur was only more damning: were not the princes often enmeshed in a network of criminal alliances and underhand payments? This was the nature of the beast: it was disguised in your own home, it was the oriental character itself, untrustworthy and mendacious, a stereotype reinforced by just about every work of literature available from Shakespeare's Shylock to Thackeray's Rummun Loll. The weight of European prejudice was coming to bear and its victims were to be those tangled up in the allegations of convicted murderers.

In this case, the three approvers all positively identified the sepoy as Booree Khan, a notorious villain who had accompanied them on expeditions seven years before in Malwa, the highland area to the west of Jabalpur. The Brahmin's name had been passed to the munshi by the mistress of a thug in Saugor Jail.

Lushington refused to accept this. He fired off a letter of complaint to Sleeman's superiors and his words were clear, direct and sensible. Where is the evidence, he demands, beyond the word of three admitted murderers who have had plenty of time to confer, plus the word of a prostitute, the mistress of another convicted villain? No one in Bharatpur, he says, has heard of Booree Khan. The sepoy is called Jhundee Khan and seven years ago he was a mere thirteen-year-old boy.

'It is of course,' he wrote, 'the object of the thug witnesses to convict someone, for on the convictions effected by them their hopes of eventual pardon rest.' He goes on to point out that men are innocent until proven guilty and adds, without naming names, that certain munshis are said to be deliberately accusing respectable wealthy men, knowing that good bribes will be paid to withdraw the allegations.

His superiors reject his objections and support Sleeman. Lushington is censured. What happened to the sepoy and Brahmin is unknown, but if they survived it was by the good fortune of having Lushington around and living in a princely state rather than British territory. The flurry of paperwork reveals the hard truth about Sleeman's campaign: the scope for injustice was enormous. Men like the sepoy could not only be damned by the word of convicted killers, but their convictions did not even require evidence that they participated in the murders. Membership of the cult was sufficient. Most of these were transported for life to the penal colony on the Andaman Islands while their families were rounded up and incarcerated in the School of Industry, there to learn how to weave carpets for their Empress.

The road out to Sleemanabad was a straight drive along boulevards of mango and jamun trees that Sleeman had planted with thug prison labour. Some were in flower, covered in a champagne-coloured froth of blossoms. Where the road kinked there would be a village, usually beside a low hill flecked with the scarlet pennants of Shiva. These were attractive bucolic places: hay ricks and lazing buffaloes, blue-washed walls, old doors and red pan-tiled roofs, all ragged at the eaves like broken pie crusts. Passing the mango groves beyond Sihora, I recalled that the thugs once strangled and buried sixty travellers in one night. Digging was going on here, but for fibre-optic cables not corpses. The families making the trench were camped in grass and twig shelters alongside the road.

Sleeman had travelled this way many times, camping in the groves long before he knew what lay beneath. Like travellers in those old days, the local bus stops everywhere, sometimes long enough to grab a handful of singara nuts or a cup of tea. Most people were farmers, planting rice where there was good water or a pump, chickpeas elsewhere. There were mahua trees dotted everywhere, its fruit popular animal feed as well as the source of local illicit hooch, but no forests. The arrival of the British had a huge effect on agriculture, starting the wave of tree clearances that have resulted in the open countryside of India today. They made attempts to improve seed stocks, just as Sleeman did with sugar cane, but there were efforts to control what was planted too, in one particular case, strenuous efforts.

The first high-level report on thuggee was written after the first batch of thug trials in 1832 by Agent to the Governor-General, F.C. Smith, and it makes interesting reading as the official line on thuggee was as yet less well defined. Buried in the reforming zeal and administrative detail of Smith's prose, I found reference to a factor that took me by surprise. Opium.

One of the first acts of the British in their new dominions was to establish an opium monopoly in the suitable upland region of Malwa to the west of Jabalpur. Although poppies had long been grown in India, the use of the drug was not widespread and not taxed. Following the British conquests of the 1780s onwards, however, there was a need to collect revenue and the answer was opium.

China had been supplied with the drug by European merchants for many years, assisted by an ambiguous legal system that allowed importation, but punished selling with public strangulation. Despite a tightening of the laws, demand was increasing and British merchants saw an opportunity: a product they could exchange for the new-fangled tea wanted back in Britain. Huge areas of land began to go under poppy cultivation in Malwa.

[157]

As China became dependent on Indian *chan du*, British India developed an unhealthy addiction to the revenue raised and, of course, the product itself. India had over 10,000 official opium dens by 1891. The system was that rich Bombay merchants would send money to buy the product in advance and they used the traditional Rokerias, a caste of treasure-carriers, to do it. Jewels, dollars and gold mohurs came pouring across India into Malwa: officially four million rupees in 1827. The time to do this was shortly after the Dessera festival in mid-October, exactly the same time that all accounts give as the onset of the thugs' 'hunting season'.

Smith's report deplores the huge losses to Bombay's mercantile classes and also their response: a system whereby they paid off thugs at annual meetings. He does not mention the people who died in famines that were a direct result of opium cultivation. When questioned by a parliamentary commission in 1871, the former British Resident at Indore admitted Malwa had become a net importer of food because of increased land use for poppies. From 1810 onwards production had doubled approximately every decade. When crops failed, the farmers found themselves unable to feed their families and in hock to agents who had forwarded money on opium.

Here, then, was the new factor in central India: the movement of large amounts of money with relatively little security under the very noses of substantial numbers of people dispossessed by British conquests. A few were hardened robbers, others were freebooters who saw a chance, some were desperate: they all needed a method of survival and that method was plunder.

John Malcolm, the first British administrator in the Central Provinces from 1818–22, saw it that way too, defining eleven types of marauders, including thugs. Malcolm states clearly that the thugs were composed of all castes and Muslims, that booty was always their first objective, that they used a strangling silken cord and that drugs might be mixed in with their unwitting victims' drinks while innocently sharing a meal.

[158]

Smith's report inadvertently makes clear what was later conveniently forgotten: the thugs were freebooters and to a great extent created by British conquests. Their opportunity for thievery was due to the opium trade. He does not mention Kali or nationwide leaders or high levels of organization.

After those first trials, 111 of the 345 prisoners were hanged. A further sixty-eight died inexplicably in prison, either before or after trial; 167 were transported for life (most to the Andamans); 32 got life imprisonment, and 22 were released on security or pardoned.

In the view of Stewart Gordon of the University of Michigan, 'It was the writing of William Sleeman and the evangelical, crusading tone of the British Indian administration of the 1830s that played up these locally-organized, small-scale marauding groups (given the name thugs by the British) into a hideous, widespread religious conspiracy, somehow typical of India and Indian "national character".'

It can be added that the drug-running East India Company also placed temptation under their noses, then hanged them without too much bothering with evidence. William Sleeman, for his pains, became a hero to the Raj.

I had asked the driver to drop us at the police thana, but he got the wrong place and we had to walk half a mile with our baggage through the straggly town that bears Sleeman's name.

The police post was set back a little from the road with a couple of tall trees on one side of the gate. It looked very much like the house given to William Savage by the makers of *The Deceivers*, a low single-storey bungalow with whitewashed walls and an uneven pantile roof stooping down over a shady veranda. To the right, almost next to the road, was a modern addition, a peculiar monument with a plaque for a murdered policeman and another for William Henry Sleeman. Under the trees on the left were parked several old motorbikes and a lorry; the policemen had also dragged their desk out there and were lounging around chatting.

I strolled over and greeted the constables, a motley crew with faded uniforms and big bellies.

'Station officer sleeping,' they said, making no move to go and wake him. It was now around two p.m.

I explained why we had come and we were shown around the post – excepting the officer's sleeping quarters. There were two empty lock-ups, a rickety desk with handcuffs and leg irons hung above it on the wall.

'Are you married?' asked one of them.

Maddy laughed. 'No! We are friends.'

We were shown the living quarters at the back. 'You can sleep here tonight,' said one, and I noticed the sidelong glance at Maddy as he said it.

It was a suggestion but was it suggestive? Maddy showed no sign of hearing anything amiss.

Back in the front yard they showed me the framed photographs of William Sleeman and Amélie, a straight-backed specimen of Victorian womanhood. I asked about the temple and one offered to take us there on his motorcycle.

It was a battered old Enfield 350, a model still made in India. He kicked it into life and waited for us to get on behind him. Maddy hesitated, I did too. The rear position would obviously be vulnerable to falling off, plus very uncomfortable. On the other hand, the middle person would inevitably be squashed against the policeman.

'Maybe we could walk,' I said.

'Too far!' cried the constable. 'Lady, sit here.'

Maddy took my suggestion as a slur on her adventurous nature and, gathering her skirts and scarves and colourful cottons together, threw her leg across like a Marlboro cowboy. The lecherous expression on the man's face confirmed what I suspected. I leaned back on the rack and gave a mental shrug. I'd known her long enough to see that she would clip her outstretched wings for no man, and no situation. But this was a backwater rural part of India where the women did not do such things. As we pulled away, I glanced across at the other policemen and there was Memsahib Amélie Sleeman, gazing back in black-and-white disapproval.

We rode along the main road for about a mile then cut east along a smooth path of hardened earth. The first village we came to was a lovely tight-packed huddle of houses with narrow alleyways lined with patties of drying cow dung. In the centre was the temple of Baba Haridas, the holy man who had known Sleeman. It was a simple place, a clean swept yard at the front and a single box-like room which the priest opened up for us.

'There was a holy man called Baba Haridas who performed a famous breathing feat in 1837,' said Maddy. 'I wonder if it could be the same man? He was locked in a box for forty days with his orifices blocked up.'

I liked the idea of Sleeman's favourite holy man surviving without breathing, but if it was the same yogi he had travelled over to the Punjab as the feat was performed for Maharajah Ranjit Singh and some British observers.

Inside the temple the priest showed us the portrait of Haridas and the brass lamp that Sleeman had given, still burning with a low camphor flame. Most of the village had turned up to view our visit and ask for photographs to be taken. We made a donation to temple funds and set off back to the police post.

It was now the time of day when the light begins to subtly change: the harsh glare of noontime dies and colour comes back to the fields. We roared into the yard to find that the station officer was still sleeping. I went to photograph the monument, leaving Maddy sitting at the desk surrounded by the constables. Their manner, friendly at first, had become truculent and leering and I knew why. Maddy's friendly nature was being misread. As I walked away I heard, 'You are very loving,' and next thing she was at my side, walking closely around the monument with me.

She would not hear the suggestion that the motorbike incident had set their pulses racing. 'I am what I am. It's Indian men that

[161]

have got a problem. Jesus, I only rode on a motorbike!' But from then on she stuck close to me and was decidedly cold towards the lecherous constables.

The typical Indian policeman, described in the 1860s as 'deferential to his superiors, but haughty and tyrannical to his inferiors', lives on. As outsiders we had arrived with the potential to be cast into either camp, but over-friendliness, as they had seen it, was a weakness. The truth of this was revealed in the moment when the superior officer appeared, a tall Sikh, immaculately groomed and elegant. His constables sprang out of their slouches; the lecherous grins were wiped clean; the one with a cap whipped it off.

'Good afternoon,' he said. 'I'm Manjeet Singh, station officer – so sorry you waited. You should have had my men wake me. Please come through to the office.'

There was the rub then: we should have marched in and demanded they call him.

The office was a new world too: green marble floor, a desk bearing a souvenir of the Golden Temple and a wall map next to an account of Sleeman's life written in Hindi. A constable appeared with a tray of tea but Manjeet Singh dismissed him with an imperious waft of the hand.

'Not glasses. Use tea cups and saucers! Ach! And bring biscuits – on a plate – a clean plate!'

For a while the police station had begun to seem a little menacing, but now the officer's civilized manners and excellent English pushed those fears away – for a while. The open stares at Maddy were replaced by downcast eyes. It reminded me of the prisoners in Narsinghpur.

I told him why we had come.

'These days we call thugs "420s" after the number of the penal code.'

'So do they still operate?'

'Oh, yes, but our main problem here is illegal distilling from the mahua fruit.'

'Do the thugs kill?'

'We have five or six murders per year in this district, usually over land disputes or old enmities.'

'Is religion an element in those murders?'

He thought for some time before answering. 'Yes, two years ago we had a case of narbali.' A human sacrifice. 'It was this time of year, close to Shivaratri full moon, and the people were preparing food in the Shiva temple at Dhira when a man came with an axe and kicked the neck of another man.' He mimed chopping. 'Four or five kicks and the head came off. He took it and laid it before the god.'

'Was the man caught?'

'He came here himself and gave up.' He gave a shrug. 'But it will never come to trial. You see the witnesses will not go to court. They say he was possessed and it was for the god, so he may not be punished.'

The tea and biscuits arrived in freshly washed cups and saucers. I asked about Sleeman.

'We are very interested in Sleeman,' he said. 'And any new information that you have.'

I showed him some pictures I had brought and he took me off to see his quarters, a small room with an old bed in the middle. 'This was Colonel Sleeman's room,' he said proudly. 'Maybe not changed at all.'

As we left the room, Maddy nudged me. 'Don't let's stay too long,' she whispered. 'It's getting dark and I don't want to be stuck here for the night.'

Manjeet Singh pointed out the peepul tree that towered over the yard.

'Sleeman hanged the thugs from that tree,' he said. 'There was no time for trials, he used to directly hang them from the trees.' He shook his head and added with a tinge of regret. 'We cannot do that now.'

Back in the office, a candle had been placed on the desk as the sun was now gone. He sat down and toyed with his desk ornament.

I asked, 'Do you think he hanged innocent men too?'

'I think that sometimes he did.'

[163]

'Could he succeed now?'

'Certainly not. Now we have human rights people who say you can only ask. Only ask!' He glared at us. 'Here we have no modern Western inventions like fingerprint section or forensic – how can we get confessions without the third degree. It's impossible.'

'What kind of third degree is used in India?'

'Slapping prisoners.'

There was a silence. In fact fingerprinting is neither modern nor Western. The idea of individual identification by fingerprints was suggested to the colonial administrator William Herschel in the late 1850s by the Bengali system of tip sahi in which fingerprints acted as a signature. The first system of criminal identification by prints was started by Sir Edward Henry in Bengal during the 1890s. (Henry went on to become Commissioner of London's Metropolitan Police from 1903 to 1918.)

Maddy had withdrawn into the darkness at the back of the office, but now she spoke. 'Can you ask your men to stop any bus heading north, please? We are going to Murwara.'

He called an order outside in Hindi. 'There is a barrier here,' he said. 'All traffic must stop.'

'Will there be a bus?'

'It is late.'

I sipped my tea and watched the candle splutter.

'There are holy men on the trains,' he said. 'They offer you prasad and it is drugged.' The same story as in Narsinghpur. 'You must be careful when travelling. There are many dangers.'

He offered a malted milk biscuit with a faint smile, and I took one and weighed it in my fingers. All through British accounts was the fear of an enemy within: tales were told of faithful servants later proven to be thugs. James Sleeman records the case of a bearer who tenderly cared for his master's children but went thugging for a month too. 'Cold-blooded human beasts with a callous disregard for the sanctity of human life for one-twelfth of the year, and patterns of virtue for the remainder.' The outrage seems directed not at the real horror – dead Indians – but at the

[164]

prospect of murderers caring for the sahib's offspring.

If the British had feared the enemy within, if that was partly what shaped their re-creation of thuggee as an evil cult of demons, then that fear was still here. Perhaps it would always exist in any human society as complex as India's, or perhaps it is something we all carry with us. Cave paintings from 30,000 years ago show the half-man, half-animal figure as the enemy; the devil that is almost as we are, the one with cloven feet hidden in the shadows. And the enemy within is always closest to you, the least suspected, be it the trusty servant or the holy man.

'Who are the most dangerous men in this time?' I asked.

He took a biscuit himself and ate it thoughtfully. 'Did you see the lorry standing in our yard? It is filled with stolen goods. A month ago three men came with this lorry and a motorbike at night. They waited for another lorry to pass then two of them chased behind it without lights on the motorbike. One man then climbed on to the load, cut the ropes and began to throw it down to the side for the third man in the lorry to pick up. Fortunately the driver realized what was happening and he stopped. We were called but the three men escaped on foot.' He brushed the biscuit crumbs from his fingers. 'This lorry was found abandoned and we believe it belongs to those three men. They are Kanjars, a criminal caste.'

'What do you mean by criminal caste?'

'They are families of criminals who are registered with the police. All of them are criminals. They have their own language, like the language of the birds.'

I was reminded of Veerappan's supposed powers of mimickry and of Ramasee, the thug argot.

'Those are the worst criminals,' he said. 'When you question them, they tell some story. If you accuse them, they shut up. They say nothing.' He laughed. 'Even with third degree, all they say is "unffff"! They never talk, even if you kill them!'

Perhaps it was the darkness, the long isolation in this unsophisticated spot, but I don't think he thought it was a mistake, or a slip of the tongue, to reveal that suspects were beaten. In the first thug

[165]

trials, sixty-seven men died in prison and the British did not regard it necessary to say why. The Indian police had stepped straight into the shoes of their colonial predecesors.

'We will catch them,' he continued. 'Those Kanjars will come back for their lorry, with some story, and we will catch.' He made a movement with his fist.

'I'd like to go now,' whispered Maddy again from the darkness.

I put the biscuit in my hand back on the plate uneaten. What would become of those thieves, I wondered, should they ever be so foolish as to revisit Sleemanabad police post.

Despite the officer's protestations, I went out and tried to see if they were trying to stop a bus or not. Within a few minutes I had arranged two seats on a crowded bus heading for Marwara. I rushed back to get Maddy and the bags.

It was with a sigh of relief we finally got moving. Maddy was squashed up on a front seat with several large ladies. I was in the back, but in the dark I could see nothing of my neighbour, only that his head was swaddled in cloth against the night air. After a few minutes he unwrapped the cloth and said to me, 'What is your topic, brother?'

I smiled. 'What do you mean: "my topic"?'

'Are you not a journalist like myself?'

I supposed he had seen that we were sitting with the police. I told him I was investigating a colonial officer and some goondas.

'You should know, my brother,' he said, 'that the police are the goondas here.' Some lights by the road revealed his face for the first time, an older man than I'd thought, with terrible pockmarks.

'We were worried we might have to stay the night there – no buses were coming.'

He chuckled. 'It is good for you that we came along. These police fellows are capable of the worst crimes.'

His home was fifteen miles away, but out in the country.

'It must be peaceful,' I said, but he made a scornful noise.

'Peaceful! Ha! It is a dangerous place full of pistols and hired pistols. This country is full of dangerous men: the police are

[166]

gangsters, the naxalites are gangsters, the landowners are gangsters. But I will not talk about it – even to talk about it is dangerous.'

And, true to his word, we chatted on innocuous topics after that despite all my attempts to draw him out. Only when we stopped at a wayside village halt and disembarked for a cup of tea did he draw me aside and return to his topic.

'I travel by bus to avoid recognition,' he said. 'My car would be too dangerous.'

'Who do you fear?'

He smiled mirthlessly. 'You can buy yourself an assassin here for a few hundred rupees. A gun will cost no more. Enemies cost nothing. When William Sleeman came here, he hanged a few hundred men from trees, some of them innocent, then the British declared the job done and went away.' He glared at me. 'The job was not even started. They blamed Kali, but the truth was that the real evil was the networks of corruption and the British could not attack that because they relied on those high people. Every thug, every dacoit and bandit, they were all linked to the landowners and maharajahs. Now we call those big shots member of parliament or police inspector or councillor, and those thugs are now Naxals and rebels and dacoits. Nothing is changed. The poor farmers, the women and children, these people still suffer.'

'What did you do to endanger yourself?'

'I wrote about it. I was a business man before, but I became so tired of this corruption, I decided to do something.'

'Do you regret that now?'

He had to think for a long time, blowing the tea in the glass and sipping noisily. 'As it may kill me, yes I do. But I would not mind dying if it would change something. But I fear it will not.'

The bus was hooting for the passengers, but he did not re-embark. 'I take another road from here.' He waved vaguely eastwards. 'About fifteen miles that way.'

As we pulled away, I saw him sitting at the tea stall, his scarf once again around his head and face.

*    *    *

The station officer had got his facts wrong. The Criminal Tribes Act 1871 was repealed in 1952 soon after Independence, being regarded as untenable in a civilized and egalitarian society. No one can now be legitimately described as of a criminal tribe or caste: those individuals and groups captured by its long tentacles were renamed Vimukht Jati, literally 'liberated classes'.

At its peak the Act is thought to have encompassed about thirteen million people, all of them criminals by reason of birth. During the period that this bizarre and unjust piece of legislation had operated, their lot had been to be told where they could and could not live, to be punished for movement outside those boundaries, to have their children taken away, their marriages controlled and their men imprisoned. The rules were so stringent, the punishments so draconian, that many honest individuals were driven into crime, a fact that was often held up as proof of their recidivist genetic tendencies. Where the officer was not mistaken was in making the link between thugs and the Criminal Tribes Act.

Back in 1830s Britain, Sleeman's success in identifying the thug menace as a specific cult had not only given readers a delicious thrill of the dangerously exotic, but it had struck a chord with evangelical and utilitarian policy-makers who had come to regard India and the Orient as a savage place requiring civilisation. James Mill's *History of India* in 1820 set the tone: 'Both nations [India and China] are to nearly an equal degree tainted with the vices of insincerity; dissembling, treacherous, mendacious, to an excess which surpasses even the usual measure of uncultivated society.' (Should anyone imagine that such views are archaic, listen to the contemporary British war historian Sir John Keegan in the *Daily Telegraph* following the events of 11 September 2001: 'Westerners fight face to face, in stand-up battle . . . Orientals, by contrast, shrink from pitched battle, which they often deride as a sort of game, preferring ambush, surprise, treachery and deceit as the best way to overcome an enemy.')

In the early nineteenth century, this was pretty much what the evangelical movement thought of India. They agreed with James Mill that at the heart of the problem was religion: 'by a division of the people into castes, and the prejudices which the detestable views of the Brahmens raised to separate them, a degrading and pernicious system of subordination was established among the Hindus ... built upon the most enormous and tormenting superstition that ever harassed and degraded any portion of mankind, their minds were enchained more intolerably than their bodies.'

The tolerance and respect for Indian society that had gone before were now being swept away. Practices that were seen as backward and pagan such as suttee, infanticide and thuggee were to be ignored no longer. Suppression and eradication was the policy. In this all the new fangled techniques of science were brought to bear. Thugs, like thousands of tribespeople throughout the empire, were, as we have seen, measured and studied. Their heads were occasionally removed for the benefit of craniologists at home. Remember the seven Dr Spry removed at Saugor and sent to Edinburgh.

The imperial nineteenth-century urge to quantify is well known when it comes to birds, flowers and animals. Less savoury was the dried human flesh that was sent back, usually of those groups and tribes seen as primitive or savage. Vast tables of data were compiled, based on parameters laid down by the Swedish anthropologist Anders Retzius in 1842, who declared that the cranial index was the measure of civilization. This ratio (of maximum cranial width to maximum length) revealed to the upper-middle-class scientists of the west that the highest and most noble form of humanity was the upper-middle-class scientist of the west, something many of them had suspected all along but had been unable to prove. At the bottom were women, children and savages (i.e. the rest of humanity).

The craniologists worked themselves up into views that were as widespread and reputable as they now seem cranky and detestable. 'Without doubt there exist some distinguished women,' wrote

Gustave Le Bon, a leading psychologist of the 1870s, 'but they are as exceptional as the birth of any monstrosity, as, for example, of a gorilla with two heads; consequently, we may neglect them entirely.'

In the appropriately named *Journal of Mental Science*, 1856, one Dr J.W. Eastwood opined, 'The lower races have the smallest amount of brain, and the Caucasian the largest.'

Like all the other craniologists, Eastwood had a cavalier approach to data, discounting peculiarities such as the fact that Napoleon had a brain smaller than a 'savage'. (The great leader's corpse was much studied and even suffered the indignity of having its genitalia put up for auction only to fail to meet its reserve. What the catalogue described as 'a small dried-up object' of about one inch in length was subsequently sold to an American urologist for $3,800.)

This passion for anthropometry was well suited to British India where the rulers believed that caste gave them a simple and verifiable ground rule for study. Sir Herbert Risley's *The Tribes and Castes of Bengal* (1891) and his later *People of India* (1911) were meticulous in cataloguing the dimensions of caste. He used nine paramount measurements for the nose alone, plus the broad classifications of broad, medium and fine (for students of archaicisms: platyrrhine, mesorrhine and leptorrhine).

Noses were a particular obsession for Risley and the rest, reflecting the desire to prove that long and thin was indisputably linked to being intelligent and officer material, while thick and broad was peasantry and servile classes. 'It is scarcely a paradox to lay down, as a law of caste organization,' he wrote, 'that the social status of the numbers of a particular group varies in inverse ratio to the mean relative width of the nose.' The Dravidians he tells us, have noses that are 'thick and broad', while their features are 'coarse and irregular' and bodies 'squat'. The nasal index is 94.5, as high as 'a negro'. The Aryans, on the other hand, have 'straight', 'finely-cut' noses, while their bodies are symmetrical and well proportioned; their nasal index is around 70 which 'can fairly bear comparison with the noses of sixty-eight Parisians, measured by Topinard'. He describes their skin as 'wheat-coloured', a term still used today in Indian matrimonial columns.

The caste system made India accessible and comprehensible to the British. Small pocket books were produced by the East India Company for training their men: a type of *I-spy Indians*. The 1837 volume, *A Digest of the different castes of India* by C.V. Ramaswamy, gave a neat summary of the eighty-three main castes with accompanying illustrations. There are no entries for criminals, though 'No. 37 dancing girl' gets the largest entry and there is 'No. 63 wild sex' too, a woman who lives in the jungle and 'knows the art of picking green spots from the foreheads and arms of women'. Most are tradespeople, cotton-spinners, goldsmiths, boatmen and so on, given brief descriptions of their dress, diet and manners. Remarks on skin colour, nose size and shape are conspicuously absent.

In the hands of colonial scientists this haphazard and rather quaint approach was soon to be superseded. The Rev. M.A. Sherring, a missionary in Benares, wrote a respected treatise on the subject in 1871. Here we find the Brahmin is 'Light of complexion . . . his lips thin, and mouth expressive . . . the true Brahmin is a wonderful specimen of humanity walking on God's earth.'

But these admirable top castes are sadly less numerous than all the ragamuffins and ruffians; we are soon down to thimble-riggers, robbers and interiors. The Reverend is much less forthcoming on the appearance of these people. The Kanjars, our lorry men of Sleemanabad, are mentioned as makers of 'kaskas grass coolers', but are 'very bold people' who commit gang robbery at night-fall. Badhaks are 'a caste of professional robbers and assassins. Formerly, they committed great havoc in the country in association with Thugs, another class of murderers . . . it is impossible, however, for such persons to indulge in such pursuits while the administration is in the firm hands of British rulers.'

In volume 2 the classes of miscreants multiply: Kul-Korwah 'are all professional gang robbers and burglars'. The women of the

Haggal Kaikya are all thieves, the men cattle-stealers. The Agadi are prostitutes when not thieving. The Pardasi are wandering 'mahomedans' who 'commit burglary' and infest northern India. The Lambani are highwaymen, kidnappers of children, coiners of false money and thugs: their faces are 'expressive and sometimes good-looking'. (It's notable that the thugs were glamorized as a worthy enemy while others were simply treated as verminous filth.) The Uchli are pickpockets and shoplifters; the Bedar are cultivators but secretly robbers; the Ramusi are watchmen who secretly commit murder and robbery themselves, they are 'hereditary robbers'. The Kathkari are nomadic 'leaving their employment without reason, and sometimes without wages'. They are 'squalid lazy and reckless; and indulge in disgusting practices'. Needless to say they are thieves. The Bheel are 'great robbers'.

Then come the thugs.

> The Gand Bigari are thugs in clothes of turmeric colour who wander about. The Tin-nami are a class of thugs, of the caste of those Gosains who mark their foreheads with three streaks of paint . . . they hold a cane in one hand, and an alms dish in the other, a bag hanging over their shoulder. They answer all enquiries by declaring they are going to Kashi [Varanasi], or Rameshwar . . . they follow them [treasure-carriers] and ingratiating themselves into confidence, often manage, like the more regular thugs, to strangle and kill them. They dispose of the corpses in round holes, the regular thugs using oblong ones; which is the chief distinguishing feature between them.

So it goes on, the divisions of caste and tribe as carefully delineated as in a field guide to ornithology, as if India had finally been dissected, understood and catalogued. And alongside the various criminal terms, the single most obvious feature of all these people is that they wander. The words wander, wandering, roving, vagabonds and nomadic appear again and again. Like the descendants of Cain, these are the peoples exiled to east of Eden. In total there are 107 recognized tribes and castes of wandering people, the vast majority dedicated to a life of crime, be it simple counterfeiting and swindling up to gang murder and thuggery. For most of this information the Reverend was indebted to Colonel Harvey, Superintendant for the Suppression of Thuggee and Dacoitee, Sleeman's successor in the post.

The thug department was instrumental in this fantastical explosion in enemies of the state. Once Sleeman had hanged a few hundred thugs, it was possible to declare the problem solved. But the witch hunt had its own momentum now and the fears and terrors thrown up were like a virus that must grow and replicate in order to survive. To the colonial officials, as they delved deeper, it seemed that Indian society had an inexhaustible supply of evil. The hunt was extending outwards, grasping at new prey, instinctively suspicious of nomadic, and so ungovernable, peoples. 'When a man tells you he is a Buddhuk, or a Kunjur or a Sunoria he tells you . . . he is an offender against the law; has been so from the beginning, and will be so to the end; that reform is impossible . . . it is his religion to commit crime.' So wrote Lieutenant-Colonel William Nembhard, commissioner in East Berar.

Francis Otway Mayne, commissioner for revenue in Allahabad, noted in 1870 that 'the fraternities are of such ancient creation, their numbers so vast, the country over which their depredations spread so extensive, their organisation so complete, and the evil of such formidable dimensions, that nothing but special legislation will suffice for their suppression and conversion'.

By the 1870s it was accepted by criminologists, as well as many colonial officials, that crime was inbred, a hereditary feature of its perpetrators, possibly detectable by measurement. Leading the field in propagating this view was Cesare Lombroso, Professor of Legal Medicine and Psychiatry in Turin, the inventor of the world's first lie detector machine, and a man of remarkable scientific views: 'Among savages crime is not the exception,' he wrote in 1887, 'but rather the general rule.'

Lombroso's seminal work *Criminal Anthropology* is a marvel of unsubstantiated bigotry dressed up as fact, all the more alarming for being widely read and cited. Plates refer readers to typical specimens: the assassin tends to wide cheekbones, the ravisher to abnormalities of the nose and genitalia, and so on. He rounds off with a defence of capital punishment on the grounds: 'perfecting the human race by means of selection and the survival of the fittest.' Little wonder that years later Adolf Hitler was impressed.

Lombroso knew exactly why people become criminals: their arms are too long. In addition his anthropometric data collected from 5,907 criminals showed they 'have outstanding ears, abundant hair, a sparse beard, enormous frontal sinuses and jaws, a square and projecting chin, broad cheekbones, frequent gestures, in fact a type resembling the Mongolian and sometimes the negro.' Gypsies, of course, 'are the living example of a whole race of criminals' and 'we know that a large percentage of the thieves of London are of Irish parentage or are natives of Lancashire.'

With theories such as these, the case for hereditary criminals was made and the Criminal Tribes Act 1871 was duly formulated. Proposing the bill to the Indian legislature, the eminent jurist James Fitzjames Stephen revealed the true extent of imperial bigotry. Criminal tribes, he said, were 'criminals from times immemorial who are themselves destined by the usages of caste to commit crime and whose descendants will be offenders against the law, until the whole tribe is exterminated or accounted for in the manner of the Thugs.'

For the marginalized peoples the Act was a disaster. Distinctions were made on flimsy evidence, often wrongly, or on the prejudices of a local official: bards, minstrels, gypsies, nomads, holy men, they were all thrown in. Under the legislation local authorities could designate any tribe criminal if they regularly committed non-bailable offences. There was no recourse or appeal, though individuals could object to being listed as members of the tribes (lists were maintained). Tribes could be resettled, forced to work and incarcerated in reformatory settlements; their members were issued with passes saying where they could live and how often to present themselves to certain officers. Rollcalls could be made and impromptu searches carried out. Breaking the rules led to six months in prison, a fine or a whipping, penalties that were stiffened in later amendments. Further changes in 1911 were to add compulsory fingerprinting. Only in 1924 and 1947 was the Act softened at all; repeal did not come until 1952.

Injustices were rife and nomadism or vagrancy was often grounds for suspicion. The Banjaras were designated a criminal tribe but they were simply people who had used pack animals to transport goods all over India for many centuries. It was the British introduction of railways and roads that made them jobless and, in desperation, some had turned to crime.

Maghiya Doms, a people whose ancestry may be the same as European Romanies, came in for particular scrutiny. They were, one district magistrate declared, 'little removed from animals'. 'Abominable,' said another. They were the lowest of the low, quite literally, being the sweepers and scavengers at the bottom of the untouchability ladder. The British officials piled scorn and contempt on them in an orgy of revulsion: 'the very scum of the lowest class of Hindus', their women were 'shameless in sexual matters', wrote C.A. Elliot, secretary to the North West Provinces. Fellow officer C.T. Metcalf, commissioner of Patna Division, was diligent in pursuing them. 'They have more the habits of wild beasts than human beings. The men do not hesitate to take human life, and the women in the commonest quarrels use the children like clubs, catching them up by the leg and swinging them round their heads,' he reliably reported in 1876.

Unfortunately the Doms did not commit sufficient crimes to be declared hereditary criminals, but such was the general revulsion at their filthiness that special colonies were made for them. Tools and livestock were provided, along with a parcel of inferior land. Interestingly, the administrator in this was the same Edward Henry who went on to use fingerprinting as a tool of detection. After some initial success, there was failure; the Doms deserted and took to crime so emphatically that in 1911 they were officially declared

[175]

criminal, thus proving to colonial officers that they had been right all along.

The idea of settlement camps for criminal tribes is said to have begun in the 1850s and soon blossomed into a programme worthy of National Socialism. The Sansiahs were one tribe of Upper India that were deemed genetically criminal with a dangerously nomadic lifestyle. In 1887 they were declared congenital criminals, along with various other groups, including our old friends, the Kanjars, with whom they were known to intermarry. They were rounded up and divided into three groups: harmless adults who were released on licence to work for local landowners, children under eighteen who were separated from parents and sent to a reformatory at Fatehgarh, and finally the hardcore criminals who were sent to a penal colony at Sultanpur. Many of the latter had never been convicted of a crime, yet their imprisonment was regarded as indefinite.

It was soon clear that allowing Sansiah women to marry criminal Sansiah men was foolish. Marriages would have to be arranged with better types from the 'harmless' group. So it was that British colonial officers found themselves working as marriage brokers, carefully cross-breeding within the tribe to eradicate criminal tendencies. Naturally, those individuals who had been imprisoned at Sultanpur or Fatehgarh attracted some negative publicity and the next step was for the government to provide dowries to overcome this.

Once 'reformed', individuals were sent to be sweepers in cities such as Lucknow and Allahabad, a life so bad that some begged to be allowed back to the prison at Sultanpur. As they were now deemed reformed, their requests were usually denied.

When this system faltered an agricultural colony at Kheri near the Nepal border was begun in the 1890s. Though less prison-like, it had strict rules: no leaving the colony without permission, no intoxicating drinks, and rules to be enforced by whippings. Unsurprisingly it suffered a seventy-five per cent rate of absconding and, rather embarrassingly, colonial officials also discovered that large numbers of inmates were not wandering Sansiahs at all, having been caught up in the fairly indiscriminatory 'sweeps' in the early days. One man, Kumbha, had been a farmer with seven bighas of land before he was arrested, not a wandering criminal at all, but he was sent to farm two bighas at Kheri. After several years he applied to go home and no one could work out why he had been there in the first place. He was released, not on compassionate grounds however, but to cut state costs.

At the close of the nineteenth century, success proving elusive, authority was passed to the Salvation Army, an organization that took to social engineering with messianiac enthusiasm and unmiraculous results. F. Booth Tucker's tract *Criminocurology or The Indian Crim, and what to do with him*, published in the 1920s reveals the tone of the settlements. The Salvation Army, he reveals, has 3,300 hereditary criminals in twenty-two settlements (two in old opium godowns). 'To find suitable employment for so large a number of unskilled workers, or rather shirkers, has been most difficult,' he says. 'We never work,' one told him. 'We only dance and sing.'

Obviously a stop had to be put to this and Tucker proudly relates how it was being done. At Gorakhpur was a settlement in four barrack blocks where 'only the most reliable settlers are allowed to live with their families'. Four years crime-free meant a settler could go off the 'badmash' register and on to 'nekmash' Bad habits, like the Dom custom of putting a coin in a dead man's hand so he could gamble as soon as he reached heaven were being suppressed. Children were separated from parents and sent to Industrial Homes and Gorakhpur had one about a mile from the main colony containing forty-five children.

There is no doubt that the institutions run by the Salvation Army and the Indian government were nothing but forced labour camps, an injustice inflicted on low-caste and nomadic peoples. In 1914 the American Baptist Mission also took up the challenge, incarcerating fifty families behind barbed wire and instituting a programme of vegetable-growing and Bible study. The settlement was near Madras and it was to the Chief Secretary there that the prisoners complained a year later. They were hungry and unhappy and begged to be allowed to go home. There were beatings and children were taken away from parents to avoid 'contamination'. Such complaints, however, went unregarded and the settlement survived until 1952 when the police were given charge. Likewise, the Salvation Army's pseudo-science 'criminocurology' did not continue, thankfully, beyond Independence, but the task of destroying unwanted cultures was done.

Reform for those convicted of thuggee murders was not considered possible, though the Raj could be magnanimous when it suited: some thugs were taken into the Punjab Frontier Force as guides. Sleeman's own School of Industry set up in the 1830s in Jabalpur saw its original convicts die out, but the sons were kept incarcerated – eighty-five were still there in 1879.

While murder was certainly being done on India's roads in the 1820s and thirties, the British reaction was partial, unbalanced and unjust. Thuggee was a social evil but it was not a religious cult: it was a threat to the opium trade. Then, once the demon of an eradication campaign was released, its history ran a similar course to any other witch hunt, be it of Senator McCarthy's Communists or Osama bin Laden's al-Qa'ida. Special powers and special laws were granted, then the exoticized and over-blown reaction to thuggee begun by Sleeman came stampeding down the decades, gathering strength from orientalism and pseudo-science and post-Mutiny hatreds, eager for new enemies to crush. (Two months after 11 September 2001, an article in *Newsweek* by Jonathan Alter called for 'an open mind' on torture for terrorism suspects and President Bush's Patriot Act was rushed through. It allows the indefinite holding of immigrants suspected of terrorist links.) The forces unleashed in India dealt blows to the poorest and most defenceless people at the bottom of the caste system; and into the very foundations of the Indian police service it laid deep veins of corruption, bigotry and injustice that continue to poison its work 170 years later.

[178]

With Independence came repeal of the laws and supposed suppression of the term 'criminal caste', but there was no respite. The Habitual Offenders Act (1952) and later the Terrorist and Disruptive Activities Act (whose powers now enable the hunt for Veerappan) have ensured that pretty much the same groups are harried and oppressed, just as before.

# 8

# The End of Thuggee

SAGAUR IS ONE OF CENTRAL INDIA'S most isolated towns, a
shabby and dilapidated place with a lovely lake set above it,
and overlooking the water, the old fort. The origins of the lake
are mysterious, but it is certainly man-made; the fort was once a
stronghold of the Peshwas, Mahratta kings from Poona.

I stayed in the lower town in a room where the mice scampered
freely around the floor when the lights went out, which they did
without any assistance from me. The restaurant was partitioned
with brown curtains, like some dismal casualty department and the
menu included such delights as 'danceing coffee, peanut, chicken
greavy, sand witch and tamato egg drop soup'.

In the morning I walked up the hill and found the court, and next
to it, Sleeman's house, a grander version of the Narsinghpur abode,
with a lovely view down over the lake and fort. There was little of
interest to be seen inside either building, but the courthouse was
besieged by petitioners, plaintiffs, defendants and suchlike. The
advocates in their shiny black jackets and whitish shirts stood in
a crowd, waiting to be retained. I liked that simplicity: lawyers

[181]

touting for trade in the open air like the plumbers and bricklayers down the hill.

'Can I furnish you with assistance, kind sir?' one of them enquired and I told him my mission.

'Oh indeedly, it was ever thus,' he said in a big loud voice more used to making himself heard on drowsy afternoons with half-deaf judges. 'You British only ever meet rogues and rascals in India.'

'Which one are you?'

He liked that and roared with laughter. 'I am most certainly a rascal.' He was playing to the crowd that had gathered, his chest puffed out and thumbs hooked in a waistcoat. 'Our Mother India, you see, is a hostess of contradictions. The rascal may be the good man you need. Look upon the holy cow: we worship the poor beast and yet everywhere they eat rubbish in our streets. Our holy men go naked and yet, if you or I were to cast off our vestments here and now, we would be arrested and severely punished.'

I could imagine this man in a painting by Charles Wade Crump, the English soldier and artist who came to Saugor and sketched a scene of a thug at trial (see plate). Crump died at Lucknow during the 1857 uprising. All the characters and colour he depicted were still here, though now dressed in the crumpled colourless clothes of nineteenth-century English law: the earnest, the crooked, the pompous, the fearful and the loquacious. Hanuman, my advocate friend, now twisted the conversation skilfully on to the subject of history, then artefacts, then old coins, then he pulled out a book of photographs of old coins and tried to sell me some.

'Collecting: my family disease,' he said loudly, adding under his breath. 'Rare items available – but later at hotel.'

I declined and asked about the fort, clearly visible at the end of the lake.

'It is a police training college,' Hanuman announced. 'The principal is a fine man. I can introduce you, of course.'

This was obviously a comment aimed at the crowd who were suitably impressed. I accepted the offer and we set off on his motor scooter, Hanuman finely attired in a pair of magnificent flying goggles and a purple knitted skullcap in addition to his somewhat worn advocate's suit.

It was curious to see how quickly his gravitas deserted him when challenged by an armed policeman at the gate. His territory, I realized, did not extend beyond that crowd outside the courthouse. Noticeably, he did not claim any relationship with the Principal either, merely announced me as 'an important British visitor'.

We hung, if that's the right word, around the gatehouse, inspecting the yard beyond.

It was a scene worthy of observation. The fort's walls are impressive and there are ancient buildings within. But what caught my eye were the huge messages painted in man-high letters on any available surface: Gandhi was there, exhorting the trainees: 'The Police that I would maintain would be a body of reformers.' There were all the hoary old clichés you might expect: 'When the going gets tough, the tough get going,' alongside the more thoughtful, 'Happiness lies in what one is and not in what one has.' But if the others might have appeared in any police college from the LAPD to the London Met, I did not imagine those institutions would have used the largest and most prominent message, 'Search within the expanding emptiness of the self not outside.' Go and put that into practice on the Mumbai beat, I thought, idling away the minutes of waiting with visions of mystical police officers, babu bobbies patrolling in the lotus position. It reminded me of Maddy, and I wished she had been with me to tell me who had said those words.

After five minutes the guard returned to say that the principal would see us. We followed him past the old magazine to the office block in the corner. The Deputy Inspector General had a large office with another motto behind him: 'It is better to light a candle than curse the darkness.'

Hanuman was almost completely dumb now, his manner servile. The DIG was a busy man and could spare only a couple of minutes and I rattled through a quick explanation of my journey.

'We still use William Sleeman's work in our training programmes,' he said. 'Of course, it is very much connected with
this town.'

I asked about Sleeman's methods.

'Now we have civil liberties and human rights on top,' he said
plainly. 'We cannot simply hang a man from a tree.'

He called an adjutant. 'Show them the museum.' He turned to
me. 'I think it will interest you.'

The museum was housed upstairs in the old magazine, rebuilt
in 1873, according to a plaque. Downstairs was the armoury
with racks of rifles and an aged armourer who found it hard to
believe that we had been given permission. Eventually, however,
accompanied by the inevitable entourage of sweepers, dishwashers
and office boys, he trudged up the steps and unlocked the door.
Hanuman was recovering his composure, out of reach of his friend
the principal.

'Do not touch anything,' he ordered, slapping his motor scooter
goggles on his thigh. 'These are precious artefacts of historical
actualities.'

This seemed pretty rich coming from a man who had recently
tried to sell me ancient coins with the air of a man pushing stolen
goods, but I ignored him and concentrated on the treasure trove
before me.

Ever since the fort became a police college in 1905, its principals
had deposited interesting items here. There were tribal weapons,
Communist shoulder pips, radios, guns, jewellery, several generations of disturbingly battered truncheons; there was a presentation
elephant tusk from Japan, a sample of heroin, a naked figurine
marked 'sex goddess', and an old rifle with a hole in the barrel
labelled 'Result of tiger bite'. Most fascinating, however, were the
photographs of dead dacoits. Here on police camera were dozens
of bandits soon after their glamorous careers were unkindly cut
short by police bullets: faces and bodies thrown into grotesque
postures, eyes sunken, cheeks sunken, foreheads blown away, only
the moustaches seemed to preserve the dignity. I did rather wish the

[184]

DIG would come up and explain the difference between Sleeman's summary justice and this modern version.

A few miscreants survived capture: there was Putli, a female bandit, a tiny slip of a woman but apparently a fearless leader and seasoned killer. Her glass bangles were under her portrait in a box.

If I had hoped for thugs' rumals and a pick-axe though, I was disappointed. The only artefact was a photograph of some clay figurines performing strangulation, an arrangement that made ritual murder look like an episode of *Wallace and Grommit*. Hanuman, however, insisted that it was real people.

'Indeedly, tugs! Caught in camera performing dastardly murder!'

'But they are pots – clay figures.'

He was outraged. I had slurred the entire Madhya Pradesh police force, the legal system and his own estimable profession. He raised a finger, back in court at last, finding his voice for the armourer and the cleaners. 'Historical actuality! Indeedly! Time to go.'

'But I want a photograph of the dacoits,' I appealed to the armourer, but Hanuman dived in.

'Certainly not! Absolutely and expressly forbidden! Principal will not allow liberties!'

The armourer wavered, but Hanuman came in with a killer blow.

'Dangerous precedent!'

The armourer shook his keys. 'Finish.'

The thugs were not hanged within the fort. They had been taken out to a gallows north of the town on open ground. All showed great courage and composure, though this impressed their executioners not one whit. Dr Spry, governor of Saugor Jail and the man who removed the seven heads sent to Edinburgh, has left us an account of a hanging.

He begins with a brief summary of how justice was done: approvers were encouraged and then 'one caste was set against the other' and raiding parties sent out. One can imagine how simmering class hatreds were brought to the boil and old scores settled. He notes with approval that unclaimed booty recovered had paid for two jailhouses in Saugor and all incidental charges. The circumstantial proofs of recovered loot and the testimony of approvers was sufficient. Then Captain Sleeman read out sentence in Hindustani:

> You have all been convicted in the crime of blood; the order from the Calcutta Council therefore is that, at tomorrow's dawn, you are all to be hung. If any of you desire to make any further communication, you may now speak.

Few did, though the doctor indignantly recalled one who shouted, 'Let me find you in Paradise, and then I will be revenged.' He continues his account:

> The night was passed by these men in displays of coarse and disgusting levity. Trusting in the assurance that, dying in the cause of their calling, Bhawani would provide for them in Paradise, they evinced neither penitence nor remorse. Stifling their alarm with boisterous revelling, they hoped to establish in the minds of their comrades, who could hear them through the wall, a reputation for courage, by means which at once proved their insincerity and belied their fortitude. Imagine such men on the last night of their existence on earth, not penitent for their individual errors, or impressed with a sense of the public mischiefs to which they had contributed, not even rendered serious by the dismal ordeal which in a few hours was to usher them into an unknown world, but singing, *singing*, in the condemned cell, and repeating their unhallowed carols while jolting along in the carts that conveyed them to their gibbets!

The gallows were in three sides of a square, each capable of hanging ten men at a time. The prisoners arrived in leg irons, but

[186]

each man would quickly climb the ladder and test an empty noose for strength. There was no delay on their part, the thought of being touched by the hangman, a Chumar or skin-curer caste, was too horrible.

> Everyone having proved the strength of his rope with his own hands – for none of them were handcuffed – introduced his head into the noose, drew the knot firmly home immediately behind the right ear, and amid terrific cheers jumped off the board and launched himself into eternity!

One can imagine few places as bleak and barren as Saugor to die. I went out that afternoon and climbed the hill a few miles east of town where an old fort stands. There was a long flight of whitewashed steps to a temple dedicated to the Monkey God, then a path leading through scrubby brushland to a ruined tower. Here I climbed up to a high ledge and sat looking out over the desolate landscape.

Sleeman worked endlessly on the thuggee problem, then dacoity. Just as one set of villains was suppressed, another arose. Like Kali slicing heads from demons, the British found their enemies becoming more and more numerous. Sleeman's health suffered and eventually, in 1849, he was allowed to move to the role of Resident in Awadh, but the department soldiered on.

Awadh was scarcely a soft posting, a kingdom riven by religious divides and caste hatreds, including one apparently less serious concern: a small mosque in the town of Ayodhya. It was known as Babri Masjid, after its founder the first Mughal emperor Babur, and there were those eccentric sadhus who claimed the Mughal had built it on the birthplace of the Hindu god Rama. Sadly for India this was a dispute that Sleeman did not nip in the bud.

In fact, Sleeman was a sick man. In 1854 he was told to leave India or die, the bouts of debilitating fever had become too much for him. Together he and Amélie travelled down to Calcutta for the last time and boarded the Indiaman *Monarch* in January 1856. But it was too late. Off the Ceylon coast, Sleeman took to his bunk and his condition worsened. At four a.m. on 10 February, he died and was buried at sea. The *Indian Mail* reported: 'India was the proper field for him, and he adds one more to the number of distinguished men, who, from Clive downwards, have there gained a reputation which, as long as either India or England has a place in history, may well be pronounced immortal.'

Sleeman had been a good servant of Empire, valiantly sweeping through the Augean stables that was the India of British perceptions. He had hanged several hundred murderers, quite likely several innocent men too. Though his own writings are relatively free of religious dogma, he had done the work of the reformers nonetheless. It was in his insistence on thuggee as a hereditary lineage of killers that the damage was done. Once this was accepted, it was a short step to the criminal tribes and castes, as fine a legal framework for prejudice as was ever enshrined.

My own journey would have to change now. I had seen the British campaign, how the witch hunt that began with visions of exotic criminality developed through pseudo-science into bad laws and worse discrimination. Now I was heading north into the Bundelkund, the area that stretches along the south bank of the Jamuna and one renowned for lawlessness. Most of all, I felt myself drawn towards Kali, the great goddess whose brooding bloody presence had hovered over my journey. I wanted to know her better, to understand how religion had become woven into this grand tale of human evil. If orientalist prejudice had made her a devil, then I had swallowed some of that delicious poison, tiny doses with every novel and history book from *A Thousand and One Nights* to rather larger ones with *The Deceivers*. Now I felt free of that, I wanted to get out of this region of hanging grounds and prisons, move away from the endless suspicion and scepticism. I wanted an Indian perspective, then to take Maddy's advice and start to see the positive.

*         *         *

[188]

I must have sat for an hour in that lonely place, legs dangling over a thirty-foot drop from a ledge in the tower. Then I turned to go.

His hand was actually inside my bag.

I froze, knee drawn up. There were white hairs on the back of his arm, each appeared so carefully delineated and some were moving in the gentle breeze. Our eyes met.

'What do you want in there?' I asked, stupidly. I couldn't believe he had crept so close without me having heard him.

There was no answer but he did not step back either. I remember thinking that I was too high to jump down without serious injury; I also wondered if he might push me. There was nothing for me to hold on to and the red sandstone was perfectly smooth. The bag was not over my arm, only next to me. I could grab it. He could pull it.

His eyebrows were white too. He was far too old for this game, long past retirement; hang up your handkerchief, I should have said.

He bared his teeth and snarled and I flung myself forward at him and he leaped back roaring and I scrambled to my feet and he came running at me, shied away, backed off. I shouted and stamped, went back at him. He was quick round a pillar, was behind me, the teeth near my calf soft meat. I kicked out madly. And then he was off, climbing agilely up the pillar and over the upper ledge on to the roof of the tower, still roaring his anger and hurt at not getting my bag and the shiny lovely things that were probably inside.

I went down those old broken stairs in a mad rush, my heart pounding and mouth dry, then I hurried away and reached the temple, itself surrounded by monkeys, and whipping off my shoes, I sat down inside.

The floor was cool marble and inside the inner sanctum sat an aged Brahmin, the strings over his shoulder and ashes of the sacred fire on his face. He nodded toothlessly at me and went back to staring into the flame of the lamp. Slowly my breathing returned to normal. On the wall I noticed an image of the Monkey God, in appearance almost human. It reminded me

[189]

of those 30,000-year-old cave paintings that show beasts become humans: their heads of apes, lions or snakes. And the hands of the Monkey God were tearing open his own chest to reveal Rama and beside him, his lost love Sita.

# PART THREE

# A LITTLE LIGHT BREATHING

*hamsa* [Sanskrit: literally, 'swan' and esoterically 'breath'] The two syllables of the word stand for the ingoing and outgoing breaths, as well as the ascending and descending currents of the life force.

Georg Feuerstein, *The Yoga Tradition*

An unjust law is itself a species of violence. Arrest for its breach more so.

Mahatma Gandhi

# 9

# Jhansi (and a day trip to Mumbai)

JHANSI IS A CANTONMENT TOWN, A place full of big villas given out to government servants and army officers. There is a big railway station that warrants a canteen where they serve meals, a curry plate, and each item is recorded on the wall, its weight, its nutritional value and its cost. The roads sweep around the town in grand but futile gestures because there isn't a lot to go within them. They look nice though, and are well kept with trees planted all along.

I rode around the extensive town in a rickshaw at sunset, looking for a place to stay, stopping at one point to allow a line of prisoners all in white to march across the road. They were going back to the prison from their vegetable gardens, a few in leg irons. It was while waiting for them to cross that I noticed the Jhansi Hotel. It was a long single-storey building with a dusty row of eucalyptus trees hiding it from the street.

I paid off the rickshaw wallah and went over. The reception was hopeful: a large curving counter, like a ship's bridge with several fancy mirrors behind it and above them a lovely portrait of two blonde-haired girls in white dresses. There was something deliciously langorous in their pose, the way they gently dandled roses in their fingers. Although it was very dimly lit, a small fluorescent tube had been conveniently mounted in the actual frame of the picture. To one side was a sign: 'Facilities avail ableat counter'. But as no one appeared I went around the curving teak screen that separated reception from 'Hunters' Bar'.

This was a grand room with cast-iron pillars supporting a high ceiling and tables laid out with checked tablecloths. The bar was at the far end and an Indian gentleman with white hair, dressed all in white, was sitting on a stool with his back to me. To his right, below the two adjacent signs 'Toilet' and 'No Admission', was a fishtank containing – I could just see as I approached – a kind of lamprey glued to the side and a plastic model of a Chinese peasant wrestling with a wastepaper basket. The man on the stool turned and nodded. He was a portly character with a good belly and jovial of face.

'You've arrived then?'

'Yes.'

'Coming from?'

'Sagar.'

'Take a peg?'

'Thanks.'

He called out and an old man in an almost white jacket came from a back room to pour two stiff whiskies. I sat down.

'I am Om Nath Mehrota,' said my benefactor, 'proprietor of Jhansi Hotel.'

'It looks interesting.'

'First hotel in the Bundelkund,' he said proudly. 'Built in 1906 by Mr Abbott.' He gestured expansively at the room. 'This was once a ballroom, you know. People would fly into Jhansi on Imperial Airways flying boat – it was on the outward run, you see, and there was a decent lake to land on. They spent a night here, cocktails, dinner, dancing, then go on to Calcutta next morning then Rangoon.' He slapped a hand on the bar. 'See this? Solid

Burmese teak taken from a railway wagon. The wagon was actually the first room but then it became the bar. Take another peg?'

I did. I liked Jhansi Hotel.

Om Nath had bought the place in 1975 but the anticipated revival of Jhansi tourism had yet to come. He was mindful of history, keeping the portraits of Abbott in the dining room, his daughters over the reception and the monogrammed crockery in the kitchen. I had my dinner there and later sat on the veranda feeling the gentle kiss of a lizard catching mosquitoes off my ankles.

Next morning Om Nath took me to the bank in his white car. He drove at 10 mph everywhere, without exception, and if anything blocked his path he honked his horn until it moved, be it man or beast. If he blocked anyone's path, however, something that occurred with greater frequency, he ignored all horns as though completely deaf. At regular intervals, realizing that driving and talking was a hazardous combination, he sensibly suspended all forward progress whatsoever and finished what he was saying, especially at junctions and roundabouts. It was a driving style that was imperturbable, grandiose and dignified; it was the driving style one expected from God on his day of rest.

The first occasion when Om Nath stopped to finish a sentence we were poised in the centre of the road at a junction near the prison.

'You are interested in Bundelkund, Kevin, then you must meet some of our rajahs!' A bus, blocked by the white car, unleashed a bombardment of hornplay sufficient to melt the wax from a moustache.

'It's rajahs – and robbers – that I'd like to meet.'

Om Nath frowned, deep in thought. 'Maybe I could arrange . . . you see, if it's rajahs you are wanting, we have so many here. Orchha state, you see, was divided by eight brothers – most are tiny bits of land. I know these people. I will ask for you.'

A policeman, striding over angrily, saw who he was about to deal with and his scowl became a smile. He turned away. Om

Nath leisurely engaged first gear and set off again. A boy on a bicycle overtook us.

'They are the best sort of people,' said Om Nath. 'Rajahs!'

True to his word, Om Nath began to gather word of where the rajahs might be and next day I was told I could visit one.

The first interview did not go as well as I had hoped. It's as well to say from the outset that in India people have a profligate and generous attitude to the word rajah. The British always preferred to nail down their terms: a thug was a caste of ritual killer identifiable by his knotted handkerchief; the rajah a kingdom-owning type with a throne, flunkeys and a political agent from Eton. For Indians this was unnecessarily exclusive: a thug was a con-man and a rajah anyone with the bare minimum of a small patch of land, fortified shed and a dead tiger nailed to the wall. My first rajah had a dead tiger nailed to the wall but little else; he was not in any case a rajah, no one is technically a rajah in India, as the princes were abolished by Indira Gandhi. Those who had actual experience of ruling, prior to Independence, are becoming fewer every year.

We went out to his ruined palace with its lovely, but crumbling, wall paintings in the temple. He was not a great talker and instead handed me small slips of paper on which someone had written snippets of information. The first contained his parents' names, the second their dates of birth. It was like learning Indian history through Christmas cracker messages.

From the temple we went and scoured the ruined battlements for his three cannons but found only two in the dry furze of grass and herbiage. Scrambling back through a broken wall we met the caretaker who was surly and claimed not to know where the cannon had disappeared. No one else came to see us, something that disturbed the rajah. 'Perhaps they do not know I am here.'

I was filled with pity for him: condemned to a nostalgia for an age he had barely known. 'They usually have some food for me, and problems to solve.' But no one came. Before we departed, he gave the caretaker a slip of paper. It was a relief to leave, the heat was intense and the rajah's mutterings less and less comprehensible. As we drove away, I saw the caretaker crumple and discard the slip of paper.

Over a whisky peg in the bar, Om Nath trawled his memory of the local nabobs and royals. 'Some have not prospered – they have troubles. But if you want a rajah who governed . . .' It took a few minutes and another peg, but we got there. 'I know! You must meet Rajah Dhurwei; he is a very elderly gentleman now, but he did rule before Independence. Actually, I should say he is the only one left now in Bundelkund. His son will be here tomorrow morning on some business. I will ask if his father can give you an appointment.'

He gave me a lift in the white car as far as the internet café which was about two hundred yards away. The journey took about ten minutes as we stopped in the road and had a think about robbers.

'Jhansi is a perfectly safe town you know.'

'I know.'

'You can go freely to wherever you wish without molestation.'

'I know.' A lorry, unable to get around on either side began, as they say in India, to horn us.

'But not at night. Not out of town – that is not advisable.'

'Because of robbers?'

'Rajahs are what you want – now those are good fellows.'

'There must be some big time crooks around – real dacoit bandit chiefs.'

Om Nath chuckled and slipped the car into first gear with a sickening crunch. We crept forward a few paces and stopped again.

'Down there you will find the internet place.'

There was no doubt in my mind that fate would provide. If I was meant to meet a dacoit chief, then Mother India would arrange it. Nevertheless, I sent out an email to a journalist in Mumbai who specialized in crime, Hussain Zeidi, could he give his Ma a nudge for me?

\*     \*     \*

[197]

Two days later I was taken out on the south side of town to meet Rajah Dhurwei. He lived in a lovely villa with a large porticoed entrance and huge cool rooms, once the home of a British army officer. When I arrived on the back of his son's motor scooter, the rajah was sitting in a cane chair wearing his best suit and gripping a sword. Though very old and frail, he had a strong voice and a ready chuckle that bubbled up whenever he recalled something amusing.

He had been just fifteen when he came to power. 'My political agent was Major Aldridge Oh Bee Eee!' For a few seconds he could only splutter with laughter at the memory of Aldridge. 'We had to say it: Oh Bee Eee. He'd come for lunch. My, that fellow relished Indian food, truly relished it, especially Bengali sweets. He was entitled to eleven guns and a flag on the car and Oh Bee Eee!' He dissolved into laughter again. They must have had great fun at Aldridge's expense.

'How did you rule? You were only fifteen years old.'

'I had my chief of police and my diwan. I would sit and listen. There is no limit to people's grievances. It was like that.'

I asked him about thugs.

'Aha! That is a very elaborate subject.'

'I read that some rajahs were in league with thugs and dacoits.'

'Oh, yes. There were so many dacoits and thugs here on account of it being poverty-stricken. Then a man might say, All right, I am going to the jungle and will start dacoiting. One day he might come to the rajah. There was one great dacoit named Pooja Baba, a very dangerous killer, he used to come and see me very regularly. He was a hardened dacoit.' His face crinkled with pleasure. 'Such funny stories he would tell. Once he stopped a palanquin of a rich man going for medical treatment. That man was bed-ridden. Then Pooja Baba held him up and put his face inside the curtain saying, "I am Pooja Baba!" That rich man, so sick, leaped from the palanquin and ran away. He was only posing as sick.' He slapped his thigh, roaring with laughter until tears started in his eyes.

'Did the dacoits become involved in politics?'

'It is easy to go from dacoity to politics,' he began to laugh, 'because both require illiteracy! Take Dudwa, he is a good example.'

I had heard of this modern-day dacoit.

'His mandate is very high now across Banda and Chhitrakot. Whatever he says they follow, all the local officials. But he is a hardened dacoit: they send armed soldiers on all railway trains going on the Jhansi to Allahabad line because of Dudwa.'

I wanted to come back to this topic – I was planning to take that train – but felt I needed some context, to approach it from the past. I asked about his own ancestry.

'Dhurwei was given to us 650 years ago by Orchha. Our forefathers were of Benares, and at that time there was a great thug, Bonachur, who ruled from a castle at Garhkundar, a place east of here. He was a terrible thug, the worst. The legend is that his father went to the temple of Kali at Brindachul in Mirzapur and sacrificed himself to the goddess.

'Some years later our own forefather went to that temple and worshipped. After completing his pooja, he took a sword and was cutting himself until a drop of blood fell, but at that moment Devi [Kali] appeared and caught the blood in her hand. He asked her for lands and she made a bird appear, a crow, and promised that where it landed would be his. It landed at Garhkundar, so we fought and defeated Bonachur.'

The tale reminded me of those Sleeman had put on his thug family trees – 'Cut his throat as a Sacrifice before the image of Davey at Brindachul' – but now I could see that anyone hungry for power and wealth might do that.

The rajah smoothed back his well-oiled black hair. 'You see Bonachur was a thug and he was Kangar caste. Even now the Kangars are the best criminals because we reduced them to the poverty line after defeating their empire. Remember though: they were once kings too.'

Rajah Dhurwei was clearly not a man to take the short-term

view, these events being several centuries old. I liked his straight-forward attitude to the criminals, so refreshingly guileless.

'What about Kali. Do you still worship her?'

'Originally for the Bundelas she was the most important deity. Bindu means a drop of blood and that was the origin of the name Bundelkund.'

I knew the word bindu had the meaning of a drop (usually of water), or a point (including the dot between the eyebrows), also that it had high esoteric value to the ancient yogis. Bindu is the echo created by the holy sound *Om* and, as such, it represents concentrated mental power.

'When I was a boy,' continued the rajah, 'every year at Dessera time we would go and sacrifice a buffalo at Garhkundar. There is a temple to Kali in the castle. Nowadays, some worship her, some do not.'

I could see the complexities now, how Kali had been the patroness of many groups, some of which time and fortune had ennobled. All she asked was blood and in return came the boon. Some groups clung to power long enough for their criminal or freebooting origins to be forgotten. They became the new aristocracy, but always with a weather eye on the new rebels coming up.

'I met Man Singh a few times,' said Rajah Dhurwei, talking of India's most famous dacoit of the 1930s and forties, the Veerappan of his age. 'He was very submissive. "Maharaj," he said to me. He had good manners as far as that was concerned.'

Man Singh was a dispossessed landowner, a thakur caste, from the Agra region who took to the dacoit's life to right injustices. He soon became the Robin Hood of the Chambol Ravines but was caught and jailed in 1928. When he came out in 1938 he found his family had been killed by a rival, so took to banditry again, this time ruling the ravines as a benevolent despot.

Perhaps a few generations earlier Man Singh would have gone on to found a dynasty and leave lots of nice palaces for future hoteliers to adopt; perhaps if he had lived in the 1980s like

Phoolan Devi he might have become a politician. But he came at the wrong time. The British had no need for such a chaotic and unreliable means of social change. They wanted the clarity of *Debrett's*: this man is an eleven-gun salute, that one an eighteen. Things were nailed down and made immutable and in the process the little fluidity available was lost; change itself outlawed.

Rajah Dhurwei had lapsed into silence, gazing out into space and smiling. Now we were interrupted by a stooping old man coming hobbling up the drive.

'Haha!' cried Rajah Dhurwei with delight. 'Major Aldridge?'

'OH-BEE-EEE!' came the reply and the two old men dissolved into thigh-slapping giggles.

It was not, however, the major himself but Dhurwei's last chief of police, now extremely elderly and bent almost double. We were introduced, then he went on into the house. Rajah Dhurwei picked up the conversation.

'You must go to Garhkundar,' he said. 'You can take a bus on the Khajuraho road and get down at Nivari. From there you will find something, a motorbike or rickshaw.' His eyes twinkled. 'Ha! That is a magical place. When you approach you will see the castle in front of you, but it will then disappear until you are almost at the gate.'

His son then appeared and announced lunch. I ate with him, but not the rajah. 'I have not yet taken my bath,' he said cryptically and went into his room behind a curtain. Over the sound of our eating and conversation, I could occasionally hear the merry tinkle of glasses and the boyish laughter of the last Bundela rajah and his chief of police.

That same day an hour before sunset I was walking past St Jude's Church (the patron saint of lost causes has a popular shrine quite close to the Jhansi Hotel) when I heard a shout from behind me. Two armed soldiers were running after me. This seemed a little odd, but perhaps they were not after me. The most innocent thing would be to carry on walking. But this caused a louder and more peremptory command to stop.

They were tough-looking guards, forage caps low on their noses and moustaches bristling. I was made to walk back up the road with them to a gateway where they stopped and indicated I should go inside.

I stepped through and found myself at the top of a short driveway. There was a garden to the right and a house with a veranda on which sat a girl of about nine years in a frilly dress. She waved brightly, jigging up and down in her chair with excitement.

'Uncle! Come for tea – oh, please.'

I turned and found the guards smiling and waving me to go down.

She had laid a place for me and was pouring tea. 'Oh, Uncle!' she said. 'Come and eat cakes.' When the tea was poured, she ran off into the house shouting, 'Daddy! Daddy! Uncle has come.'

I sat down, a little stunned by the realization, the awful truth: I had been kidnapped by the Violet Elizabeth Bott of Madhya Pradesh – and no sign of a William Brown coming to the rescue. I looked at the gate and received an indication that I should drink my tea. I did.

The girl reappeared with a school atlas and her daddy, a benevolent, smiling man who obviously enjoyed indulging his precocious child greatly.

'Your daughter has kidnapped me,' I said, getting to my feet and smiling. 'One day she'll be a hardened dacoit.'

A shadow seemed to pass over his face. 'My daughter, a dacoit? It is impossible. I am the prison governor.'

There might have been an embarrassed silence then, but Violet Elizabeth slammed her atlas on the table. 'Now, Uncle. Are you London or New York?'

'London.'

She began flicking through the pages.

Daddy's indulgent smile returned. I was thinking that I couldn't believe my luck, now I'd get to interview a few bandits in his jail.

'I suppose you have plenty of dacoits inside your prison?'

He wobbled his head. 'Many notorious dacoits are there but most inmates are simply users of charas or ganja.' This is one of the contradictions of India, like the revered cow eating rubbish in an open sewer, its prisons are full of drug-users, but its holy men openly use charas (hashish) and ganja.

'Could I visit the prison?'

He frowned. 'That is impossible. We have received instructions that no foreigners can visit. Some prisons have recently had unscheduled visits from nosey-parker foreigners and now we must apply to Bhopal for permission.'

I nodded. 'Terrible people – nosey-parkers.'

Violet Elizabeth had tired of searching for London and held out her hand. 'Give me your coin, Uncle.'

'Sorry?'

Her father beamed with pleasure.

'Give me your coin.'

I fumbled in my pocket for a few rupees, the girl was completely brazen. But no, this wasn't it.

'Your coin. The coin of your London.'

The father chuckled. 'She is very advanced in mathematics. Don't you have a coin for her from London?'

I rummaged in my bag, hoping I would not find anything. It felt as though I was being mugged – by a nine-year-old in a party frock. I did not have any coins.

'I must have left them in the hotel.'

'Go! Uncle. Go and fetch!'

Her father smiled. 'Maybe Uncle is busy?'

'Yes, I am very busy.'

I escaped up the drive pursued by Violet Elizabeth screeching. 'Bring your coin! Bring your coin!'

The guards at the gate were grinning under their moustaches.

\*     \*     \*

The road out of Jhansi to the south-east, into the heart of Bundelkund, passed through dry woodlands where the flame of the forest trees were coming into flower – brilliant arterial sprays of colour against the grey furze. Vultures hung on the thermals above or squatted on the piles of grey boulders that interspersed the fields.

At Nivari there was a heated debate among the population as to which castle I really wanted, until I had the insight to say the name Rajah Dhurwei had given me: 'Bonachur?'

Whereupon all debate ended, everyone grinned and said, 'Ah! Maharaj Bonachur. Thug!'

I chose a rickshaw man with a good-looking machine as we had about twenty-five kilometres to do on what I suspected would be very bad roads.

It was a clear day and a lovely ride through rural India. In the simple villages the houses had traditional arched and scalloped niches each side of gnarled wooden doors. Children made speed bumps out of the scarlet cotton tree flowers or ran alongside us by the stubbled fields. The hills enclosing these agricultural lands were no more than piles of boulders a couple of hundred feet high, splattered with flame of the forest and vulture guano, perfect hiding places for snipers, robber bands and strangled bodies.

It was through a gap in two of these stony hummocks that I first caught a glimpse of the castle, a dark massive curtain wall with several towers. It made me catch my breath in excitement. But as quickly as it had appeared the place went and, try as I might, craning my neck out of the rickshaw, it refused to reappear. We bounced along for mile after mile and I was convinced we must have passed it, or veered away on some new route, when we breasted a low rise and there it was, grim and magnificent, on the next hill.

The *Penguin Guide to the Monuments of India* gives a brief description of the castle: 'in a wild and forbidding tract of country renowned for dacoity. It was founded in the late 12th century, by Khub Singh of the Khangar clan, a ferocious tribe of war-like Rajputs ... In the 14th century they were annihilated by the Tuqluq forces from Delhi, and at the siege of Garhkundar the entire garrison of women and children committed voluntary self-immolation.'

It was indeed wild and forbidding: a defensive wall surrounded a broad hilltop compound and inside was a massive stone fastness, its dimensions deliberately exaggerated by tapering perspective. We parked in the tiny hamlet at the foot of the hill. There were only about six houses, but I soon had an entourage of three guides. They did not recognize the name Khub Singh but Bonachur drew a big reaction.

We set off at a brisk pace up the stony track, curling up to the right-hand corner of the outer wall and a gatehouse. Passing through this, we crossed the hot barren hilltop to the inner door and entered the castle. It was dark, cool and, safe to say, rarely visited. I know this because a swallow hit me squarely in the face just inside the door. The youths with me gestured to a narrow staircase and we went up, higher and higher within the wall and then to the top of the highest tower.

From this eyrie Bonachur had enjoyed unequalled panoramas of the Bundelkund: a hard stony vista of bouldered crags with squares of yellow fields slotted between. There were occasional shrines and suttee posts dotted across the landscape, memories of that disastrous siege. The existing castle, a Bundela construction, was abandoned in 1531. Quite why it has survived so long and so well is not clear. Perhaps the memory of the fearsome thug king had kept visitors away, certainly the locals had maintained a reputation for volatility and crime. The youths took me to the north side and showed me the pool where, they said, Bonachur had used to bathe with his wives, now a brilliant green pool where parakeets clattered among the munda mehel trees. Possibly some of the features do survive from those pre-Bundela times but the architecture is fifteenth century, similar in style to the later palaces at Orchha.

[205]

In the centre of the courtyard, they pointed to a pile of rubble and whispered, 'Kali Ma.' There was nothing left of the temple structure, but this was where Rajah Dhurwei had been brought every year by his father to honour the goddess who had granted their boon.

I left the youths in the courtyard, discussing the holes made by treasure-hunters and went and sat in a breezy window up in the tower, watching the vultures wheel overhead. What was Madhya Pradesh coming to? Not a single dacoit in sight, even in this prime territory.

That evening in the Hunters' Bar, Om Nath expressed disapproval of my next plan: to visit the notorious town of Jalaun on the edge of the Chambol Ravines, plus a few small places along the way.

'Sumthur, yes, I do not know the rajah personally, but I hear he is a good fellow. Jalaun has no rajah – I say give it a miss. Take a peg?'

I did.

Jalaun was said to be dacoit-infested territory. In *Confessions of a Thug*, Meadows Taylor has the Rajah of Jalaun capture the hero, Ameer Ali, and his gang. Two of the thugs are then trampled to death by elephants.

Om Nath called someone and arranged a car and driver. 'If you are visiting Rajah Sumthur, how can you arrive by bus? There is protocol.' He had not really approved of me heading off to Nivari on the state bus.

But Rajah Sumthur was not at home in his lovely palace on the fringe of a quaint old market town. His syce showed me around the temple with its marvellous frescoes of religious and military themes, then waved goodbye from the gate.

In the countryside, the fields were filling up with Rajastani sheep guarded by men in white dhotis and pink turbans, a seasonal migration to graze the flocks on the stubble. Harvest had brought other itinerants too, such as the Lohar tinkers in their fantastically hefty chariots. They pulled up in the towns, slung out an awning, lit a fire and were ready for business. There was a feeling of a society that was old and steady in its rhythms, and the wandering peoples could follow their trades, moving back and forth with the seasons.

Traffic on the roads was light, perhaps because further north Kanpur had been sealed off by communal riots. We saw a Jain holy man, walking stark naked towards the troubled town, his face ecstatic. He had two acolytes with him, one bearing a parasol, the other sweeping the ground in front with a peacock's feather, lest he tread on a living creature. It was as though he had been sent to quell the battling Muslims and Hindus.

At Jalaun my driver became nervous for his car, refusing to leave it unattended. I visited various temples and grand houses, knocking on doors and chatting to everyone I could find. Two fruit-sellers showed me a subterranean swimming pool once used, they claimed, by Nana Sahib. It was a strange place, out of town a short way, next to a ruined palace where a family were camping out. Nana Sahib had been the arch-devil of 1857, the man the British blamed for the massacre of women and children at Cawnpore (Kanpur). His swimming pool was a deep dark brick-lined slit and, as I leaned over to look down, I kept a wary eye on who might be behind me. But there were no incidents, nor any revelations. Jalaun was quiet and sleepy that day. On the way back I stopped in the village that Sleeman claimed was Feringhea's birthplace. Despite my attempts, and the driver, we could find no one who had heard of the thug leader.

Om Nath commiserated with me and tried to deflect my growing disappointment with a new rajah.

'Datia – now that man is a good fellow. Very charming. Exquisite manners.'

But I knew what I wanted now, and nothing else would suffice: I wanted a baddie.

Then, right on cue, I got one.

\*　　\*　　\*

When I checked my email next morning there was a message from Hussain Zeidi, the Mumbai crime reporter. 'Call me.'

I did.

'There's someone I could take you to meet.'

'But I'm in Jhansi, heading east next.'

Hussain was adamant. 'You take the overnight sleeper train, you spend three hours with me, then you take a sleeper train back. No problem. It's just a day trip to Mumbai – you will not regret it.'

Fifteen hours later, my luggage still in my room at the Jhansi Hotel, I was disembarking in Mumbai and taking a familiar black and yellow taxi across town.

We met at the office of Hussain's newspaper, *Mid-day*, a smart place tucked away from view in an old cotton mill. On the wall behind the receptionist was the paper's motto, 'He who thinks, speaks and acts with God as his witness will never feel afraid of doing the right thing.'

Hussain was a chubby young man with a friendly smile and seven years of Mumbai crime reporting under his belt. 'If you're interested in crime, then shouldn't you meet one of the dons?' He grinned.

'But they're all abroad, aren't they?' The dons being the big-time gangland bosses of the Mumbai underworld.

'There is one: Arun Gawli. He lives nearby here.'

I had read about Gawli in the press, noting one particular report with interest. Court sessions in Mirzapur, it declared, had been interrupted by the fatal shooting of a prisoner in the dock. It was the mention of Mirzapur that had attracted my attention, close to Brindachul and the Kali temple. The accused, the report noted significantly, had once tried to assassinate the brother-in-law of Arun Gawli, notorious Mumbai gang leader. A follow-up report announced, with some irony, that Mr Gawli had become a 'social worker' following his release from prison on weapons charges. I mentioned this to Hussain who gave a sceptical laugh.

'Gawli says that he's changed. Anyway, you can see for yourself. Let's visit him.'

'What, just knock on the door?'

He stood up. 'I had a tip-off that he might say yes.'

Out in the street there were plenty of taxis around, but every time Hussain gave the address they shook their heads and drove away.

'Gawli's a don though he claims not to be any more,' explained Hussain, waving valiantly at taxis in the chaos of rickshaws, carts, pedestrians and lorries. 'He's just doing some work on his image.'

Here was a man attempting to manipulate the social process whereby villains became heroes and then respectable bastions of society; that interested me. The difference was that this was an urban version of the process that had swept dacoits like Bonachur, Man Singh, Phoolan Devi and dozens of others to the top, the process in which Veerappan is unwittingly engaged. This was a new variant of the phenomenon.

We found a taxi at the fourth attempt. It was not a long journey, but we didn't spend the time concocting a cover story. Hussain wouldn't hear of it. 'We will see. He may be there and he may see us.' Instead he told me a few details to help my questioning.

Arun Gawli, 'crooked to his bones', had been released from Thane Jail only a few days before after charges of 'harbouring gangsters' were framed against him. It was this that prompted Hussain's email: Gawli had been sequestered and might be feeling side-lined. A little media attention might go down well for once. The gossip on the street, he explained, was that Bal Thackeray, supremo of Shiv Sena and notorious agitator against non-Hindu pollution like St Valentine, had wanted Gawli out of the way for some elections.

'So is Gawli a political force to be feared?'

'Very hard to answer that – his gang is certainly to be feared criminally.'

There had been setbacks for Gawli, Hussain explained. Several members had been gunned down, both by police and by the henchmen of his rival Chhota Shakeel. Now he was regrouping with new 'sharpshooters' and preparing to go back into the extortion rackets. This was a simple game where builders and developers were forced to hand over a proportion of their proceeds: either as cash or as real estate.

I asked Hussain about the other dons, the ones who had gone overseas. 'Daud Ibrahim is the biggest crime boss with at least a thousand men on his payroll here. I haven't met him though; he lives in Dubai under a pseudonym. We've spoken several times on the phone. He's a big enemy of Gawli.'

Daud had started out in the middle-class Bombay neighbourhood of Dongri, Hussain told me. The son of an honest policeman, he had not committed his first crime until he was twenty-one and that had been 'a small bank robbery'. It was then the late 1970s and the crime bosses of Mumbai were mainly Afghans. Their empire was soon to crumble, however. The wily Daud learned quickly how to manipulate the system, buying cops and politicians while dealing with opponents ruthlessly. In 1984 he had fled to Dubai where he is rumoured to have invested much of his $500 million wealth.

'He is very softly spoken,' said Hussain. 'He uses flowery language but never raises his voice. He called once and asked me to stop writing stories linking him with drugs.'

'What did you say?'

'I told him to stop reading the newspapers.'

'Was that wise?'

He shrugged and laughed.

'So how does he make his money?'

'Traditionally it was gold smuggling but the latest is Bollywood. In the late 1980s producers went to him because they were desperate for money. The problem with Bollywood has always been raising venture capital and he had plenty of that, plus he liked the pretty girls.'

'And the other dons?'

'Chhota Rajan's brother invested in a film, *Vaastu*, which was a big hit. Chhota Shakeel is involved too.'

'Where do they live?'

Hussain was leaning forwards, directing the taxi driver to the side of the road. 'Shakeel lives in Karachi, as for Rajan, no one knows right now, maybe Malaysia.'

We were pulling up outside a high metal gate. Hussain pointed out the perimeter wall. 'You see how a man has to live when he has Daud and Shakeel as enemies. All this compound is Gawli's.'

The two guards at this gate were a little perplexed by our arrival but showed us through to the yard. There was a single shabby apartment block of five storeys, some other buildings and a large yard containing several new cars. Hussain was all smiles and bonhomie as we approached a crowd of about a dozen men hanging about at the entrance to the apartments.

'Gawli is here?'

A smooth young man in a white shirt came across. 'What is it you are wanting?'

Hussain held out a hand towards me. 'My friend from England is writing a book about crime in India and he wants to talk to Gawli.'

The man gave me a thin smile. 'Mr Gawli is a social worker.'

'Hey!' said Hussain, chuckling. 'Gawli is a don. That's why my friend needs to see him.' He waved up at a second-floor window. 'Look, that guy!' A face smiled down at us. 'Gawli once did two years for illegal ownership of a gun and I did a story about how he ran his gang from inside. That's the guy I spoke to.'

There was a sense in which this was a game, a hugely cheerful, no offence taken, game. Not like cricket, that was war.

The old contact came down and there was some good-natured banter in Marathi before they switched back to English. Hussain explained our presence once again. The man said he would ask if we might have fifteen minutes of Gawli's time.

We stepped back to wait, out of earshot of the crowd of men. 'Is Gawli the real thing?' I asked. 'It seems so relaxed.'

'Don't be fooled,' said Hussain. 'I remember once interviewing an old man, a nice old man, who had alleged that Gawli had had his son killed. Before it came to court, the old man withdrew the allegation and when I asked him why, he said, "I only have one more son and I don't want him dead too."' He turned and pointed to the gate. 'See the new gate? Well, Daud's gunmen sprayed the old one with machine gun fire not so long ago. Gawli has several charges of killing and extortion against him. He'll tell us he's retired, but there's no evidence of that.'

The young man came bounding down the stairs. 'You say you are a writer. What books have you written?'

I told him the titles.

'Published in London?'

I nodded.

'Proper London?'

'Yes.'

He disappeared up the stairs again. The other men were slouching against the cars, no longer interested in us. The young man came back, now sweating from his exertions. I deduced that Mr Gawli occupied the top floor. An order was given in Marathi and we were searched, with many apologies. First our bags – Hussain's mobile phone was taken off him, but my camera was allowed – then they frisked us and we were led inside.

I counted three metal gates on the way up. Long dark corridors with laundry on poles: it was not the penthouse swankiness I had half hoped for, though I knew that in India wealthy men often keep their gotten gains well-hidden. Old strings of mango leaves were suspended above doorways; women in brilliant saris shuffled past and there were stains of purple on the walls where children had printed their hands during the Holi festival. It was a tenement, a village stood vertically inside a concrete frame. I half expected to see a buffalo shambling along with a mouthful of grass.

On the top floor we turned left and walked to the end. I got brief glimpses of shabby rooms and men sitting idle. Then we came to what was obviously a reception room: low glass-topped coffee table with chrome legs, banquette seating around two sides and above, dominating the room, large posters of Indian gods and goddesses. Naturally, Kali was there among them.

The room was otherwise empty and we sat down to wait.

'Is he religious?' I whispered to Hussain.

'All the dons are,' he said. 'You need a pretty big shoulder to cry on when you're as bad as they are.'

We fell silent and I thought of all the time and energy I had put into getting close to Veerappan; now I'd waltzed in here without any effort whatsoever. There was a flurry of activity along the corridor and Mr Gawli arrived, flanked by six men. We stood to greet him. He was a small man, only a fraction over five feet tall and slightly built, wearing loose white trousers, long white shirt and white Nehru cap. He was barefoot. He did not, on first appearance, look like a gangster – he looked like a milkman.

Mr Gawli sat down on my right, next to Hussain; his lawyer sat on my left and the rest remained standing. The lawyer perched forwards on the seat, his manner both servile and nervous while making the introductions. Gawli was impeccably courteous, though his eyes were strangely lifeless, almost drugged, in their slow watchfulness. On his left hand a diamond ring sparkled with a five-carat stone. A servant came in and placed two glasses of dark liquid, Coca-Cola or the Indian version, Thumbs-Up, one in front of me, one in front of Hussain. Neither of us moved to drink.

'Where were you born?' I asked first.

The lawyer translated Gawli's replies, but the gesture said it. 'Here.'

'What did your father do?'

'He sold milk.' I smiled a little to myself. 'We had many buffaloes here in the yard when I was younger. We milked them and took the milk out on the cart, selling it to local people.'

Milk carries much significance, of course, but nowhere more so than in India, a cow-worshipping culture where idols are washed in milk.

'What happened to those buffaloes?'

'The authorities banned us from keeping cows inside the city.'

[213]

I watched his calloused toes play with the leg of the table. It was a very rural kind of dispossession. I wondered if they had been urban cows, the sort that munch cardboard boxes at the traffic lights, but no, he said, they were proper buffaloes. I could imagine them down there, where the gleaming Landcruiser now stood, their mouths gently chewing, backs steaming in the mornings and the slow measured breathing.

'So what did you do?'

'In 1968 I joined the Shiv Sena.'

He was an early convert. The banning of cows from the city was a perfect issue for Thackeray's organization, as it was both anti-Hindu and anti-Maharashtrian culture.

Gawli had begun by organizing rallies and security. I could see Hussain was smiling more than usual and could not bear to stay out of this.

'There are twenty cases against him,' he said to me. 'With Shiv Sena he became involved in political violence, then crime.'

Gawli clearly understood more English than he was letting on. He denied Hussain's allegation, delivering a long speech which the lawyer translated as 'never crime'. At all times Gawli spoke in a soft even tone, not once raising his voice or becoming animated. Hussain winked. I decided to push harder.

'Why does Daud Ibrahim hate you?'

He smiled gently. 'Since the Shiv Sena days Daud has hated me for being a Hindu.'

'Has he tried to assassinate you?'

'Once the gate was sprayed with bullets.'

Daud is known for his violent behaviour against Hindu extremists. He was widely held responsible for the bombings that came in the wake of the destruction of Babri Masjid in Ayodhya by members of Sangh Parivar, a militant Hindu group. Although Daud is far away in Dubai, just as Veerappan is isolated in his jungles, the Indian gangster is never far from the issues of the day, or his community.

Hussain put in again here. 'Gawli's brother was close to a

journalist who published stories about Daud's gang. As a warning Daud had the brother killed in 1989, and Gawli went into crime to avenge his death.'

There were two driving forces here: the dispossession of his father's trade and vengeance. Gawli, however, did not comment; instead he waved his hand towards the drinks. Neither of us moved to drink.

'Have you ever killed anyone?'

He smiled sweetly. 'Never.'

The lawyer began to speak to me, but forgetting himself used Marathi. Gawli cut him off with a swift rebuke. Hussain dipped his head and I followed his gaze to the lawyer's hands. The piece of paper he was holding had begun to tremble.

'Mr Gawli runs an organization called Akhil Bharatiya Sena Party,' said the lawyer. 'He founded it four years ago to do social work and run blood donation camps.'

I saw the amusement in Hussain's eyes.

Gawli put in here. 'I am retired from the underworld.' We all laughed dutifully. He added, 'There is no evidence I am a goonda. Charges were filed, but no evidence.'

He smiled gently, obviously satisfied that the point was proven.

'Are you a religious man?'

He moved his head in agreement.

'Which gods do you worship?'

'Krishna is my favourite.'

'And Kali? You have two pictures of Kali, only one of Krishna. Isn't Kali the goddess often worshipped by gangsters and criminals?'

'Yes. She is a symbol of power. We worship power.' He broke off to mutter something to the lawyer. From its tone, I gathered it meant, 'Say your piece, what do I pay you for?'

The lawyer started off again, the paper now trembling more. 'Mr Gawli's party has 80,000 members and their contributions are his only funds for this operation. The symbol of his party is the cow, which animal symbolizes the goodness of milk and holiness. Mr

[215]

Gawli has built a new temple for worship in his compound, the doors of this temple are of solid silver.'

Mr Gawli nodded, a half smile of pride on his lips. The old buffalo yard had become his urban castle, a rajah's stronghold complete with defensive wall, castle keep, temple and sepoys. He patronized the arts, led the prayers; he had a lawyer to sing for him and a butler to buttle. Under the shabby concrete, the electrical cables and chrome, this was a modern Garhkundar in downtown Mumbai.

As if to reinforce his regal generosity, Gawli indicated the drinks once again and said in English, 'Please, take something.'

Hussain ignored the offer. Gawli turned to me. 'Please.'

'Please to accept Mr Gawli's hospitality,' said the lawyer with an unctuous smile.

'Please,' said Mr Gawli.

There was an awkward silence. The row of flunkeys staring at me, their hands together like schoolchildren about to be reprimanded. If Hussain would not drink, I thought, then maybe I should not. Journalistic solidarity.

'I'm sorry,' I said. 'I never take Thumbs-Up.'

'Soda,' said Gawli. One of the row turned and went out. Gawli's eyes were totally without expression. I didn't like the pressure.

'Do you own a gun?' I asked. I could feel the heat coming off the lawyer now, and it took a moment for him to translate the question.

Gawli smiled. 'No.' His bare toes stroked the chrome of the table leg.

'But you were convicted of owning a sten gun?'

'The charges were framed. There was no evidence.'

'But you went to prison for two years.'

'The charges were false. I am not a goonda.'

The servant appeared with a glass of soda water and replaced the Thumbs-Up.

'Please,' said Gawli.

'I'm not thirsty.'

[216]

The lawyer squirmed. 'Please be accepting Mr Gawli's generosity.'

'Please.'

I glanced at Hussain, hoping he would save me. He did not move. They were all looking at me. It was Gawli, I knew, imposing his will on me. Perhaps a punishment for the impertinent questions that he had taken with such sang-froid. His hand with the diamond ring moved, a gesture of the open palm, of hospitality. 'Please.'

And I found myself leaning forward to pick up the glass.

'Would you like a picture of Mr Gawli?' Hussain interrupted me just as the glass touched my lips.

I put it down slowly. 'Yes, I would. Is that possible?' I glanced at the lawyer. 'A photo of Mr Gawli?'

I rummaged in my bag and took out my digital camera. When the picture was taken, I showed it to Gawli on the small screen at the back. The issue of the drink had been forgotten.

'Mr Gawli would like to finish now,' said the lawyer. 'Do you have any last questions?'

I shook my head and thanked Gawli for his time.

We were shown the solid silver doors on the temple before we finally escaped. When we were safely out in the street, Hussain was full of contempt for Gawli: 'He says 80,000 members but no one has seen the party lists.'

'So the stuff about social work is all rubbish?'

'He is a gangster – no question.'

Gawli's conversion to righteousness then, was no damascene affair, more a political convenience. But I could see him in five years, running for office, a poor bad boy made good. This man might not make his money sticking up trains and hiding out in the ravines, but his rise had all the hallmarks of dispossession, criminal fight back and, finally, a bid for real power and respect. Perhaps one day he would make that last leap to rulership and, just like Bonachur, the people would start to say he had received a boon from the goddess herself at Brindachul.

\*   \*   \*

The day after meeting Gawli I was back in Jhansi. All around the countryside was dying in a blaze of glory as the trees burst into flower. The hour before sunset was the best when the colours were richest. At Barwa Sagar Lake, I stood on the hill and watched a yogi stand waist deep in the water doing his pranayama, alternately pressing each nostril and counting his inhalations. It was a moment of utter peace, the surface of the water still and the colours of the sky painted there.

Prana is life force, Maddy had told me, and yama is cultivation. By this means the hatha yoga texts claim that a strange alchemy will overcome the body, there will be a change in the cellular structure. Then the yogi or yogini will have mastery of the body. Some practitioners are then buried in the earth, the seven orifices blocked. Time can pass, many days, long enough for wheat grains scattered over the spot to germinate and grow.

This yogi had only one arm. He poured water over his head to finish, then saluted the setting sun and came towards us. His arm had been lost just below the elbow which made a hook to hang his bucket on. His only clothing was a cloth around his waist.

'Pranayama?' I asked and he smiled, answering in Hindi which the driver translated.

'I do it every night at sunset pooja, then asana in the temple. For seventeen years I have been here.'

He pointed out all the ancient stones around the lake. 'Some were serais for travellers. Where have you come from?'

I told him about Garhkundar. 'Do you know about thugs,' I asked. 'Phansigar?'

He wobbled his head. 'At night I see them here – old Maharaj Bonachur and his fighters on horses, riding through the lake with their swords ready.'

'Ghosts – djinnis?'

'Yes. They come to this place. Four years ago a villager from Nivari came and slept in the temple. During the night he felt the rumal go around his throat. He opened his eyes to see a terrible giant. Huge! As tall as those palm trees over there. The villager begged for his life, saying he would never come back to this place, the giant's lands. The giant said he would allow him this one chance, then he released him from the rumal and disappeared.'

'Aren't you afraid to sleep here?'

He laughed. 'Why? I am a poor babu. The thugs have no business with me.'

'Why do they stay in this place?'

'It is their place. The Bundelkund is theirs from the time before even the Bundelas arrived. These ruined serais were where the travellers came, the people they murdered.'

We left him alone there at his temple, alone with his visions of thug kings galloping across the lake.

It was time for me to move east as I wanted to visit the sangam, the holy confluence of the Ganges, Jamuna and Saraswati rivers, then head east to Brindachul, Varanasi and Kolkata. If this was the land of thugs, then these were the cardinal points in the world of Kali, their goddess.

# 10

# Mother Ganga

JHANSI RAILWAY STATION AT NIGHT. Sadhus in fresh white socks and saffron robes, their hair in matted dreadlocks, brass tridents in hand with lemons on the prongs (ascetic acid?), all awaiting the Bundelkund Express. Families sitting on their bags. An Indian lady who had come from Rishikesh talking to me. 'God is One,' she said, adding mysteriously, 'like a banana.' Then a tax collector. 'They say we are unruly people but at the Kumbh Mela, thirteen million people took bath in one day!' Everyone was talking religion, everyone was on a pilgrimage, or planning one, or had just finished one. They had penances and observances and ceremonies and gurus. My own itinerary was perfectly comprehensible to them: stop off to see the sangam, the holy confluence of the rivers Ganges, Jamuna and Saraswati at Allahabad, continue to Kali Temple at Brindachul, then Varanasi and finally Kali Ghat in Kolkata.

The tax collector's guru was Mamaji, the hugging guru. People line up for hours to get a hug from her and so far the taxman had managed five. The lady from Rishikesh had been given thirty-five minutes' daily breathing practice to do by her guru, also a hugger,

Mamaji had even been known to hug lepers, the taxman said, even to lick their wounds.

The train was late. I walked down the platform to the end and looked back at the people. The taxman and the Rishikesh lady were deep in conversation. They all wanted to be touched, I thought. In this country where untouchability chokes human empathy, where the social dynamic of those in power is to separate and divide groups, there is still a force bringing people together. You could become a great guru merely by prescribing indiscriminate hugs.

We were soon clanking along in the darkness, guards with rifles at each end of every carriage. Dudwa, the dacoit, and his cohorts were considered a very real threat as there had been several train hold-ups in the previous weeks. Passengers were busy locking their bags to any available iron stanchions, a common enough sight on Indian Railways but I had never seen quite so many hefty chains.

I managed to push my way through the throng to the door where the guard stood. The taxman was there exchanging opinions with anyone who wanted a chat. 'Dudwa will not attack a train,' he said. 'He is too big for such goings on these days. He is heading for politics. Mark my words, he will be a member of the Lok Sabha before long.'

The guards laughed. They obviously didn't agree, but the taxman pointed out that Phoolan Devi had made it. I told them that I had been in an internet café in Jhansi and found a government website that stated clearly and with surprising candour: 'Politics [in Madhya Pradesh] are highly criminalized.'

Conversation soon drifted back to religion. An elderly gentleman was pointed out to me.

'He is going to Varanasi to scatter his wife's ashes in the Ganges there. Other people may take the body itself and burn it on the ghats.'

I told them I planned to get out at Allahabad to visit the sangam.

'You should get down at Naini, before Allahabad,' said the

taxman. 'Then you can take a rickshaw to the river and a boat directly to the sangam.'

The night passed with no hijacks, nothing worse than berth-jackings in fact: the ancient Indian art of perching on someone else's railway berth until they give up and let you share. I pushed them off until I fell asleep, then woke before dawn to find two extra people in my bed.

There were plenty of people around on Naini station, there always are in India, not least because many poorer folk share their rooms and do shifts on the sleeping space. The rickshaw men were bundled up against the cold damp chill and I woke one to take me down to the river. We clattered downhill, through tendrils of mist and packs of sleepy pariah dogs, then stopped at the head of a steep track down on to the hardened pale mud of the riverbank. I had no idea what to expect: during the Kumbh Mela, up to thirty million people cram themselves on to these banks and try and bathe at the sangam, but at less auspicious times I imagined there would still be a crowd, the real die-hards.

I followed a small group of pilgrims down the lane and out on to the bank. It was an ethereal sight, a vast shimmering panorama of white sandbars split by the broad flow of the Jamuna. Far beyond in the haze of dawn was the Ganges. But there were no massed ranks of holy men, no smoke rising from their fires. Thirty million had been here just weeks before, bathing and praying and hoping to wash away their sins in the sangam; thirteen million were said to have bathed at one time, but now they were all gone. It was empty.

At first I felt intense disappointment. I sat on the sandbank and watched the sun rise as a red ball in the mist. The truth was, I reflected, that I had come with a voyeuristic outlook: I wanted to see the sadhus covered in ashes, the great tents of successful export gurus, the fabulous feats of breath control and subsequent burial. Now what I had was the essence, what all of those people had come for: the sangam. It was a lesson from Mother Ganga.

I attached myself to the group of pilgrims and we boarded a large

[223]

rowing boat. Now I had got used to the scale of this place, I could see that there were people on the far side, most of them standing on the riverbank opposite a line of boats. This, my companions told me, marked the line of the sangam: the point at which the waters of the muddy Ganges and clear Jamuna meet, plus some invisible additions from the legendary Saraswati. By some trick of topography and hydrology the two waters slide against one another, creating a distinct line and it is this natural phenomenon that for thousands of years has been revered.

As we approached, we began to hear the distant hubbub and other boats appeared bearing more pilgrims. Soon we could hear the splashing and the incantations of Brahmins, the poojaris who help the pilgrims through the complexities of ritual and recitation. Boys carrying plastic billycans were doing a good trade for those who wanted to take away a litre or two. Others were selling camphor lamps made of dried leaves to set afloat with a prayer.

As soon as we had tied up to the line of stake boats, all the people on board threw off the towels and blankets in which they were wrapped and stepped off into the water which was only waist deep. This was the great moment, the moment when all sins were washed away, and yet there was no displays of ecstasy, simply a quiet devotion. They pressed their hands together under their chins, closed their eyes and quickly dipped down three times. Some used pots to help bathe each other. Old ladies clucking around their menfolk. The boats next to me were filled with the murmurings of Brahmins. Coconuts were smashed, offerings offered, pastes pasted and flames lit. A skein of seagulls came by, stealing the food offerings.

I lay on my back, not wanting to leave the warmth for the water, enjoying the sense of single-minded activity all around. I had a sense of the vastness of India, the millions who came here, who had been here in all the centuries. The Ganges had carried so many sins down its course and out into the Bay of Bengal, along with ashes and bodies and general rubbish and sewage. The river is a god in the pantheon and its broad

[224]

back can carry many burdens; now I had one more for it to take.

My journey so far had been trawling through murder, prisons, criminality, through the darker regions of the human psyche. In its evil, the British victimization of innocent millions as 'criminal castes and tribes' was a long way behind the undoubted murders of the dacoits and thugs, but its evil was undeniable. Sleeman and colleagues had constantly expressed amazement at the guilt-free demeanour of their prisoners, yet few colonial officers had ever shown the least remorse for the horror of treating a newborn child as a criminal. True evil, I reflected, does not know itself; good intentions pave the way down. And we all suffer those delusions in our own lives, the unwitting consequences as we blunder blindly forwards.

One night in Jabalpur, Maddy had told me that it was all maya, that this was a world of illusions and that the sadhus and sannyasis were brave individuals setting out to break through those barriers. Her guru had sat for two years in a charnel ground, had eaten the flesh of corpses amongst other things, all in the process of discarding the veils and breaking through maya. Then, free of worldly ties, he moved beyond good and evil.

But fed up with the mystical jargon and tie-dye philosophy, I'd said, 'Rubbish. Fairy stories – I never liked them.' And a chilly silence came down between us. I was so far into the subject of criminality, and the suspicion that came with the territory, that I no longer even tried to hear her. Somewhere along the way I had picked up the virus of mistrust and scorn. With it, her open mind became nothing but gullibility and I felt some devil in me, sending me on to the attack. I only had to hear a phrase like 'floating in the cosmic egg', and I'd be snarling with derision. 'That'd be the scrambled one, I suppose?'

'I've noticed,' she said, after one of our long frosty pauses, 'that just before you say something like that, you stop breathing.'

I leaped into action, ready for a fight.

[225]

'Don't you tell me how to breathe! I've managed long enough without any bloody yogic help on that, thank you very much!'

What stung hardest was that, even in my anger, I had noticed that my breathing stopped for a moment before I spoke.

As I lay on the sangam, the memory came back to me and I concentrated on breathing slowly and steadily. I was tensed up and I didn't know why. Anger and resentments from other times perhaps, now inflicted on the present. Maddy made me realize how closed I had become; if I heard her words and those of others it was only to extract what I wanted, what proved I was correct. I wrote it down and took it away and made a story that suited my purposes. But I had stopped listening, stopped breathing.

It is not for nothing that the sangam is a holy place: the two rivers become one, the dark-watered Ganga joins the bright-watered Jamuna, and on the very meeting place, you can wash away your sins. (The Saraswati exists only in Legend.) It wasn't sin I wanted swept down towards Varanasi: it was the dust of the journey through the criminal heartland and the mistrust and suspicion it was breeding in me. If the traveller carries devils within, and the nineteenth century had its own, then here were mine. All the sadhus were charlatans, all their musings hokum, and all their western followers dupes. But I wanted to go forward with an uncluttered and open mind, not with that devil on my shoulder.

I should have dived fully clothed into the divine waters, filling my mouth with its sweet inspiration, but I was too chilly for philosophical dunkings. I landed on the riverbank and went in search of some breakfast first, pausing on the way to note a beggar who had bent his knee back and painted it to look infected. It reminded me of Jaahiz and his ninth-century recipes. (Tie up limb till it swells, then paint it red with Dragon's Blood resin and add a liberal smear of butter.) It was good to see an ancient tradition kept up.

I returned that afternoon with two posh ladies from Mumbai. I met them at the place I was staying in, a rather better option than my usual fleapits, and they had a private boat complete with butler.

'Shall I wash away for Selwa?' one asked the other as our oarsman manoeuvred us in. 'She did ask me to, but she didn't say exactly what her sins were.'

While they were discussing what Selwa might have been up to, I slipped into the sangam and dipped myself three times.

At dawn two days later, I crossed the river in a rowing boat and took a train east, along the south bank of the Ganges towards the spiritual home of all thugs: the temple at Brindachul (now also known as Vrindyachul).

There was a station there, a few miles west of Mirzapur, and I got down, enjoying the sight of a typical country halt with its old-fashioned ticket machine issuing dockets of thick card and a stack of brass lamps by the stationmaster's chair. The temple was a couple of miles away in the hills and I took a rickshaw.

We rattled along the roads, a pleasant breeze in my face, and sunlight flashing between the trees. It was there, a mile before the temple lane, that I began to see the monkeys: not any normal, tree-climbing, banana-stealing primate, but men dressed as monkeys in brilliant costumes of red, blue and gold, with long tails attached. One was loping along on his knuckles, oblivious to our passing and with no one near. Then in the narrow lane that leads up to the foot of the hill and the temple, there was a man covered in blood, his face covered and clothes splattered.

The temple is nestled in forest near the base of the Vindhya range of hills, the site, it is said, where Kali's left breast fell to earth when she was sliced apart by the angry Vishnu. It is a single-storey stone construction around a courtyard with a well. Next to one corner was a tree in which a man-monkey was crouched, behaving much like the langur monkeys who were crouched at the opposite end. A popular penance is to adopt a monkey's life for a year, as homage to Hanuman. I could imagine such characters had long inhabited the temple; perhaps

[227]

impersonation of animals was the first kind of mummery, the first deception.

In the centre of the frontage was a flight of steps up to the door and, after taking off my shoes, I went inside. There was a small throng of people standing waiting while the bell was rung and the Brahmins performed the mysterious rites. Then the doors were thrown back and the people pushed around in front of the idol.

It was certainly not terrifying: a low flat face with two staring eyes and a gaping red maw almost disappearing in the dozens of garlands, but the women in the crowd threw themselves face down on the floor and prayed fervently. More people came rushing in now, ringing the temple bell furiously. There were still too few to create a crowd but there was something different to other temples, an urgency and excitement, the faces full of animation.

When it was over, I sat outside on the wall and after a while the Brahmin came and sat with me. He was a mild-mannered man, dressed simply and with a mouth full of paan.

'The Kali temple here for two thousand and forty-eight years,' he said in a mix of poor English and Hindi, not helped by the betel. 'This building was raised by Rajah Vikramajit.'

That would put it in the early sixteenth century. Vikramajit, I recalled, had once owned a great and famous diamond, possibly the Koh-i-Noor. I asked the Brahmin about sacrifice and he pointed to an unobtrusive stone near where the langur monkeys were sitting. 'That place.'

'Is it used now?'

He waggled affirmatively. 'For sheep or goats. But long time back the dacoit Man Singh killed a man there.' This was more likely an ancient Man Singh than the twentieth-century bandit – there have been a few, including a noted rajah of Gwalior.

'And the thugs and dacoits? Do they worship Kali here?'

He didn't like this question. 'Bengal men say it is dacoity temple, but for us it is only for Kali. When Man Singh killed a man, the blood drops fell on the earth here and every drop became a dacoit. So Kali takes the blood in her mouth to stop dacoits borning.'

Here was the central mystery of Kali: she both creates and destroys; she eats demons and creates men-demons instead; she both lusts for blood and hates the demons created in the spilling of it. Kali is a mother goddess, but not motherly; hers is the female intensity of Macbeth's witches, a crazed, wild-haired woman in communion with her nature. In one legend she was born from the forehead of Durga, a mother goddess, but her cult has outgrown the parent. Kali is wild female power, shakti; when she dances, the world is threatened with destruction. Her most common image is the Smashan Kali, the goddess in the charnel grounds. Around her neck are fifty skulls, around her waist a girdle of human hands, her mouth and tongue are scarlet with blood. No wonder the first westerners to see her image regarded her as an Indian devil. But it was a misunderstanding: the fifty skulls represent the letters of the Sanskrit alphabet and so mental work, the hands symbolize the labours of this life. Kali herself has four arms: in the left hands are a bloody knife and a severed head, in the right she gestures to offer boons and courage. In this symbolic way she offers to cut her followers free from their earthly labours and troubles, if they only dare to go with her.

The good and evil of the human world are of no concern to Kali: she offers an escape from those unsteady and unreliable values. Little wonder that a land of so much injustice and servitude should produce a deity that expresses the human desire for some power above right and wrong, a deity that captures the passionate desire for life and death, the mystical yearnings and violence of the dispossessed and powerless. Kali is perfect for millions of Indians, perfect for the thieves and criminals driven to their trade, perfect for the age we live in.

# 11

# Kashi

'VARANASI IS THE PLACE,' MADDY HAD said. 'I heard there are men, aghoris, who are following that way of Kali: they call it the left-hand path of god and it's dangerous – many of them go insane.'

I left the Kali temple and walked up and around the hilltop where there were further temples to various incarnations of Kali. Some devotees had made images of her and were begging, others used photographs of her most famous temple in Kolkata. At sunset I left and returned to the station.

If there is one city in India where the chaos, the filth, the noise, the overwhelming sense of compressed ant-heap humanity makes sense, it is Varanasi. Arriving at dawn, I rode by rickshaw down through the new town, then walked through the alleyways of the old. I wasn't looking for a hotel and I didn't need to ask directions: I was going where everyone goes, to the river.

Even at this hour, or rather especially at this hour, people were heading down, bearing brass ewers and offerings, all wrapped in shawls against the chill. Some men were bearing a small bier adorned with flowers and joss sticks, but it was not a child, as I first assumed, rather a dead monkey that had been electrocuted on the wires overhead. Further along an elderly lady in widow's white placed a single marigold on a Shiva lingam, a stone phallus, next to which lay a sleeping dog, its fur completely destroyed by mange and its greyish skin twitching with dreams.

I came down a narrow lane, squeezed past some buffaloes, went under an arch and then, from the head of a long steep flight of steps, spotted the water. A few seconds later I emerged into the sunshine on the ghats. Two hundred yards away across the shimmering silver water was a white featureless sandbank. This is the marvel of Varanasi: on one riverbank is the teeming, visceral madness of the city, on the other, nothing. Between the two glides the river, the borderline between those two contrasting worlds.

The sun rises from across that white shimmering expanse of nothing and you can see why, five millennia ago, someone thought it a good place to build a town. As I sat there, the sunlight warmed the whole crescent of the riverfront, all the temples and towers of ochre and red, and the haze gave it depth and mystery. Below me sadhus were washing their saffron robes and a naked man was sitting astride a wallowing buffalo giving its head a vigorous shampoo with soap and water, singing to it gently. In the air was a faint spicy tang, slightly acrid, a smell one never quite escapes in Varanasi; in all the churning vital life, it is death, the scent of cremation from the burning ghats.

I walked south along the steps of the ghats. All the sadhus were camped here, with simple canvas or plastic sheeting tied up and a bed roll each. In front of the camps were the dhunis, the sacred fire, more often than not with a trident standing in it. Some sadhus were naked except for ashes, one or two were well blessed with gold jewellery donated by wealthy admirers, but most satisfied themselves with a necklace of rudraksh seeds.

I passed their camps and moved on, past a water tower and came to the final ghat, Assi Ghat, named after a river that once flowed into the Ganges here. Under a tree women were pouring libations of Ganga water over the Shiva lingam and barbers were busy trimming moustaches. This would be my favourite spot in all Varanasi, a place where the village life of timeless India is best observed, a place beside the river where the people wash clothes, bathe, eat, drink tea and gossip for hours. Searching around, I found a small guesthouse with a rooftop terrace overlooking the ghat and took a room.

It did not take long for me to appreciate that I had landed in the perfect spot for my purposes. Shashank, the owner, was a cultured man: his living room a poised and artful space with portraits and maps on the walls, piles of books on low tables and interesting artefacts dotted around.

'Doesn't anything ever go missing?' I asked.

He looked surprised. 'Never!'

I sat on the sofa drinking tea, he at his desk in the corner.

'But Benares was famous for thugs.'

He laughed. 'Even our friends from outside say they never get the better of us for we are Benares thugs.'

'The old-time thugs strangled travellers.'

'It is true, they sometimes did that, with a rumal, a handkerchief.' He leaned across and delicately took a book from the table. 'You see there is a tradition of embroidery with the rumal. It was used to cover offerings to the gods.'

It is astonishing, I thought, how religion permeates every aspect of the tale. Shashank showed me various examples of the rumal art. For him beauty was a passion. He had turned the family home into a shrine to it: building ornamental pavilions on the roof, organizing lectures on art, and producing elaborate dinners. As a result he knew everyone who knew anything about his beloved Kashi. (Varanasi is the official name of the city, though Benares is still used. Kashi is the ancient name, also still used.)

'You should meet Professor Anandkrishnan,' he said, writing down a phone number. 'His family are very well known here – his father founded the museum at the University.'

[233]

\*      \*      \*

That night was Shivaratri, the night of Shiva, and all the sadhus had come down to keep the vigil. At sunset there was a huge arti ceremony at Dasaswamedha Ghat, and hundreds of people sent lamps floating down the river. I managed to get through the crowd and close to the main temple, but it was barred to foreigners and heavily armed police were in position. Propelled by the crowds I went down through the lanes and emerged on the burning ghats.

The air was thick with smoke and the taste of scorched flesh stung my mouth. Gangs of pall-bearers were charging down through the crowds towards the burning ghats, as though it were a matter of life and death, rather than just the latter, chanting, '*Rama nama satya hai!*' God's name is truth! Under the spangled shrouds the bodies were pathetically thin. Boats piled with wood were tied up waiting to be unloaded: there was even, incongruously, a lifeboat. On either side of the steps were two charnel grounds with fires burning. Death and destruction is not hidden here: feet protrude from the flames, a head pops with the heat, men with long bamboo poles carefully fold up the corpse as it is consumed, making sure the ashes are neatly gathered ready for disposal in the river. And the dead keep coming, pouring down the alleyways towards this curious door into the next life, a stream of bodies swollen by those who came from other parts of India, even overseas, to die in the holy city of Shiva. The buildings all around the ghat are filled with elderly people, praying and fasting, preparing themselves for the journey ahead. And there are those who cover themselves in the ashes of the burning grounds and sit in the small temple next to the steps where, casually thrown on a window ledge, were two skulls, one wearing a cheap pair of spectacles. The old sadhus inside were completely gaga, staring at me in puzzlement, speechless, motionless, mouths ajar, as though someone had just popped out and not yet returned.

I could understand their baffled inertia. The frenetic movement of death all around, the stench that made eyes water, the sheer staggering unreality were too much. The internet café, for example,

[234]

should that have been there, at the end of the universe as it were, its monitors flecked with the ashes of corpses?

There were others like myself, attracted by the drama and spectacle. I wanted to observe unseen, but that is rarely possible. A group of medical representatives from Kolkata collared me. They were on pilgrimage, but their minds were on other matters.

'What is the comparison of Indian and English female beauty?'

'Both are good,' I said, watching a corpse have its leg broken at the knee, releasing a shower of sparks as though a welder were at work.

'But English is sexier?'

'I think that television makes you think that. There are beautiful women everywhere.'

This was taken as a tremendously wise saying. Two of them clapped me on the back. 'You are right-speaking,' said another. 'I am proud of you. Come and meet Guru-ji.'

I was glad to get away from the heat and fumes and into a room off one of the lanes.

Their guru was a medical rep, just as they were, and in all that strangeness I could somehow accept this as normal. He sat cross-legged on the floor, beaming beatifically at all the world, his beard long and straggling, wrapped in simple robes. The devotion shown by the others was touching, but slightly sinister too – though this perception could have been influenced by television.

I sat next to him and he smiled gently for quite some time before speaking. When he did, his voice was tiny, with great long pauses between his words and barely a whisper. 'What – is – God?' he said, rocking himself.

'I don't know, do you?'

'God – is – nothing. God – is – everything. You cannot know – if water is hot – or cold until – you place your hand – in it. Same like God – you must experience Him. God is in that door – that light – God is in you. You are God. We worship you. Yes, we worship you.'

[235]

The medical reps who had been hanging on every word chimed in. 'We worship you.'

They laughed with me. 'Do not think to be boastful,' said one, cheerfully. 'We are all gods too.'

'You have many gods,' I said. 'I doubt you need another.'

The sage wobbled his head. 'You are quite incorrect. Think of milk. It may be curd – or ghee – or rasmallai [a sweet] – but it is all milk. Same like god – god is one – and god is many.'

'Or cheese,' added one earnest and excited acolyte.

'Indian people,' continued the guru, 'we are not inspired – by commodities and whatnots – look how we measure a man. Gandhi, for example, who had nothing.'

'Does anyone in India care about Gandhi now?' I asked, perhaps with a slight holding of breath beforehand. 'I see lots of people rushing to get qualifications on computers and buying new cars and mobile phones.'

'There is a difference,' said the guru. 'Here they – are happy. In England, not.'

'Have you – been there?' I was catching the halting disease. I tried to imagine him in Europe and failed.

'I was in – Hartlepool in 1963.' He smiled gnomically, perhaps recalling the good old days in the northern town. 'In Hartlepool people do not see – that life is illusion, maya. There was – one poet of Benares – Kabir – *maya maha thagini ham jani* – were his words. Illusion is like – the female thug. Life deceives you. Yes?'

I suppose I had heard this many times before: the oriental viewpoint, life is an illusion, not so much that the hand in front of your face might not exist, but that the senses, the culture, society, they may all delude us. Even good and evil are relative.

'And how to break through the maya?'

'There are many roads.'

'The sadhus are on the road?'

'Some of them – are. But others are – not.'

'And aghor. What is aghor?'

He blinked, very slowly. 'That is one – way to salvation. Aghor means Not Horrible but – only horrible things they do. Then maya is defeated. More I cannot – say. They do not tell us.'

Sadhus have become the most colourful and prominent part of the human landscape of India. Looking back at photographs, from the first taken in the 1850s, it is easy to see why. The wonderful jewel-bespeckled maharajahs and their cohorts have disappeared, likewise many of the tribes and more bizarre professions. Yet the sadhus remain the same: in the albumen prints and daguerreotypes of early photography the sadhus are there, seated in lotus position, naked, covered in ashes from their sacred fires, dreadlocked hair piled up in tasteful buns, exactly as they appear now. Strangely, for anyone who has visited India, the eye flicks over them too quickly and rests longer on the memsahibs in their bustles and parasols: those paragons of English middle-class conformity have become the more unfamiliar exotics. While other aspects of Indian life have gone, the ascetics have endured and archaeology suggests that their heritage is as long as any in the country. A seal found at Harappa in the Punjab dating back to 2000 BC shows a horned god seated in padmasana, the lotus. His three-pronged headgear resembles the trident and he is portrayed in the jungle, surrounded by wild animals. Undoubtedly, the pose and situation is typically ascetic, some have even proposed it is a precursor of Shiva.

What became of that Indus Valley civilization is not known with any certainty. Nineteenth-century European scholars were sure that it was conquered by the Aryans, a people from the west who spoke a language that would spawn Sanskrit as well as most European tongues (and give their name to Iran). The anthropometrists noted with satisfaction that these fine-nosed Aryans (nomadic/horse-riding/martial) conquered flat-nosed peoples (sedentary/plough-pushing/gormless), thus confirming that Europeans and Brahmins were best and always had been.

Sadly for the racist agenda, there is a tricky time gap of about two hundred years between the fall of Harappa and the rise of new Aryan culture. With the fall of western imperialism has come revision: extreme Indian nationalists have even claimed that the Aryans were indigenous, a position that ignores linguistic problems. (The new arrivals had to borrow words for agricultural artefacts and practices.) Whatever the truth, India had certainly acquired new masters and the beginnings of a caste system – one based on parameters that have persisted ever since.

Early Vedic scriptures written by the Aryan priests, the Brahmins, show contempt for the ascetics and the phallus worship of the conquered tribes. They preferred fire-worship and complex sacrificial rituals, sometimes of humans but usually cows or horses. Dasaswamedha Ghat translates as 'ten-horse sacrifices' and the spiritual merit gained by the ancient king on the riverbank is said to pass to anyone who bathes here today. Yet, with time, the more 'primitive' traditions were embraced and the wild-haired, jungle-dwelling god who drank from a human skull became Shiva, the most powerful in the pantheon.

Shiva's control of the 'inner fire' generated by his yogic austerities echoed the Brahmins' fire worship, while his erect penis made him acceptable to the aboriginal phallus worshippers. (Twelve stone linga dotted around India today are accepted as divinely made, while the estimated thirty million others are manufactured to strict guidelines.) In these two paradoxical facets Shiva's character resolves the duality of ecstatic lover and celibate yogi.

A legendary teacher, Shankara, is said to have first organized and sytematized the ascetics around AD 800. Some had traditions inimical to the Brahmins, human sacrifice among them. These kapalikas, literally 'skull-carriers', offered human blood and flesh to Bhairava, Shiva in his most terrifying form as a licentious entranced lunatic. Some related cults were also known as worshippers of Shiva's female counterpart, the power of shakti, deified as the Great Goddess, and usually in her most terrifying incarnation as Kali. Gradually these practices were expelled from the mainstream, but they have never been eradicated.

*    *    *

I walked back along the ghats, enjoying the spectacle, stopping now and again to sit with groups of sadhus and, inevitably, I would be invited to smoke a chillum, a clay pipe stuffed with ganja or hashish.

'Hold the pipe like a rose offered in love,' said one. 'Then grab that hand and breathe through the space between thumb and forefinger.'

When I tired of that, I headed off. I was looking for a place Maddy had told me about where a friend of hers, Bhaskar, stayed during Shivaratri. I wondered if he would know where she was.

I found it eventually, a ramshackle house on the ghats, totally unobtrusive and unmarked. Up some steps through two doors, I came out in a courtyard filled with old trees and stone benches where three men were lazing. One was Bhaskar, long-haired and bearded, dressed in tee-shirt, waistcoat and a lunghi.

'I've been coming to this place for years and years for Shivaratri,' he said when we had introduced ourselves. 'After this, all the sadhus head off and Varanasi gets hotter and dustier till monsoon begins.'

He explained how all the festivals fitted in with the lunar cycle: Dessera, Pongal, Holi, Shivaratri, Navaratri, and so on. For most of India these were the rhythms that governed life and he liked to keep to them too, despite being a busy television producer in Delhi. We went up on the roof and looked out over the crowds below to the river. At night Varanasi seems like the edge of the world: all the bright lights of a border crossing and then nothing, just darkness and a kind of violet phosphorescence over the river.

'Aghoris are outside the main sadhu traditions,' he said when I asked. 'They have no specific texts, only a process of initiation and meditation.'

'Is it secret?'

'There are plenty of self-promoting types of sadhus – you must have met a few walking along the ghats? Aghoris are not of that type.'

I told him what I had heard. Of aghoris worshipping Kali and

[239]

living in charnel grounds and eating corpses, all in the attempt to break the chains of maya.

'You must find out from those people themselves,' he said gravely. 'Not accept what is said by those who may know nothing.'

Sound advice, considering what I had discovered on other matters. I explained my interest in Kali.

He stood up. 'Come. I'll take you to meet someone.'

We went down and on to the ghat. At Assi the riverbank curls away slightly, leaving a mudbank where the boatmen tie up and wait for customers during the day. At night there are restrictions on river travel, but we found one old boatman slumped over his oars apparently sleeping. When he heard Bhaskar's shout, he swung his head up in a crazy uncontrolled arc.

'I like this boatman,' said Bhaskar. 'He is always pissed though. I have to pay his son not him, otherwise he'll drink the lot.'

With some cursing and singing we set off, propelled largely by the gentle stream. The boatman waved the oars in the air, then fell over sideways banging his head on the gunwale.

'The number one reason women go to the sadhus for prayers and advice is to stop their husbands drinking,' said Bhaskar. 'This guy's wife is always there asking advice.'

'And men – what do they ask about?'

'The clap – venereal disease.'

'So sadhus have a role socially?'

'Oh, yes. Especially out in the villages. There you get them doing all sorts of things – some are even hitmen – yes, really. Don't forget the akaras, the sadhu fraternities, started as mercenary monks.'

While we talked, by some unfathomable magnetism, our boat drifted to the place where we were to disembark. As the boatman clearly had nothing to do with it, I could only assume that the boat itself knew the way.

We left the man singing lustily and drifting further down. Our destination proved to be a house just behind the ghats. 'The doctor is an aghori,' said Bhaskar. 'I'll introduce you then leave you to talk – I have some people to see.'

[240]

If I had expected a naked fakir with dreadlocks and a necklace of human bones, I could not have been more wrong. The doctor was dressed in a neatly pressed shirt with a Brut monogram, jeans and a necklace of rudraksh seeds. He had the build of a wrestler and, it transpired later, had trained regularly as a young man at a local wrestling gym. We sat in a courtyard under the dark shadows of trees with an oil lamp to light us. There was a little stone box for a deity and inside some marigolds and a trident next to a burning joss-stick. He had a strange manner, his eyes unfocused, but his initial grilling of me was detailed. Who was I? What did I want?

I was careful with what I told him, not wanting to imply aghoris were criminals. As it turned out, I need not have worried. He began to relate his life story.

'When I was a boy my brother was a goonda and a schizophrenic. Things were so bad with him that my poor mother did not know what to do. In desperation she took him a hundred miles away and abandoned him.' The doctor sat straight on the stone bench, staring up at the night sky, never looking at me.

'I ran to the ashram near our house crying to the baba, "Please, help me. Lord Shiva, for once, show your curative powers." And the baba scolded me because I asked for help for my brother, not enlightenment for myself.

'The next night I drank rum and went dancing, but as I passed the ashram the baba called to me, "Hey, you, son of a pig!" He always spoke to people in that way, even beating them with sticks. But this time I went to him and he reached into his hair and brought out a seed, a one-faced rudraksh seed.'

The rudraksh seed is normally a five-sided pith, revered for its association with Rudra, an early form of Shiva. Occasionally a variant occurs of which the single-sided form is most auspicious – some believing that possession of such a seed is a guarantee of a favourable rebirth.

'He gave that seed to me and I still have it.'

I noticed that the doctor's eyes had filled with tears as he recalled this incident. 'Was that baba an aghori?'

'Yes, from the ashram. He became my guru.'

'What practices did he give you?'

He did not answer for some time – when he did it was enigmatic. 'There are many steps to the roof and the guru gives what is necessary for the next step alone.'

'Was there a mantra?'

'We concentrate on one thing: Kali, to then be free of all bondage.'

'What bondage?'

'Of this life.' He thought for a while. 'Our guru may test us. Myself, he sent one girl of sixteen years to me, full-bosomed.' His hands described the shape. 'That I resisted.'

He described how his parents had insisted on a marriage for him and he had reluctantly agreed. Four or five days after the wedding he told his wife that there would be separate rooms and no 'secretions': his religious practice precluded such things.

'Thank goodness I am blessed with no children.'

I understood that his guru had recognized his particular need to transcend sexual desire in order to progess. Had it worked?

'I have a beautiful house, worth ten lakhs ruppees – all from the goddess.'

This, I reflected, was where the twisting of human nature must start. His desire for selflessness seemed to have a rather selfish twist: his wife had had to forgo children, no small sacrifice in Indian society.

I asked about more extreme practices such as eating human flesh.

'The guru decides what is necessary. There are many steps to the roof but we see only the step we are on.'

'There were, many years ago, a group of thugs who strangled travellers, and some people said that the victims were a sacrifice to Kali.'

He nodded gently. 'Thugs: those holy fellows, that was their destiny. It was their practice and their inner god told them to follow it.'

I must say, I sat up straight then: it was the first time I'd heard anyone express sympathy for the morality of murder. 'Those thugs did what they did to support their families,' he continued. 'Who gave them their hunger and who gave the idea of how to satisfy that hunger?'

Now he jumped into another subject and I couldn't follow his reasoning. 'At my clinic prostitutes of Varanasi are coming for treatment and I say only to them, "No work in the waiting room."'

I waited and he stared away, eyes watering constantly as though he was in thick smoke. Perhaps he meant that he did not judge the methods of others. The excesses of aghor, the eating of faeces and flesh, are all excesses that are self-sacrifices; they destroy the discrimination of earth-bound human criteria. There can be no good or evil remaining because they are man-made.

But now he jumped somewhere else. 'You know, for me Ravanna was no goonda or thug.'

I recalled that Ravanna was the monkey king of Sri Lanka who kidnapped Sita, Rama's wife.

'Ravanna was wanting salvation, but he wanted it in a hurry. He kidnapped Sita for his mukti. That is why I have a soft corner for Ravanna and in the south they worship him.'

Mukti means liberation and Ravanna is generally taken to be a malicious and frightful figure. Here was the sleight of hand, the moral shifting required; the demon king could become the hero and achieve liberation through theft of a woman.

'You wear ordinary clothes,' I said to him, 'not long hair or ashes.'

'True aghoris do not feel the need to be seen. Look along the ghats and see those fellows with their big hair and robes and beads and you think maybe he is a great saint when all along he may be a big thief or rogue. The aghori is not attracting attention like that. The aghori moves among the people and they do not know him.'

Like the thug, I thought.

\*　　\*　　\*

[243]

Bhaskar didn't want me to take just the doctor's word on aghor. When we met the next day, I told him about the doctor's attitude to thugs and to Ravanna.

'Ravanna had ten heads and he got it wrong ten times. You cannot achieve salvation by thievery – that was his mistake.'

After the doctor's strange ramblings, this was sense. Bhaskar followed Kali, but remained rational and human.

'OK, your next step is to visit the aghor leper colony. Take a boat down the river to the railway bridge – not the drunk, you'll never get that far – then get out on the far side and walk inland for about a half mile.'

I had the feeling I was being shown each step at a time, just as the doctor had described.

That night there was a note waiting for me at the guesthouse when I returned. 'I'm in the Baba bag shop waiting for you, love and laughter for ever after – Maddy.'

I had no idea where the Baba bag shop might be, neither did anyone I asked. I waited on the terrace, but nobody came. Then I paced up and down outside the guesthouse, feeling sure she would appear, but there was no one there but Deko.

Deko and I got on well immediately. For a start he had the most outrageous Brooklyn accent and the kind of starry-eyed vivacity one associates with a young Liza Minelli. He was waiting for a friend who hadn't showed up.

'Do you think gay men exist in India?' he asked. 'Cos I got my gay-dar switched on and I'm not getting any beeps!'

He had come to India, not cruising, but on a pilgrimage after a friend's death from AIDS. 'My God, Varanasi! Isn't it amaazzing? Burning, bathing, burning, bathing. I went down the ghats and got all smoke in my hair. You know I was in that shower so long with so much shampoo singing, "I'm gonna wash that Ram right outta my hair!"'

'Let me do your cards,' he said, pulling a wadge of large playing cards from his little bag and holding them out for me to choose.

'Those tarot cards are kinda scary, dontcha think? And people see the skeleton and just freak. So I got myself these.'

I turned my choice over.

'All raiiight! Beaver. No, ple-ase! Beaver is industrious and hard-working. You're on some kinda mission, right? And the card is telling you stick with it. Choose again.'

It was a furry alsatian dog. 'Loyalty. OK, remain loyal to your mission and it's better.'

He put the cards down. 'You don't believe in cards, right? You know, I came to India because the cards told me to. They said I'd work with children and meet a great guy. Then the day after that happened, an old girlfriend rang me from Nepal and said come and work with me in this children's home, so I thought, this is it! But when I came, she had left for some reason and now I'm here and no great guy appeared yet. Now the cards tell me, go easy, go with the flow, take the pilgrimage. This is a pilgrimage for me but I ain't got that feeling right yet.'

We gave up waiting for our respective friends and went up on the roof of the guesthouse with a paper bag full of Guru beer bottles. Deko was a natural entertainer, a chef who did private parties for exclusive and wealthy New Yorkers.

'But I gave it up, you know, I mean it was too crazy. I was working for this couple who were Wall Street, serious money. But they never stopped working to make more money. They couldn't accept they had enough for the rest of their lives and several other lives too. And there I was: swimming up and down their pool, butt naked, sun-bathing, making some sandwiches, and they'd be sitting with their laptops, writing business reports, making more money. And I got like: what is wrong with this picture, huh? I started doing AA, NA, DA and CA.'

'Deko, hold on. I understand AA, but those others?'

'Narcotics Anonymous, Debtors Anonymous, Co-dependants Anonymous.'

'You had all those problems?'

[245]

'Nooo. I had no problems. I needed a problem. I was sooo normal, sooo blessed. Do you understand? This is America I'm talking about. I had to get in touch with my inner Woody Allen and that's led me here – to Varanasi.'

# 12

# Slowly Across the Ganges

SOMEWHERE IN THE LANES GOING OUT to visit Professor Anandkrishnan the rickshaw was brought to a halt by a procession of
men wearing baggy brown shorts, white shirts and Nehru caps.
They were carrying iron-tipped stathes.

'Khaki-wallahs!' said the rickshaw man, grinning.

It was the first time I had seen the cadres of the right-wing
Rashtriya Swayamsevak Sangh (RSS) party on the march, a party
whose support is vital to the ruling BJP and yet comes with a muddy
back catalogue – the murderer of Gandhi was an RSS supporter
and their founders were fascist sympathizers inspired by Hitler and
Mussolini. These men were clerks and shopkeepers and government functionaries, not soldiers. They did not look especially
menacing as individuals, but as a group they had something,
the kind of power one sees looking back at early photographs of
Hitler's followers. These were the simple, law-abiding little people
bearing the stathes meant for skull-cracking and that was what
intimidated. Little India was on the march.

My rickshaw man waited on the verge patiently, one or two of
the men smiled but most ignored the people they had pushed to

one side and stared steadfastly ahead. When they had gone, the people next to the rickshaw smiled at me, the sort of surreptitious look people exchange when they see something faintly ridiculous but nonetheless menacing.

The professor had arranged some tea and snacks on his patio, a verdant spot overhung by a large tree where a gang of monkeys sat, eyeing the food greedily. The sun was setting behind the house, a sturdy old bungalow set above the street a little and surrounded by garden. There were mulseri and jamun trees, long established, with flowering bushes beneath and uneven paving stones patched with lichen. In these last few moments of daylight, small stripy squirrels were bustling about, while the garden seemed to ooze a deep damp smell of earth.

I asked the professor about his family history and he explained they had once been revenue officers for the Mughal emperors, vastly wealthy in their time. Clearly those great days were past, but I had the impression that the professor did not set much store by wordly wealth anyway – it was ideas, art and history that got him excited, even though he had officially retired from academia.

We started talking about caste. 'Once again it has become important to know your caste,' said the professor, pushing the round spectacles up his nose. He had a gentle manner with a ready smile. 'Like when I was a child. But times have changed, you know. In my childhood in the 1920s there was one day in the year when we would wash our servants' feet and treat them like kings. Such customs were beneficial, but now they have gone.'

He paused while a gardener came past us, a wiry old man with deep-set eyes and a home-made haircut. The professor asked him to chase the monkeys away as they had come dangerously close. 'They do bite,' he explained.

The man fetched a long pole and waved it at the monkeys who ignored him disdainfully.

'Look at this fellow.' The professor paused, thinking. 'I wonder if I dare say to him . . . but no.'

I was intrigued. 'Dare to say what? Maybe I can dare – stupid foreigners can say things that a local cannot.'

He laughed. 'Well, that would not be suitable.' We watched the man put away the pole. The professor continued. 'You see he is of what they call a criminal caste.'

'But they don't exist now, do they?'

'It is embarrassing to say that they do in the culture, if not officially.'

'Can we ask him what he thinks?'

The professor thought. 'It would be interesting – if I dare.' We sipped our tea and wondered, but the gardener slipped away, precluding any questions for the moment.

'India has so many varieties of thieves and robbers,' said the professor. 'There was a group of sadhus who used all the names of Vishnu as their secret language – to warn each other and so on. The British exterminated them. I remember as a child being told tales of thugs by the household servants. They were bogeymen for us. One story my father's maternal uncle told was that when the family lived in Allahabad, a party of travellers came and camped on their land waiting for a boat next day. There were some two hundred of them and all from a wedding party with a bridegroom and horses. But there was something suspicious about them and an advisor said they should be offered food. You see, it is known in India, even today, that once you "take the salt" of your host, treachery is impossible.' I was reminded of Arun Gawli and his insistent requests for me to accept his hospitality.

'But when they were offered food, they refused, saying it was a special day for them and they could only eat sweets. Then halva was prepared for them and brought. They ate and one asked, "Did you put salt?" When they were told yes, they jumped up shouting, "You have betrayed us and our devotions."

'But my great uncle then accused them, saying, "Is it not true that you are thugs?" Eventually they admitted this was true and they had intended to rob and kill, but now, after taking salt, they would not.'

[249]

Religion and superstition were so intertwined with every facet of crime, they provided cloaks of disguise, the language of deceit, even the subtle defences of vulnerable victims.

The gardener reappeared and threw something up at the monkeys who slowly got to their feet and moved along the bough a little. With a grin to me, the professor called him over and asked him in Hindi, 'What do you know of thuggee?'

The old man had a hank of old coconut fibre in his hands which he tore apart as he spoke. Now the sun had set it was difficult to make out his face in the shadows of the trees. The professor translated his replies. 'I knew one of those men once. He showed me how they picked pockets and prepared the datura to drug people.'

'Were they stranglers?'

The gardener smiled to himself and ripped at the fibre. 'There are three kinds of thug now. Some use magic to make sterile women pregnant, another type make counterfeit currency, and the last turn brass into gold.'

The professor added to me under his breath, 'These are common matters; I want to go deeper.'

But again the gardener had gone, melting silently back into the shadows. I saw his figure against the gate as he passed through. The professor sighed. 'It is a tricky subject.'

The monkeys had given up waiting for a chance to steal our food and decided to move off in search of more profitable pastimes, crashing through the foliage then across the rooftops.

'There was a tribe called Mus'har,' said the professor, 'derived I should think from musna, to rob, and har, to take away. Then the British declared them hereditary criminals and they were unpopular. People joked about their name, calling them musa, meaning mice or rats.

'With that nickname it was not long before rumours started that they ate rats and mice. When independence came and Gandhi said criminal tribes could no longer exist, they recast themselves, literally, as Rajputs and not only that but chuhan, a high-caste

Rajput clan. Why they chose that particular caste? Because chuha means mouse or rat!' He chuckled. 'But now another twist has come with BJP government. There are benefits to being a Scheduled Caste, you see, so they want to go back and rejoin the lower orders, but socially they want to be known as kshatrias, warriors.'

Perhaps some groups are able to do that, working the system to their advantage. But if governments could create advantages to being low caste, just as they could once create criminal tribes, they could not take away the stain. Some of the settlements managed by the Salvation Army have survived, though everyone is now free to come and go as they please. Academic studies have shown that the inhabitants are still disadvantaged despite some benefit from the Army's education programmes. One study (by Y.C. Simhadri in 1979) found that local police, politicians and businessmen can even push individuals and families into crime in order to extract from them bribes or a share in loot.

The professor turned and called into the darkness and there was a rustle of dry leaves. I hadn't noticed his return, but the gardener was there.

'Come,' said the professor gently, 'come and tell us of the thugs.'

The man shuffled awkwardly. 'Some women here are called natinee which means skirted. They are casters of spells and thieves.'

'He does not say of his own kind,' the professor added to this in a whisper.

'I heard of a goldsmith who was a thug,' said the gardener, stepping into the dim light though his face remained hidden. I slapped at the mosquitoes that were biting hard. 'His clerk was also thug and he cheated his boss just as the two of them cheated the people. One night they were staying in the serai outside of Kashi and the goldsmith was sick and dying. His final words to his clerk were that family tradition demanded that after death a wooden stake be driven into the mouth so the soul might be released.

'The goldsmith died that night and the clerk did as he was asked, driving a wooden stake deep into the mouth. Then next day cremation was prepared but the wooden stake was noticed and the clerk accused of murder. The case went to the rajah who declared that the clerk was guilty and must die, by the same means as the goldsmith. As this punishment was announced the corpse of the goldsmith was heard to laugh.'

The professor waved his hand at me excitedly. 'Now he's warming up!'

But the story over, the man had stepped back into the darkness and the professor had to summon him back. 'Wait! Tell us of Kali-ma, did not the thugs worship the goddess?'

'Kali is most powerful. Many worship her for that, not only thieves and robbers. A believer can cut off his own head and Kali will cause another to grow. Truly, there is no limit to the power of the goddess.'

The professor nodded. 'This is how they fool people. No one really wanted to offer his own head, only that of others.'

It was an endless game of bluff and counter-bluff, with deceivers in every camp. The higher castes conning the lower by religion; the lower fighting back with fake gurus and sadhus; the thugs moving among them all; little wonder that the western mind had seen only mendacity and cunning, this shifting surface of treachery and shadow. I thought of my experience in Madras, how I had been warned that I was entering a maze where there would be no black and white, only grey. Indians used the orientalist fantasy of exotic dangerous east too, another weapon in the armoury. But it was only a surface.

The professor was quoting the fifteenth-century poet Kabir, just as the medical rep guru had done. '*Maya maha thagini ham jani.*' Life's illusion is a great enchantress and a thug.

'You know there is a story of Kabir's death,' said the professor. 'All along Kabir had refused to be categorized as a Muslim, a Hindu, or anything. And when he died they began to wrangle over his corpse as it lay under the shroud. The Muslims wanted to bury him, the Hindus wanted to burn him.

'At last debate became so heated that the shroud was torn off the body – except there was no body, only a faint scent of flowers. Kabir had outwitted them all.'

No foxy paths then, no weird practices, just simplicity and honesty and a refusal to deviate from the straight road, that had been Kabir's ultimate weapon and the means to his salvation.

'Now I think we can ask,' said the professor, turning to the shadows under the tree. 'His caste are Jeraim, a word of Persian origin, I think.'

But there was no answer, only the rustle of a squirrel as it dashed across the patio. I looked across at the gate but there was no sign, no shadow falling across the step as he passed. Like the poet, the gardener had given us the slip.

On Panchaganga Ghat under the Alamgir Mosque there were many bamboo poles for yogi shelters. One of them glared at me. 'If you take my photo, I'll steal your soul,' he said and I laughed at him.

The poet Kabir had sat here on the steep steps, waiting for his guru, Ramananda, to accept him, despite being repeatedly rejected. I'd been weeks in Varanasi now. The heat had come down on the city and many of the sadhus and their followers had gone away. In the middle of the day there was scarcely any activity at all, though the elderly died with endless and increasing frequency. One morning I came across a trolley laden with marigolds and in among them, stretched out as if he had fallen from a great height, was the corpse of an old man, flat on his back and face utterly serene. He had died secure in the knowledge that he would be cremated in Kashi and his ashes would go in Mother Ganga.

There was a second yogi there on Panchaganga Ghat, near the unfriendly one, sitting in the lotus position. Over his loins he had a scrap of dirty cloth and his long straggly white hair had none of the elegant dreadlocks that the other sadhus boasted. He was old, very old, his nose eaten away by leprosy, and a pair of broken spectacles, much bound around with sticking tape, sat awkwardly there on the slight bony hump that remained. But, despite his age, his spine

[253]

was as straight as a pick handle and he was breathing, taking long slow inspirations and counting off his mantra on a string of prayer beads. I sat and watched and found my own breathing going into rhythm with his.

Kabir had found an unusual patron in Ramananda. The guru scorned three things: the caste system, meaningless ritual and the Brahmins. Among his students were said to have been an untouchable, a barber and, most astonishing of all, a woman. Likewise Kabir became an iconoclast, heaping ridicule on holy books and places. His poem 'Maya is a great enchantress and a thug' continues,

> She is the idol for the priest
> she is the water in holy places.

He developed a system of controlling the breathing and the senses, denounced social injustice, greed and luxury, but also religious rituals, the smearing of ash, the fasts and the pilgrimages. When he was dying, despite having lived all his life in Varanasi, he moved outside to an insignificant rural town just to show what he thought of the notion that dying in the holy city would bring liberation. The town he chose, Magahar, was considered so lowly that the Brahmins said anyone dying there would be reborn as an ass. I liked Kabir.

When the old yogi finished his mantras, he unfolded his legs easily, stood up and walked away. I liked him too. No interest in me. No requests to bring hashish for a chillum later. Just doing his breathing by the river, then going.

I met Deko the next day at lunchtime in the Italian–Indian restaurant that made their own mozarella and dough.

'This place just saved my life. The food is just great!'

I told him where I was going that day and he exploded with laughter. 'Aw-right! Great pizza, let's do the leper colony. Can I come too?'

[254]

We took a boat from the ghat and made our way idly down-stream, under the railway bridge where a man was fishing for coins with a net made of little magnets. 'I wonder what caste he is,' said Deko.

On the far bank we set off walking, not really knowing where to go. Eventually we were directed across the road and railway into a grove of trees. There, inside a high perimeter wall, was the leper colony and at the gate we were met by an old man wearing a lunghi and shirt. He was a teacher, he told us, and an admirer of the aghori baba, Ram Das, the man who had founded this place.

We strolled along the leafy paths and inspected the dispensary and the dormitory. It was occupied by a crowd of silent shuffling old men who followed us down to the house of Ram Das, now a shrine as he had died of kidney disease in the USA in 1992. The large garlanded photograph showed a strong face with a rough-shaven chin, not the usual beneficent smiler, rather more like a French mercenary.

'He was born in the lotus position,' said the teacher. 'He was a great soul and could have healed himself easily. But he chose not to. He chose to die.'

'What does aghor mean?' I asked.

'The meaning of aghor is Ganga,' said the teacher. 'Think of all the dirt going in the Ganga, but the water is clean.'

We strolled on, keeping pace with the slow, silent old men. Time had no meaning here. No one wore a watch, there were no clocks. In Kashi they say there is no bad time to die, it is always auspicious whatever the stars say. But this was not the city, this was a limbo land beyond the river.

'And the baba – what did he believe?'

'That the Goddess Kali gave birth to many poor people, but they do not have to be sorry. He believed that the leper is a human being and all men and women are equal whatever the caste or creed.'

The same simple message of so many sages in India. And all came up against the same rock of caste and prejudice. In this there was a strange affinity between a man like Macaulay who lambasted Hinduism for its unjust caste system and a man like Ram Das.

We left and were rowed back along the ghats at sunset. Deko was consulting his cards and I lay on the prow looking across at the people on the ghats and how the lights and smoke faded into the vault of fading blue that stretched over and down to touch the barren shore. Suddenly I said, without thinking, 'Let's swim the river.'

I was feeling let down now Maddy had not appeared and then there was the curious nature of the aghoris, the moral slipperiness of it all, the constant smell of cremation; I wanted something reliably elemental with an identifiable goal, like the far side of the river. I wanted to dive in and swim over there, to leave behind all the muck and confusion and head for the pure white riverbank out there.

'Did you say swim? No, come on. I am sure there are crocs.'

'Read the cards. Go on.'

He picked them up and weighed them in his hand. 'I don't know. Maybe they'll tell me to go – and I don't know if I want to. I ain't a great swimmer.'

'Do the cards, Deko.'

I took one and he did too. The first was an otter. Deko groaned, 'Oh, shit!' The second was a cougar. 'Like double shit!' This, apparently, meant there was no option but to swim the river.

'Please not now,' Deko begged. 'Not in the dark.'

'At dawn,' I suggested.

I met Bhaskar for a last time that night as he was heading off for Delhi the next day. 'There is one baba you should meet in Kolkata,' he said, jotting down a few details. 'He is different to all the others – worth meeting, and he's near Kali Ghat where you'll be going, won't you?'

At sunrise I was there by the river, wondering if Deko would show. The women were fetching water to pour over the Shiva lingam under the tree and I had seen Shashank come down and do the pooja that he had done every day of his life in Varanasi, his homage to Mother Ganga.

Dawn in the city is a holy time. The river seems broader and the same pearly white as the sky and the far riverbank, all curling around each other to make the broad rusty flanks of the temples seem like bulwarks, ramparts of the last fort of the empire, beyond which lie the empty badlands. A dead cow floated serenely past. Something else rippled the surface. I watched carefully, wondering what might be down there. The possibility of dead things had been in my mind, but now the possibility of live things that fed upon them occurred.

Deko came down wrapped in a fluffy robe. 'Now you gonna swim with me, sweetheart, 'cos I ain't so sure about this.' He pulled the cards from his pocket. 'Don't say anything. I'm just checking.'

I took a card and he did too. This time mine was the otter and his was the cougar. 'Holy shit! I don't believe that.'

I turned away, back to the river, and at that moment the smooth grey water erupted and a long-snouted curling shape leaped free and seemed to hang there for an instant, looking across. A river dolphin, the susu, *platanista gangetica*.

Deko was still staring at the cards. The dolphin disappeared leaving an opening flower of ripples.

'What?'

I was grinning. 'Nothing.'

We left our clothes with a boatman and went to the edge. The water was cool, moving steadily away to our left, spinning with marigolds thrown in upstream. It became deep very quickly. We began to swim, breast-stroke, very gently. The current took us away but it was not strong and we kept pace with each other, not talking at all. In the entire crossing we did not exchange a single word. There was only silence and far away, but clearly, we could hear the singing in a temple somewhere along the ghats. The water was silver and smooth like transparent skin. All the rubbish they throw in, I thought, all the millions of people along its way, the filthy dirty cities and the corpses and ashes and deceased cattle and sewage, yet all we see is clean water and a constellation of marigolds. I didn't want the e.coli rating, or the depleted oxygen levels – they'd be bad enough – here was the Mother that absorbed everything and always remained the same, who took all the vagaries and reversals of life in her broad unchanging stride. It was no more than anyone wanted, constancy, something rarely found in others and more rarely still in ourselves. But maybe old Ma would give it, in whatever one of her great incarnations, as Durga, Bhawani, Ganga, Sita or Kali – however she came out. Ahead was the saffron sun and the shimmering white shoreline.

When we reached the far side, we sat for half an hour on the whitened mud looking back at the city and listening to its noises: voices, clankings, bells and snatches of music – village noises of India. Then we waded out through the squishy silt again and swam back towards all the noise. It felt like swimming back down to earth.

# 13

## Ma's Message

THE NIGHT TRAIN TO KOLKATA AND I did not have a reservation, simply jumped aboard trusting to luck. Almost immediately I got talking to a senior conductor who was travelling alone but had a whole section to himself, three spare bunks for his wife and children.

'It is perk,' he said gruffly. 'In case family are coming, but missus decided not to accompany. You take upper berth.' He spoke like a railway telegraph of old and, when I enquired, it transpired he had started out as a bookings clerk in the days when reservations were telegraphed ahead. 'Telegraph was superior and faster. "Mr Kevin. Joining Mughal Serai. Berth secure. First-Class Howrah." See? Simple.'

We were rolling now, leaving Varanasi across the iron bridge with a last look back at that wonderful stretch of riverbank, the smoke hanging in a pall around the burning ghats and the temples lit up while we plunged into the darkness.

'Are you Christian?' asked the senior inspector.

I told him I had been brought up that way but no longer believed.

'It is bad time for Christians in India,' he said solemnly. 'Many attacks and church burnings.'

He undid a small bundle and took out some glass vials, a syringe and a tourniquet. He handed the latter to me. 'Tie for me. Here.'

He drew up some insulin and jabbed himself while I held the tourniquet above his elbow.

'India is all corruption now – since Mandal politics came.'

This was a reference to the Mandal Report of 1990 when Scheduled Castes were recommended quotas in government posts. Acceptance of this by the government led to serious rioting but, more importantly, it ushered in a whole new era of Indian politics, coinciding with the decline of the Congress Party and the rise of the BJP.

'Are the railways affected then?'

'All India is affected. Who is to help Christians, Muslims and other non-Hindus?'

We were interrupted by a team of inspectors come to pay their respects to a senior colleague. Extra pillows were provided, 'bed-tea' ordered for the morning. I paid the extra for the berth.

When they had gone, the senior inspector returned to his theme. 'Corruption is not simply taking of bribes,' he declared. 'The archaeologists now spend their time looking for proof that Hindu temples are under every Muslim monument. Some of those fellows even want the Taj Mahal to be declared a Hindu temple. It is corruption of mind. Better the British return. Then things were straightly.'

He popped two pills in his mouth and lay back on his bunk, grunting and sighing. 'Mr Kevin, you inform pantry car of any needs. I will sleep now.'

And with that he closed his eyes and was almost instantly snoring gently. I moved over to the window and, switching the lights off, stared out. It was undoubtedly true that India was at a great time of historical revision: at Ayodhya, once part of Awadh where

Sleeman had been Resident, Hindu extremists had demolished a mosque which they claimed was on the site of Rama's birthplace. Now the threat of Hindu extremists forcibly building a temple on top of the ruin is the greatest internal challenge to India's stability. School textbooks were being rewritten, turning Hindu defeats at the hands of Islamic invaders into victories. Suttee had begun to recur. Even recent history was being altered: right-wing extremists who had connived in colonialism were now to be anti-colonial freedom fighters. (No doubt they will start to queue at the railway ticket office window reserved for freedom fighters.) The founder of the fascist RSS, Kashav Hedgewar, a man inspired by Nazism and Mussolini, was to be a pivotal figure in the battle against the Raj when he had done nothing. Why? Because the RSS were allies and soul-mates of the BJP. And, I might add, thuggee was never a cult, its eradicators not heroes, and the Criminal Tribes and Castes Act was not an attempt to help the fallen, but a vicious folly. The Raj needed its share of revisionism. Was there to be no solid ground? All the angels of history can be devils, and all you have to do is travel with them long enough to see them transfigured.

The senior inspector snored louder now and I knew his breathing would keep me awake, and all down the carriage others had taken sleeping pills too, and their snores echoed his. I pulled the blanket over me and waited, feeling the train sway softly from side to side as though it were breathing too.

Kolkata is the city of Kali, her image is in every taxi and in the greatest temples. Shops stock her picture from all the famous temples around the country: the Kali Ghat temple where her toes fell to ground, Dakshineswar in north Kolkata where the mosquitoes are said to never enter her sanctum but stay in the VIP lounge, and Kamakhya in Assam where her vagina landed and the earth is said to menstruate every July.

The city deserves a far better reputation than Mother Theresa and the Black Hole have given it. The streets are broad and well laid out, the transport system (modern underground trains, fine old trams, hand-pulled rickshaws) actually gets you around quickly and cheaply, and there are generous acres of parkland. I walked through the centre, admiring the old colonial architecture and the eccentric cacophony of shops: surgical supplies next to cast-iron hand pumps, books beside bathroom tiles (a smashan Kali for the shower, sahib?), shipping clerks and shop-fitters, it was impossible to guess what might come next. The Rabindranath Tagore Museum was closed so I took a rickshaw to College Street, then went up some shabby stairs and sat in the cavernous Coffee Shop. In the 1940s this was the home to radical intellectuals and it still looks like a scene from Conrad's *Secret Agent*: nicotine stained and institutional with conspiratorial gangs of callow university youths. Now, however, although the boys were still learning to smoke lungbusters, they preferred to talk about girls rather than proletarian uprisings.

I did not stay long. My smoking days were over, I had decided. I was dedicated to breathing. Nevertheless, I still walked across to a place full of people who had stopped altogether: St John's Church and graveyard.

When built in 1787, the church was not considered an architectural success, mainly because it started to sink and they couldn't put up the spire they wanted – one modelled on that of St Martin-in-the-Fields in London. There were those who might have said it was not the land alone that was suspect: the grant was by a Hindu; the congregation led scandalous lives, and the chaplain retired home the following year with 350,000 rupees, a vast fortune for a man of the cloth.

Yet it has survived and its cool airy interior is a treasury of history. Plaques recall deaths both glorious and ignominious: 'buried in the Indian Ocean', 'died when his horse was struck by lightning', died 'for want of proper nourishment' during the siege at Lucknow in 1857.

Out in the garden is an octagonal mausoleum to Job Charnock, the founder in 1690 of English Calcutta, and a man of legendary strength and energy. For all his faults, and they were many,

Charnock was a man of action, direct and simple: in 1679 he rescued a Hindu widow from the funeral pyre and married her. They had several children and, when she died, he erected the mausoleum over her remains, sacrificing a cockerel there every year until his own death in 1693. He was typical of a breed of merchant adventurer who came before the Raj and all the reformers and politicians. They lived rumbustous lives full of incident and excitement; drinking and carousing to excess, sometimes immoral but never dull. Their world ended when the Company conquered the Mahrathas and ushered in a new era, the time of Thuggee Sleeman and reform.

Buried next to Charnock was the woman who best represents the female side of those early English adventurers in Calcutta: Begum Johnson. In his early days in Calcutta, Sleeman had visited her house, finding a lady of eighty-five years who still threw parties every night. As a young woman she had been captured by Siraj-a-Daula, the invader who created the infamous Black Hole: her beauty saved her life and her pregnant condition saved her from the harem. In the drawing room, behind crimson protective cloths, were portraits of the several husbands she had outlived or sent packing. At one gathering she confessed that she couldn't immediately remember all their names. (Parry Purple Templer Esquire was one; the last was the chaplain who had departed with a pretty fortune.) The plaque recorded that she died in 1812 when eighty-seven, the oldest resident of Bengal and 'universally beloved, respected and revered'. With her went the spirit of a more exuberant age and in came the worthy and more arrogant Raj. Government became more objective, more organized perhaps, but the individuals less colourful. If I had arrived in Kolkata fully disillusioned with the British in India, I could salvage something here. Sleeman himself recorded the mood of that earlier time.

> There is, I believe, no society in which there is more real urbanity
> of manners than in that of India – a more general disposition on
> the part of its different members to sacrifice their own comforts

[263]

and conveniences to those of others and to make those around them happy, without letting them see that it costs them an effort to do so ... They pay no taxes [and] religious feelings and opinions are by common consent left as a question between the man and his Maker.

It's hard to imagine a more sensible prescription for human society than that.

The temple of Kali at Kali Ghat is on the south side of Kolkata. I dropped off the tram and walked past the line of stalls and shops selling all kinds of souvenirs: postcards, masks, balloons, votive trays, handkerchiefs to cover the offerings – yes, the rumal was there still – and huge trays of hibiscus flowers, Kali's blood-red favourite.

The temple itself was in the centre of a large paved square, almost entirely hidden by the stalls and shops clustered around. Crowds of excited people swarmed in carrying garlands of hibiscus, a queue came out of the gate and wound around the building like a cobra's tail. Guides and pundits were grabbing anyone they could – help with your devotions, for a fee. But I did not enter immediately. I walked past the temple, turned the corner where the Little Sisters of Mercy have their hospital, then took a narrow paved lane down towards the river.

It was a residential area, densely populated: women washing clothes, buffaloes strolling and naked children scampering around. Towards the end, a few yards before a low archway, was a temple. Not a huge one like that back up the lane, this was a simple room with a tiled floor, a Shiva lingam, a brass snake, a brass urn full of ashes and a couple of grass mats. There was no one here, however, the open frontage was sealed off with one of those cantilevered barred gates.

'Is it the Baba you are wanting?' a voice asked and I turned to find a tall elderly man wrapped in brown shawls.

'Yes.'

He indicated that I should follow him and led me on through

several alleyways, each narrower than the last. A man taking a bath in an aluminium tray had to stop soaping himself to let us past; scabrous dogs and bold cockerels were driven before us. Finally we came to a tall building that had been divided into apartments. The division was clear because a concrete wall had been built in the middle of the front door, splitting the entrance hall neatly into two narrow squeezes. We entered, sideways, to avoid touching the walls which were dripping with water and green algal gunk. There were sounds all around – the high chatter of women, bangs and clatters, the sizzle and spark of an electrical fault – but there was little light. My guide took my wrist and led me through a maze of dishevelled concrete.

It was almost impossible to see where the original building had been in this morass of shoddy additions. Mezzanine levels that were not level grabbed space from corridors, forcing us to bend double; random supporting pillars rose like crusty stalagmites from the floor; cock-eyed beams were balanced on breeze-blocks. In one place it opened up into what passed for a light well, and I looked up, past the forlorn washing line with its threadbare sarong and a home-knitted balaclava (in this heat?), past concrete lintels and projecting rusty reinforcing rods, all the way to the little square of sky. This was certainly the bottom of the well: a place for the people thrown down by modern life, as surely as any thug ever threw down a strangled corpse.

We moved on, squeezed between two pipes and came to a low plywood door where my guide knocked. There was a shout from within, then some conversation about 'the British man' and 'the Baba'. The door opened and my guide showed me in, around a tatty curtain of sackcloth. He did not follow and the door was rapidly closed behind me, then bolted by a slim young man in a sarong. The damp heat and the smell of ganja fell over my face like a warm wet flannel.

I'll admit to a stab of nervous energy at that moment, some fear even. It was a room so low that I had to bend my head, it was at most ten feet wide and as many deep, lit by a naked low-wattage bulb that hung low down one side on a tattered cable. There were no windows and just one item of furniture, a huge high bed that occupied the full width of the room and came within a yard of the door. It was covered in a patchwork of blankets and shawls, several overflowing ashtrays, a pile of playing cards, perhaps three dozen empty beer cans and nine half-naked men.

I think they must have been as surprised to find me there as I was. They stared in disbelief, check sarongs around their waists and torsoes bare and glistening with sweat, playing cards in their hands. One had a huge ramshackle spliff in his mouth. Their faces were villainous, no doubt, especially lit from below like that: the dim golden light cutting up through grizzled chins and moustaches to hooded wary eyes.

'*Kamon achew*,' I said, my first attempt at Bengali. Nobody moved.

The one with the spliff was older than the others. He now slowly took the smoking giant from his mouth and spoke.

'English,' he said, nodding gently, then added something in quick Bengali.

One of the others jumped down off the bed and took my bag from me – I let it go feebly – then he bent down and removed my shoes.

'Come,' said the older man, patting the bed next to him.

I crawled across the covers, weaving my way around the remains of a fish curry and all the other things, then sat cross-legged next to him.

Almost simultaneously I heard the wall say something. Just a whisper, but it came from the scabby top corner of the room. The older man leaned around me and, taking hold of a tab on the wall, he yanked open a small duct. I could see a tiny smudge of daylight. It can hardly have been more than five or ten minutes since I had left the sunshine outside, but I had that feeling you get as a child when you leave the cinema after a thrilling film and are shocked to find night has not yet come.

[266]

One of the other men rummaged under the bed covers, then put a small package in the duct and shut it.

'Ganja,' said the older man to me without being asked. 'We selling ganja and charas – good one – from Bangladesh and Assam.'

'You're a gang?'

He showed a glint of gold tooth. 'No, we are gangsters.'

I don't suffer from claustrophobia. In fact, I quite like confined spaces: my writing room has always been a den or a cave. Once I made the mistake of trying an attic with a lovely window overlooking a pleasant rural scene, but I ended up in the walk-in wardrobe. Lack of air, however, is another thing and that room was hot and suffocating.

'The Baba?' I asked. 'Is he coming?'

They shared a joke at that.

'Baba not here,' said the boss, the only one who appeared to speak anything but Bengali. He gave some orders and a beer can was pressed into my hand, then the spliff into my mouth. It was so acrid I choked and passed it on. They gathered around in a circle with eager faces.

'Fish curry?' asked Boss. I pressed my hand to my heart and shook my head. The fish glared.

Silence fell as if we were waiting a signal. The youths were watchful, most with one knee drawn up, one cross-legged.

'OK, English,' said Boss, slipping me an evil, sidelong grin. 'Time to play gin rummy.'

The packs of cards were the cleanest items in that room. He shuffled with casual dexterity, drawing out a series of great slithering arcs, then violently smacking them back together into his palm before dealing.

It was quite some time since I had lain on the bed in Hogenakkal with Jayapalani and learned gin rummy with all its originals and duplicates. Now I had some Bengali variations and a little pressure, yet I won the first round. My deal.

I was clumsy and smiled too much. When I picked up my hand,

I could see instantly that my shuffling had been cursory, but no one complained and I had a great hand. I won again.

Losing the third was clearly an imperative and I started with an unpromising set of cards, but I got some breaks. Initially there were wry smiles and some laughter, then frowns and sharp intakes of breath. Eye contact ended. I wiped a bead of sweat from my nose and wished I had not given up smoking, at least I could have offered them nicotine. The third came my way, a narrow victory from Boss in second place again.

I knew I had to lose the fourth. It was probably compulsory in Bengali gang law. I picked up and saw nine of clubs, eight and seven. They might make me eat the fish curry.

And ten. They might make me smoke the compost heap again. We started and I was throwing away good cards and making Boss frown. But it worked, I managed to come last with a huge points tally. On the next hand Boss took the lead and I wondered if perhaps I was playing only as well as the other men. By the fifth and Boss's victory I knew I was not the only one who had snatched a great defeat. We were all very happy then and the smiles returned.

I was handed another beer and let off the fish curry and compost heap. Things seemed pretty relaxed now so I ventured some enquiries about their business. Boss was happy to talk.

'These two boys go to Bangladesh for ganja.'

'Is it difficult?'

'Oh!' He translated and they all laughed. 'Very dangerous. Policemen searching.'

'And if they find it?'

'No. Never finding. Maybe jail, maybe pay money.'

'You go with a passport?' I had to explain a bit before he understood.

'No, no passport, no papers. Secret business.'

'And you sell it in Kolkata – who to?'

'We sell to all peoples. Workers, students, businessman.'

'Holy men – sadhus and sannyasis?'

Boss smiled. 'For sadhu we give freely.'

[268]

It's one of those paradoxes India has: everyone knows that holy men smoke ganja and they need it to be holy, but those who bring ganja to holy men are criminals and must be locked up for long periods.

'Do you live here because of the temple of Kali?'

'Kali is our mother. If you neglect your mother, what kind of man are you?'

The younger gangsters wanted me to learn some Bengali.

'*Tumi kotai jave?*'

'*Kali ghat jachhi.*'

They fell about laughing, upsetting some beer cans. I was wondering how I was to get out when a telephone rang. They hauled it out from under the bed and handed it to Boss, a huge blue plastic thing with a grubby white dial. He spoke briefly then replaced the receiver and gave some orders.

I was ushered off the bed and told to put on my shoes. Then, after some heartfelt goodbyes and promises to visit again, I was led by one of their number back out into the world of daylight.

When we reached the temple there was a small crowd of people outside who parted to let us through. Inside, reclined on the grass mat, was the Baba. He was a tiny man, very old, but with a bright mischievous look in his eye.

'Ah! British fella. I am so sorry I was not here when you arrived.'

He moved to let me come and sit beside him. His hair was grey and straggled halfway down the loose purple waistcoat that he wore along with a dhoti.

'That's no problem,' I said. 'This young man and his friends looked after me.'

The Baba grinned. 'Oh, they are very good boys though they are undoubtedly miscreants! They look after me.' He translated for the benefit of the crowd who all smiled indulgently. The young gangster came and touched the Baba's feet, then settled himself there like a contented dog. At the same time a small package of ganja was passed up to a helper who began to prepare a pipe.

'You came to see the Mother?'

I nodded.

The Baba touched my arm. 'Wait until tomorrow and come early morning. There will be a great ceremony tomorrow.'

'You live here because of the Mother?'

'Yes. Thirty-three years ago I gave up my possessions to devote myself.'

'What did you do before that?'

'I had many positions: government service for some years, then I had an engineering business. That developed into a successful thing – offices all over India, but I handed it to my sons and retired. Now I am ninety-one and I have no regrets.'

'Did you wander?'

'I am not sannyasi. To be sannyasi one must never stay more than three days in a place. I went to live in the smashan – you understand? The burning ground. I stayed seven years there.'

I thought how wonderful India was, that a businessman could throw it all up and live as a destitute in a crematorium without anyone raising as much as an eyebrow.

The pipe had been carefully prepared, all rough pieces removed and the leaves shredded. Now it was lit and passed to him.

'Why the smashan?'

'It is a place to concentrate and forget the trivial things of life.'

He put his hands together and pressing his mouth to the space between finger and thumb, pulled hard twice, then handed the pipe to me. I drew a mouthful of smoke.

'I am not aghori,' he continued. 'I have no special teachings to give, no secrets. I have need of nothing. I just do my japa [his mantra].'

I told him about the thugs and what the aghori in Varanasi had said about them being blessed. He smiled.

'According to their system, they were correct.'

'But murderers?'

'Miscreants.' He passed the pipe to the gangster and watched him smoke. 'This boy is a miscreant, but he is good to me. I look in his heart and see a good boy. I don't ask him what he does, I suppose he smuggles ganja and sells it and according to our law that means he is a criminal. In the British time, you know, abortion was a serious crime, punished by seven years in prison, and now the government pay people money to do it. Night for day. In the old times we looked for a husband for our daughters: a boy with many brothers and strong parents – that was enough. Now they search for a boy who knows computers, without brothers and parents deceased. Night for day.'

'Things change – even morals?'

Another pipe was being prepared.

'All you need to know is that if you put padi, you will get padi – not wheat. As you sow, so you reap. In Gujarat they burned down the churches of Christians and now they have had a terrible earthquake. Is there a connection? By science, no. But I think if there is something bad in your heart, bad things will come to you. And good will bring good. It is very simple – no secrets, no special teachings. Thirty-three years ago I gave everything away and walked from the house with empty hands. Since then I never use money and yet I am never hungry. How is that?'

He took the second pipe and, leaning forward, drew on it. As he did so, a lock of his grey hair came across and dangled in the burning ganja. Seeing this, the gangster put out his hand and, with great tenderness, gently pushed the lock away, behind the Baba's ear.

I stayed that night at the Tollygunge Club in order to be at the temple early and, despite the luxury of a comfortable bed, I was up in good time. Only I was delayed. Coming down from my room I ran into a horde of men with sideburns, wearing grey Edwardian drape coats and toting machine guns. Further on, by the indoor pool, lights were being set up and a film director was talking to a star. I knew he was the star because he had a similar Edwardian drape coat to the others, except it was canary yellow.

Thinking that this was a wonderfully appropriate scene to kick off the day, I sidled up to one of the more evil-looking gangsters. Like the actor in canary yellow, he looked vaguely familiar.

'Who's the star?'

'I don't know – it is a Tamil film.' I realized then where I had seen the star, on posters around Madras all those months ago.

'Do you always play gangsters?'

He shuffled uncomfortably. 'No, it is first time for me – don't you recognize me?'

'Yes.' I squinted at him. 'Were you in *Chori Chori Chupke Chupke*?'

He laughed. 'No, sir, I am your room boy. They needed one more gangster and I was chosen.'

I waited to see the first take of the day – nothing more exciting than watching a man in a canary yellow coat eat a sandwich – then I left and jumped on a tram. It was a big day for the Muslim community too: Eid al-Adha, the celebration of Abraham's sacrifice and his son's reprieve. I had planned to be here on this day but not calculated that it would a big day for the Hindus too. It was not dawn, as I had planned, when I jumped down from the tram at Kali Ghat but nearly eight o'clock.

The police barriers were up and manned, and the crowds of excited pilgrims were hurrying towards the square, bearing huge garlands of scarlet hibiscus. Ignoring the touts, I went through into a small central plaza next to the sanctuary itself which lay under a square tower adorned with floral tiles and rounded off with a dome. A long queue already reached all around the inner sanctum, down the steps, wriggled around a large open-sided hall, also full of people, and out of the gate. Dogs were fighting, people shouting, pundits grabbing at their charges and hurrying them through their devotions while holding baskets of hibiscus aloft. I was glad when a flower-seller made a space for me to sit next to him on a high step in the shadow. From there I could take it all in.

At the main gate, just beyond the lintel, I could see a team of barbers shaving the heads of a group of youths.

[272]

'Lariki Brahmini,' said the flower-seller. 'Today special.' He gesticulated at the string that all Brahmins wear over their shoulder, the nine-threaded string that is a symbol of their caste. It was the ceremony to tie those strings, a knot that would never be undone, unless of course they renounced their caste.

Inside the gate and to one side was a small gazebo where a priest sat before a fire and a garlanded trident. There was a flock of black goats tethered there, one innocently helping himself to a hibiscus garland while the Brahmin looked away. Opposite this, on the other side of the gate, was an area at the end of the hall, surrounded by a chest-high wall and a sign that read: 'Photography of the Sacrificial Area is Prohibited.' Inside were two wooden structures rather like small wishing wells with two posts either side of a block. The posts were smoothed and blood-stained, while one block was laden with garlands, candles and a clay pot of coins.

The crowds were growing by the minute and I realized I would have to join the queue quickly so out I went and took my place. There was an atmosphere of feverish intensity among the devotees, a few looked deranged to me, others were normal families, next to me was an intellectual. I know that because he told me.

'Kali attracts many followers,' he said when I commented on the range of people. 'Even intellectuals like myself.'

I asked if he could explain what the imagery meant to him. 'Her necklace of skulls represents knowledge, her white teeth on her red lip represents purity and inner peace triumphing over danger. The hand offers blessings to the good man.'

We pressed through the gates, tension mounting, then up a short flight of steps to a balcony that ran around the inner sanctum. Here a Brahmin sat above us on a ledge and there was a brief glimpse over the mass of heads into a chamber where a neon light was flickering madly. The queue had disintegrated into a surging crowd and over it the Brahmin seemed to hold a magical power, drawing the upturned foreheads to him, then daubing them with blood-red juice from a bowl, in return for a few coins in his basket. If someone annoyed him, he slapped at them angrily.

[273]

Around the building we went, squashed together into a single snake of humanity, then through a door. Now the noise rose so you had to shout to be heard, noise bouncing off the tiles. All was metallic and hard, like an abattoir. Flickering light, metal steps and down there in the centre of the seething mass of people, a single cage holding the goddess. She was covered in hibiscus garlands, the floor sticky with the blood-red juice that dripped from them, a man-high hulking stone barely visible under the tributes. We were shoved around to face her, the Brahmins up there on ledges like vultures, grabbing at the money in people's hands, then pushing them through. The more you paid, the more time you got before the goddess. I chucked my garland on with the rest and saw her three eyes. There was no time to consider what had brought me here, I only wanted to fight my way out and breathe some air.

But there was no release from the crush outside. Conch shells were being blown, men were spitting on the ground, women were ululating. My intellectual friend had got lost somewhere. I followed the people down the side of the hall, through the sacrificial area and into the hall. Here the young Brahmins were sitting with their fathers, taking lessons on the Vedas and the etiquette of various rituals. Offerings of foods and bolts of red and white chequered cloth were laid on banana leaves beside flickering camphor lamps. Other items were laid there, all neatly arranged: a brass pot containing the hair that had been shaved off and a pair of wooden sandals with a spigot for between the toes.

I stood in the doorway watching and the intellectual came alongside.

'Look,' he said. 'My brother is making sacrifice with the goat.'

I turned to see a big-bellied man in a white sarong come into the sacrificial area. He was carrying a large cleaver. Crowds of people surged up and inside, hoping to see. Now two small frightened goats were dragged in. A drum began to beat and the flames on the block were put out and a garland of hibiscus wound around the posts.

[274]

'Come,' said the intellectual, pressing me forwards. 'There is my brother.'

I stood there next to the block and felt the long thread of human history, stretching all the way back to the first murder, done out of jealousy over offerings to the god.

Now the drum was hammering and the first goat was dragged forward, bleating pitifully. A bare-chested man picked it up, pulled the kicking forelegs back beside its body and put the head on the block. An iron pole was brought down to hold it steady, then the man leaned back, stretching the neck out. The kid screamed twice and was silent. The watching people, too, became still.

The executioner took the cleaver up; it was about as long as his arm and a hand's width, hooked slightly at the tip. His lips moved, whispering some words. Then with a single fluid motion he brought the cleaver over and down. The drum stopped.

There was a thud as the knife hit the block under the head which sprang forward, propelled by the force of blood, two arcs of scarlet, jetting five feet out, them pumping and dying down. The head slithered sideways under the feet of the crowd, the tongue flickering out a few times. The body fell off the block, legs jerking wildly, sending the dying beast in a spin with blood gushing out over the people's bare feet.

The crowd came to life even as the kid died, pressing in towards the block. The brother was muttering to himself and now placed his own head between the posts. 'Whatever is bad in his head,' said the intellectual, 'those bad thoughts, the demons and devils, he will cut them free now. The goddess will release him from those things.'

The brother stood up and the executioner dabbed blood from the blade on to his forehead. The intellectual did the same, closing his eyes, hands on the posts beside the block, then daubed with blood.

'Now you.'

I hadn't expected that. His hand propelled me. I put my head down a short way and felt the hairs on my neck go up. I could see the executioner's feet but not the blade. I closed my eyes.

[275]

It took me by surprise, the power of that moment, the connection back through all the thug ritual I had unearthed, through the Sunday School mornings of boyhood learning about sacrificial lambs, burnt offerings and the blood of Christ, all the way to Abraham's son Isaac who had gone to the block but was reprieved. I imagined all the demons going out, the negativities and anxieties that plagued me. Hinduism does not have a Devil; the demons are within us and we project them out and give them names – Veerappan, thugs, Kali – whatever we want. Better cut them out. I thought of the Baba and how he had emptied his life of everything, then walked on and found all he needed. Stop the worry. Like Isaac, be reprieved.

The finger touched the blood on to my face and I jumped back. Two small sons of the brother were brought to do the same, both in their best suits with blue bow ties, and their eyes as wide as they could go. The executioner ran water down the blade, washing the arterial red blood down and people were there with jam jars ready to catch the blood and hurry away. The bare-chested man who had held the kid touched his right hand to the bloodied stump of neck and began daubing the crowd.

Now the slaughter had begun. A second kid was sacrificed, and a third. The blood covered the floor, splashed the walls, was dragged out into the courtyard when the carcasses were taken away. The meat was now holy food, prasad, to be given away: for most devotees, usually vegetarians, this was the only meat they would ever eat.

There had been a catharsis in that first death, but now I felt sickened by the relentless numbers and the smell of blood. I pushed through the people, suddenly desperate to get out. Beyond the gate, I found a step to sit on and, with a hand holding the nape of my cold neck, I began to take some deep slow breaths.

The intellectual came outside after some time and, seeing me, he came across.

'It is very intense,' he said, smiling. 'But somehow brings peace.'

I nodded weakly: I did feel tranquil. This was theatre in the classic Greek tradition, drama as catharsis, bringing your life to a stormy crisis, thereby sailing into calmer waters beyond. One did not have to believe in Kali to see the psychological benefit to the ritual.

'I came from Trivandrum,' volunteered the man. 'And it is definitely worth the journey.'

I made an effort to talk. 'With your brother and family?'

'A whole party came. From all walks of life. The goddess is there to help anyone, no matter what their caste or background.'

Kali cared nothing for those man-made divisions; she welcomed all into her fold. There were all kinds of people in the queue before me: fat and thin, rich and poor, deformed and beautiful, old and young. Some were Kolkata folk, others had come hundreds of miles. Now the intellectual was telling me he would go next month to see Mamaji, the hugging guru, the woman who would touch the untouchables. Then his brother and family appeared and he said his guru was in Bangalore. 'I see him once a year; also he is hugging all his followers and giving some instruction. I have breathing exercise to do every morning.'

When they had left me, gone on their way back to Trivandrum, all excited and contented, I had a vision of India, a country struggling to breathe, struggling against the rumal of its taboos and its caste and communal hatreds. There was so much here to choke the life from a person and those in power exploited that fact remorselessly, as much now as before Independence. But the people struggled. I saw them all out there, on the trains and buses, rushing towards their gurus and their goddesses, some of whom were genuine. But the people were united in their travelling, and they were trying to learn to breathe, trying to learn to love themselves and one another, and they were doing it, despite all that was set against them.

[277]

# Glossary

| | |
|---|---|
| areca palm | *Areca catechu*, the nut of this palm is the active ingredient of paan |
| asana | literally seat, more commonly used to denote a posture of hatha yoga |
| aghori | literally 'not terrible', but these ascetics haunt cremation grounds and perform extreme penances. Aghora is one of Shiva's names |
| akara | the associations of sadhus |
| arti | the fire ceremony |
| babu | a respected man in Hindi, but for the nineteenth-century British a derogatory term for an Indian clerk or official who had a superficial knowledge of English |
| betel | see 'paan' |
| bhil | the hill people who lived in the forests of Malwa |
| bigha | unit of land measurement in India varying from one third of an acre to one acre |
| charas | the resin of the flowers of the cannabis plant |
| chat | a snack food made from savoury tidbits plus a choice of sauces and chutneys |
| chillum | pipe used to smoke charas |
| chuhan | a kshatria, or warrior, caste |

| | |
|---|---|
| crore/crorepati | a crore is ten million (or 100 lakhs); a crorepati is a person possessing that amount of money – wealthy, in other words |
| dacoit | an armed robber or bandit |
| datura | the thorn apple, *Datura stramonium* of the nightshade family, containing a narcotic alkaloid capable of rendering a person unconscious |
| dessera/dusserah | the tenth, and last, day of Navaratri (cf), a festival associated with goddess worship. Traditionally Indian military campaigns began on this day, as did those of the thug gangs |
| dharma yuddha | holy war for Hindus |
| dharmshala | a resting place for pilgrims |
| dhosa | a crèpe made with rice flour |
| dhuni | the sacred fire of Shiva |
| ghat | a flight of steps up to a riverbank or landing place |
| ghoor | unrefined sugar or molasses |
| gingelly | a natural oil derived from *Sesamum indicum* |
| goonda | orig. Hindi 'rascal', hence a mobster or hired ruffian |
| idli | dumpling made with rice and lentil flour |
| jamun | *Syzygium cumuni*, an Indian wayside tree bearing a purplish-red fruit |
| japa | recitation of mantra |
| kapalika | 'skull-bearer'. Those sadhus who carried a human skull as their food bowl |
| kshatria | the warrior castes |
| kurta | orig. Persian. A loose shirt or tunic |
| lakh | one hundred thousand. A word often used to mean an indefinitely large number |
| lariki | orig. Hindi, 'boy'. Hence, perhaps, the Australian slang 'larrikin', a rowdy lad |
| lathi | an iron-bound stathe of bamboo |
| lunghi | sarong |
| mahout | an elephant-driver |

| | |
|---|---|
| mahua | *Madhuca latifola*, a tree that has edible flowers and oily seeds |
| maya | the illusion of the phenomenal world, also the supernatural power wielded by the gods |
| mohur | orig. Persian. A gold coin used in India from the sixteenth century onwards |
| mukti | orig. Sanskrit, 'release', also *moksha*. The release from the cycle of incarnation and the bliss associated |
| narbali | human sacrifice |
| navaratri | festival of nine nights associated with the goddess Durga and her various manifestations |
| Naxalites | Maoist revolutionaries, or extortionists, depending on your viewpoint. They take their name from a village in West Bengal where they began. Now operating in that state plus Bihar, Orissa and Andhra Pradesh |
| paan | Hindi for 'leaf'. The collection of betel leaf, areca nut, lime and spices that is chewed in India. Also called, incorrectly, betel nut, and in India, chunam and supari (from the Sanskrit word meaning 'pleasant') |
| pranayama | lit: extension of the life force, used to denote the breathing exercises of hatha yoga |
| rumal | the large square handkerchief that has so many uses, to whit: covering food offerings in the temple and strangling fellow travellers |
| sadhu | a holy man |
| samadhi | orig. Sanskrit, 'joining'. The state of complete meditation where identification with the divine is experienced |
| sambal | a vegetable sauce. The word 'curry' is not widely used in India, but sambal approximates to vegetable curry |
| sangam | confluence of two or more holy rivers |

| | |
|---|---|
| sannyasi | orig. Sanskrit, 'laying aside'. A renunciate or ascetic who wanders |
| sati/suttee | orig. Sanskrit, 'faithful woman'. The immolation of a Hindu widow on her husband's funeral pyre |
| shaivite | devotee of the god Shiva |
| shakti | lit. power, commonly used to denote power of the mother goddess |
| shalwar kameez | loose trousers and shirt |
| Shivaratri | the festival of the night of Shiva |
| smashan | a charnel ground |
| susu | orig. Oriya, 'śuśu'. *Platanista gangetica*, the river dolphin |
| Thakur | a chief or lord of that caste of Rajputs |
| thana | orig. Sanskrit 'place or station'. A police post |
| thirtankars | the holy saints of Jainism. Lit. 'ford crossers' |
| thug | orig. Sanskrit, 's'thag'. A member of that group of stranglers demonized by the British as religious cult |
| uttapam | a type of sourdough made from the flour of chickpeas and rice |
| vanniyar | a low caste into which the bandit Veerappan was born |
| Vedas | oldest extant Hindu scriptures |
| wada | a crisp doughnut made with lentil flour |

# Bibliography

Booth, Martin, *Opium, a History*, Simon and Schuster, 1996.

Bosworth, C. E., *The Mediaeval Islamic Underworld*, Brill Academic, 1997.

Brantlinger, Patrick, *Rule of Darkness: British Literature and Imperialism 1830–1914*, Cornell University Press, 1988.

Gordon, Stewart, 'Scarf and Sword – Thugs, Marauders and State-formation in 18th century Malwa', in *The Indian Economic and Social History Review*, vol. VI, 1969 no. 4.

Gould, Stephen, *The Mismeasure of Man*, Norton, 1996.

Hobsbawm, Eric, *Bandits*, Penguin, 1969.

Irwin, Robert, *The Arabian Nights, a Companion*, London, 1994.

Keay, John, *A History of India*, HarperCollins, 2000.

Lombroso, Cesar, 'Criminal Anthropology', in *Twentieth Century Practice Encyclopedia* vol. XII, London, 1897.

Malcolm, Sir John, *A Memoir of Central India and Malwa*, vol. 2, first published 1825, Calcutta 1880.

Masters, John, *The Deceivers*, Michael Joseph, London, 1952. (The thug myth at its pinnacle.)

Potter, Harry, *Hanging in Judgement – Religion and the Death Penalty in England*, Continuum, 1993. (A spell-binding account of capital punishment in English history.)

Sleeman, James, *Thug: A Million Murders*, Sampson Low, Marston & Co. Ltd., London, 1933.

Sleeman, Major William Henry, *Report on the Depredations committed by the Thug Gangs of Upper and Central India*, Calcutta, 1840. (Aimed at fellow officers from the witchfinder general.)

Sleeman, Major-General W. H., *Rambles and Recollections of an Indian Official*, Constable, 1893. (Reprinted 1844.).

Sleeman, Major W. H., *The Thugs or Phansidars of India*, Carey and Hart, Philadelphia, 1839. (Contains the *Ramaseeana*, thug vocabulary, which was also printed separately.)

Stokes, Eric, *The English Utilitarians and India*, Oxford, 1959.

Sue, Eugene, *The Wandering Jew*, Chapman and Hall, London, 1844.

Taylor, Col. Philip Meadows, *Confessions of a Thug*, first edition Richard Bentley, London, 1839. Still in publication.

Thornton, Edward, *Illustrations of the History and Practices of the Thugs*, London, 1837. (A readable gloss of Sleeman's material – the legend begins.)

Tuker, Lt-Gen. Sir Francis, *The Yellow Scarf*, London, 1961. (Hagiography Sleeman.)

Yang, Anand A., ed., *Crime and Criminality in British India,* University of Arizona Press, 1985. (The chapter by Sandria Freitag is particularly interesting.)

## Papers in The British Library relating to thuggee

Sleeman's Records, MSS Eur 305.

'A Memoir of Service in India', The Bowring Bequest, MSS Eur G91. (Bowring travelled with the Viceroy in 1860 and visited thug prisoners in Jubbulpore Jail.)

Papers of James Paton, Add. MS. 41 300. (Paton was one of Sleeman's British assistants on the thug hunt.)

Fraser Collection, MSS Eur E258/5. (Letters from Sleeman to his friend Charles Fraser.)

Drawings and watercolours of Charles Wade Crump, WD 3089 ff 12, 38–40.

Selected Records Relating to Suppression of Thuggee, MSS Eur 1188. (Contains Smith's first report on the trials of thugs, various letters and the account of Lushington [f 152].)

The Indian Opium Revenue, 1874, in 'Ethical Tracts 1870–1902', catalogue 8425 E16.

The Phrenological Journal and Miscellany, vol. 39, Edinburgh, 1839. (Henry Harpur Spry's account of the seven thug heads sent back to Scotland.)

## Books and papers in The British Library relating to the Criminal Tribes

Cole, Simon A., *Suspect Identities: a History of Fingerprinting and Criminal Identification*, Harvard University Press, 2001,

Criminal Tribes Act 1924, MSS Eur F161/158. (In which the government assume powers to separate children of 6–18 years from their parents.)

Lalitha, V., *The Making of Criminal Tribes*, Madras, 1995.

Pimm Smith, H., *Capturing Crims for Christ*, Salvation Army Press.

Simhadri, Y. C., *The Ex-Criminal Tribes of India*, Delhi, 1979.

Smith, Soveig, *By Love Compelled*, Salvation Army Press, 1981.

# Index